'Ronald Harwood is one of our most interesting playwrights. Sinewy prose and hand-carved dialogue makes his work a pleasure for the ear as well as the mind.' *The Times*.

Ronald Harwood's plays include *The Dresser*, *Interpreters*, *Another Time*, and *Reflected Glory*. He is also the author of *Sir Donald Wolfit, CBE: His Life and Work in the Unfashionable Theatre*, and a history of the theatre, *All the World's a Stage*. He is the Editor of *The Faber Book of the Theatre*. He was visitor in Theatre at Balliol College, Oxford, was President of English PEN from 1990 to 1993, and has been President of International PEN since 1993.

By the same author

fiction
ALL THE SAME SHADOWS
THE GUILT MERCHANTS
THE GIRL IN MELANIE KLEIN
ARTICLES OF FAITH
THE GENOA FERRY
CAESAR AND AUGUSTA
ONE. INTERIOR. DAY.- ADVENTURES IN THE FILM TRADE
HOME

biography
SIR DONALD WOLFIT, CBE: HIS LIFE AND WORK IN
THE UNFASHIONABLE THEATRE

plays
COLLECTED PLAYS
(A Family, The Dresser, J. J. Farr, Another Time)
THE DELIBERATE DEATH OF A POLISH PRIEST
INTERPRETERS
IVANOV
REFLECTED GLORY

television
ALL THE WORLD'S A STAGE
MANDELA
BREAKTHROUGH AT REYKJAVIK
COUNTDOWN TO WAR

films
ONE DAY IN THE LIFE OF IVAN DENISOVICH
OPERATION DAYBREAK
THE DRESSER
THE BROWNING VERSION

edited by
A NIGHT AT THE THEATRE
THE AGES OF GIELGUD
DEAR ALEC
THE FABER BOOK OF THE THEATRE

RONALD HARWOOD
PLAYS: TWO

Taking Sides,
Poison Pen,
Tramway Road,
The Ordeal of
Gilbert Pinfold,
After the Lions
and *The Guests*

faber and faber
LONDON · BOSTON

First published in 1995
by Faber and Faber Limited
3 Queen Square
London WC1N 3AU

Photoset by Parker Typesetting Service, Leicester
Printed in England by Clays Ltd, St Ives plc

All professional and amateur rights in these plays are strictly reserved and
applications for permission to perform them must be made in advance to Judy
Daish Associates, 2 St Charles Place, London, W10 6EG

A CIP record is available from the British Library
ISBN 0–571–17401–9

2 4 6 8 10 9 7 5 3 1

CONTENTS

INTRODUCTION

Although I write in English, and have lived and worked in
England for more than forty years, I do not regard myself as an
English playwright. Given my place of birth, South Africa, and
the fact that all my grandparents had as their mother tongue
either Russian or Yiddish or Polish, this, it seems to me, is not a
contentious conceit but a statement of fact. But it is also a fact
that because I was born in a British Dominion I inherited the
English language and was thereby given free use of a vast treasure
house which has made my way of life possible.

I do not and never have written about contemporary English
society. This has created difficulties for me because it is often the
case that, in this century at least, playwrights are expected to be
critics who diagnose social ills without prescribing a cure.
Moreover, the more parochial a play (or a film or a novel), the
more universal it seems is its appeal. But I have been drawn to
subjects of another kind: some autobiographical, others which
mostly deal with the creativity and courage of artists – actors,
musicians, novelists – and that they are sometimes set in England
is incidental. In every way I feel myself to be outside the
mainstream of the contemporary theatre. I am, however, often
accused of writing well-made plays or West End plays. I take this
as a compliment.

I treat each new play as if it were my first. I try not to write the
same play over and over again, not only because I am easily bored
but also, and perhaps more importantly, because I believe there is
nothing more destructive to the creative impulse than a wilful
desire to try and reproduce past successes. This is not, I know, a
fashionable view. In contemporary drama, critics, academics and
even audiences seem to have a need, bordering on the neurotic, to
cultivate sonar listening devices in the hope of picking up the
'voice' of the playwright. I have always reacted against this
tendency and taken a perverse pride in being unpredictable.
Nevertheless I hope that the range of interests which has worked
on my theatrical imagination will be respected. I am sometimes

described as eclectic: this I also take as a compliment.

In general, I write about people who feel rather than about people who think. The characters I create seem to be able to laugh and cry with great facility. That is not only because I myself laugh or cry with great facility but also because I perceive the world as being unbearably funny and unbearably sad.

The six plays in this volume cover a period of writing from 1974 to 1993. The earliest, *The Guests*, a piece for one character, was written after I had seen, through the window of a flat in Barnes, a woman seated at a dining table laid for six, conducting an animated conversation with imaginary guests. The play was originally presented on television and I was fortunate to have the Woman acted by Margaret Leighton. Some years later, the version in this collection was produced in the theatre in Italy and Poland. The other plays collected here represent my attempts at writing plays specifically for the theatre.

The Ordeal of Gilbert Pinfold, a play based on the book by Evelyn Waugh, was important to me for several reasons. It was the first time I was able to free my imagination from the tyranny of the proscenium arch and from the political correctness of the 1960s. This was almost entirely due to the shape of the then newly-built Royal Exchange Theatre in Manchester where the play was to have its first performance.

My association with two of the Artistic Directors of the Royal Exchange, Casper Wrede and Michael Elliott, began when I was employed by them as a small-part actor in their 59 Theatre Company at the Lyric Theatre, Hammersmith. My first plays for television were directed by Wrede and because of him I joined a group of like-minded friends and colleagues who included Elliott, the actor James Maxwell and the designers Malcolm Pride and Richard Negri. We used to meet, all through the 1960s, to discuss the state of the theatre, to voice our discontents and our hopes and to attempt to seek solutions. Personally, during that decade I felt entirely isolated from the medium I most loved – which is, I now suppose, why I mostly wrote novels then. While I have always admired and marvelled at the great theatrical explosion detonated in Sloane Square at the Royal Court Theatre in 1956 with John Osborne's *Look Back in Anger*, I was not, nor could be, part of it. I was not and never have been a 'committed' playwright – to use the buzz word of that time – and I had no interest in writing about the English class system which, as a foreigner, I barely understood, but which most of the highly acclaimed plays of that period seemed to be about. This, I readily admit, may be wholly subjective and taste of sour grapes, but it is how I felt at the time and still feel. The group born out of the 59 Theatre Company offered a refuge and in due course a home.

Although many made a contribution to the concept of the Royal Exchange Theatre, Richard Negri was finally responsible for its magical design. It is a theatre-in-the-round, intimate and versatile. On first seeing this new playhouse, I was mysteriously liberated and determined to write a play that would explore and use the space as interestingly as possible. By chance, while on a visit to Helsinki, I came across a copy of *The Ordeal of Gilbert Pinfold*. I read it in one sitting and I was convinced that an adaptation for the theatre was possible. *Pinfold* provided me with my first success, largely due to Elliott's production and to a stunning performance by Michael Hordern.

It was the first time I worked with Michael Elliott. (He was later to direct *The Dresser* and *After the Lions*.) He was a great director, and I use the adjective advisedly. I have now worked with and, of course, observed a good many directors and there is no doubt in my mind that Elliott was the most gifted of his generation. No one in my experience so combined theatrical flair, intellectual vigour and a sense of service to the play. He was a complex man, quintessentially English, and although he was offered great theatrical prizes in London he chose to work in Manchester as if to dramatize his own sense of isolation. In no time at all, he and his colleagues had turned the Royal Exchange into an important theatrical centre. He died in 1984 at the age of fifty-two after an unsuccessful operation for a kidney transplant.

The genesis of *After The Lions* I owe to Margaret Leighton. Shortly after the transmission of *The Guests* she was diagnosed as having multiple sclerosis. My wife and I went to visit her. Although already finding it difficult to walk, she was in great form, courageous, witty, gloriously foul-mouthed and looking astonishingly beautiful. She said, 'Write me a play in which I'm in bed all the time or wheeled about in a chair. And do it quickly because God knows how long I've got.' I remembered Sarah Bernhardt's request to Edmund Rostand: 'Write me a play for a woman with one leg,' which Maggie had inadvertently echoed. The subject of Sarah Bernhardt's triumph over adversity seemed ideal, but by the time I had finished the piece Maggie, alas, was dead. Sarah was played with great energy and subtlety by Dorothy Tutin.

Of all my plays that have not succeeded with audiences, *Tramway Road* remains my favourite. Ostensibly it is about apartheid. But I wanted to extend the image of the outsider and hoped that the two expatriate misfits, Dora and Arthur Langley, based on a couple I remembered from my childhood, would help to dramatize the theme of alienation and of frustrated promise I was trying to explore. With hindsight, I realize that, in 1984 when the play was first performed, the savagery of apartheid was too immense to have attached to it an extended metaphor for any other sort of isolation.

In *Poison Pen* Tom Courtenay gave one of the best performances I have seen in the theatre for many a year. His misfortune was that I decided to direct the first production myself. I was of little help to him and the rest of the fine cast. I was told later by a friend that I didn't really understand the play; when I saw the first foreign production at the Stary Teatr in Krakow, I came to realize my friend was probably right. It was a great disappointment to me because, despite the clumsiness of the director, audiences seemed to be taken by the story and intrigued by the conflict of the creator and critic contained in one being.

At the time of writing this introduction, *Taking Sides* is about to go into rehearsal, which means I have neither heard the lines spoken nor, of course, seen the play with an audience; it is, therefore, impossible for me to know much about it. A play is not a play without an audience. To watch for the first time one's own play in the presence of an audience is to experience the piece quite differently: one sees, hears and feels it with the audience's perceptions and sensibilities and one knows very quickly whether or not it is working. All I can say, then, is that my intention was to focus on a dilemma which seems to belong hideously to the

twentieth century: the artist and the totalitarian state. Wilhelm
Furtwängler, to me, personifies that dilemma.

Ronald Harwood
London, January 1995

TAKING SIDES

For
Bernard Levin

Wilhelm Furtwängler (1886–1954) was the outstanding conductor of his generation, rivalled only by Arturo Toscanini. He was at the height of his powers when Adolf Hitler became Chancellor of Germany in 1933. Many of his colleagues, because they were Jews, were forced to leave; others, non-Jews, opponents of the regime, chose exile as an act of protest. Furtwängler decided to stay; as a result he was accused of serving Nazism. This was and still is the principal accusation made against him.

He came before a Denazification Tribunal in Berlin in 1946 which was conducted by his fellow Germans who questioned him for two days. He was cleared of all charges but was never able to cleanse himself entirely of the Nazi stench that still clings to his memory.

The Tribunal's evidence had been prepared in the first instance by the British, then taken over, apparently, by two groups of Americans: one, in Wiesbaden, which assisted Furtwängler with his defence; the other, in Berlin, which was responsible for building the case against him.

Little or nothing is known of the motives and methods of this second group which is the focus of *Taking Sides*. What is undeniable, however, is that Furtwängler was humiliated, relentlessly pursued and, after his acquittal, disinformation concerning him appeared in American newspapers. This may or may not have been justified. It all depends on the side you take.

CHARACTERS

MAJOR STEVE ARNOLD
EMMI STRAUBE
TAMARA SACHS
HELMUTH RODE
LIEUTENANT DAVID WILLS
WILHELM FURTWÄNGLER

The action takes place in Major Arnold's office
in the American Zone of occupied Berlin, 1946.

ACT ONE
February. Morning.

ACT TWO
Scene One: April. Night.
Scene Two: July. Morning.

SET

Major Arnold's office is an island surrounded by the rubble of a city flattened by Allied bombs. The room is in a former government building. Not everyone visiting the office need pass through the rubble. The office may also be reached from unseen approaches. The room is barely furnished but, incongruously, there is an ornate desk which Arnold uses. His German secretary, Emmi Straube, has a table, a typewriter and a field telephone. There is another smaller table with a record player and a pile of records.

Between Arnold's desk and Emmi's table stands a plain upright chair which is for those being questioned. Nearer Arnold's desk there is a rather more comfortable chair for visitors. There are double doors that lead to a waiting room. Another smaller door leads to a cupboard-like room which in turn leads to a back way out of the building. This room has a second telephone.

In Act Two, central heating radiators are in place and the telephone system has been streamlined.

Taking Sides was first performed at the Minerva Theatre, Chichester, on 18 May 1995 with the following cast:

MAJOR STEVE ARNOLD	Michael Pennington
EMMI STRAUBE	Geno Lechner
TAMARA SACHS	Suzanne Bertish
HELMUTH RODE	Gawn Grainger
LIEUTENANT DAVID WILLS	Christopher Simon
WILHELM FURTWÄNGLER	Daniel Massey

Directed by	Harold Pinter
Lighting by	Mick Hughes
Designer	Eileen Diss

The play (under the title *Za I Przeciw*) was performed on the same day in Poland at the Teatr im. Juliusza Slowackiego W. Krakowie with the following cast:

MAJOR STEVE ARNOLD	Marcin Kusminski
EMMI STRAUBE	Joanna Jankowska
TAMARA SACHS	Urszula Popiel
HELMUTH RODE	Mariusz Wojciechowski
PORUCZNIK DAVID WILLS	Marek Sawicki
WILHELM FURTWÄNGLER	Michal Pawlicki

Directed by	Tomasz Zygadio
Translator	Michal Ronikier
Designer	Jerzy Rudski

ACT ONE

*February. Just before 9 a.m. Freezing cold. One miserable wood-
burning stove. All wear overcoats, gloves, scarves. From the
gramophone in Major Steven Arnold's office comes the sound of the
last minutes of the final movement of Beethoven's Fifth Symphony,
conducted by Wilhelm Furtwängler.* ARNOLD *is asleep, his legs
stretched out on his desk. He could be any age, between thirty-five and
early fifties.*
EMMI STRAUBE *is at her table listening to the music and watching*
ARNOLD. *She is in her early twenties, pale, almost nondescript.*
In the bomb rubble, heavily wrapped up, like a vagrant, sits TAMARA
SACHS, *fortyish, waiting.*
HELMUTH RODE, *late forties, wearing threadbare clothes and a
Balaclava, enters the bomb-site. He starts rummaging for anything he
can find. Then he hears the music but cannot identify its source.*
LIEUTENANT DAVID WILLS, *aged twenty-four, enters purposefully
through the bomb rubble.* RODE *scuttles away.* DAVID *passes and
disappears around the back of the office.* TAMARA *barely glances at
him.*
The music continues. ARNOLD *sleeps.* EMMI *listens and watches. The
office door opens and* DAVID *reappears. He sees* ARNOLD *asleep and
retreats. After a moment, the music ends and* EMMI *takes off the
record.*
EMMI: Major Arnold, the music has ended.
    (*He doesn't stir; she gently shakes his shoe.*)
    Major Arnold?
    (*He wakes with a start, as if from a bad dream.*)
    The music has ended, Major.
    (*He breathes more easily.*)
ARNOLD: I wish you'd call me Steve, Emmi.
EMMI: You fell asleep.
ARNOLD: That's true, Emmi, I did.
EMMI: It is very difficult for me to understand how you can fall
    asleep during Beethoven's Fifth Symphony.
ARNOLD: Then I'll explain, Emmi. I fell asleep during

7

Beethoven's Fifth Symphony because Beethoven's Fifth
Symphony bores me shitless.

EMMI: You are joking again. Are you joking? I am never sure
when you are joking. I think you are always joking when you
are being coarse.

ARNOLD: No, Emmi, I am never joking when I'm being coarse.

EMMI: I don't like it when you are coarse.

ARNOLD: Then you must be having a really bad time of it, Emmi.

EMMI: You should listen to Beethoven carefully, Major. My
favourite is the Eighth Symphony. But you should listen
especially to the Ninth. Beethoven wrote it in his last years.
It is one of the most beautiful pieces of music ever written.
You should listen to it, Major.

ARNOLD: Is it the same length as Number Five? Or as he got
older did he write shorter?

EMMI: Yes, you are joking, but you must listen to it, Major.
That's why I have brought these recordings so that you
should know with whom you are dealing.

ARNOLD: I know with whom I'm dealing. (*He goes to the stove,
warms himself.*) I knew another band leader once. Name of
Dix Dixon. Small time. Alto sax. Not bad. Not good, but
not bad. Played one night stands in Illinois and Michigan. A
house he owned, where he and the band used to stay, burned
down. Lost everything. Well, almost everything. But I got
him. You know how? Because there's always one question
the guilty can't answer. Get a sign writer, write it big:
THERE'S ALWAYS ONE QUESTION THE GUILTY CAN'T
ANSWER. In Dix's case, it was, 'How come, Dix, everybody
lost everything except you? You've got your clothes, your
sax, how come?' Couldn't answer. He was dumb. Boy, was
he dumb. Owed the bookies. You understand, don't you,
Emmi? He burned down his own house for the insurance
money. We used to call that Jewish lightning.
(*He chuckles; no response from* EMMI.)
How many people do I have to see before the big boy's due?

EMMI: (*Consulting a file*) Just one. Helmuth Rode. Second
violinist, 1935 to the present. Also, there is a request from
Wiesbaden that you see a Mrs Tamara Sachs. I have talked to

her on the telephone and she will be coming at two o'clock.

ARNOLD: Anything from Wiesbaden's got to be bad news. What's this Mrs Sachs want?

EMMI: She wouldn't say. Oh, and, Major, a young officer put his head round the door a moment ago, saw that you were asleep and then disappeared. I suppose he knocked but I didn't hear him. The music –

ARNOLD: Who was he?

EMMI: I don't know. I have never seen him before. (*Consulting a message pad.*) And two other messages. Captain Vernay may visit later. Colonel Volkov will not be attending.

ARNOLD: That's a relief. Nothing from the British?

EMMI: No.

ARNOLD: Where's that young officer now?

EMMI: I don't know, he came and went.

ARNOLD: Go find him, will you, Emmi?

(EMMI *exits.* ARNOLD *adds wood to the heater. In the rubble,* RODE *re-appears, crosses the bomb-site, stops to pick up a cigarette butt and then hurries off towards the rear of* ARNOLD'S *office and disappears.* TAMARA *sits and waits.* EMMI *re-enters, holding the door for* DAVID *who comes to attention, salutes smartly.*)

DAVID: Lieutenant Wills reporting to Major Arnold. Sir.

ARNOLD: For Chrissakes I hate that shit, cut it out. My name's Steve. What's yours?

DAVID: (*Slightly disconcerted*) David. David Wills.

ARNOLD: Who are you?

DAVID: I've taken over from Captain Greenwood. I'm your new liaison officer with Allied Intelligence.

ARNOLD: What happened to Hank?

DAVID: Captain Greenwood was ordered to Nürnberg. Seems they need more interpreters at the trial.

ARNOLD: So you're dealing with the British now.

DAVID: Yes, sir.

ARNOLD: You call me sir again, I'll make you listen to Beethoven. (DAVID *only half smiles.*)

You seen that Limey major yet, the one who talks like he's got ice cubes in his mouth? I can't tell if he's speaking German or English, what the hell's his name?

9

DAVID: Major Richards.

ARNOLD: Yeah, Alan Richards.

DAVID: I talked to him this morning but he was just rushing off to an urgent meeting.

ARNOLD: An urgent meeting. Yeah, the Hinkel Archive.

DAVID: Yes.

ARNOLD: Do you know what's in the Hinkel Archive?

DAVID: No.

ARNOLD: And if it turns out to be important, you think the British are going to share it with their allies?

DAVID: Major Richards said he'd telephone the moment a decision has been taken. He said he was very disappointed. He wanted to be here today. Especially today.

(ARNOLD *eyes him up and down*.)

ARNOLD: We recruiting children now?

DAVID: (*A smile*) I guess so.

ARNOLD: Where you from?

DAVID: I was born here.

(ARNOLD *smiles, waits, gives no help*.)

Not in Berlin. In Hamburg.

(*Still no help from* ARNOLD.)

I escaped in '34. When I was twelve.

(*Pause*.)

My parents sent me to my uncle in Philadelphia. They were to follow. But they delayed and delayed. They did not follow.

(*Nothing from* ARNOLD.)

Our family name is Weill. But that doesn't sound well in English. My uncle changed it to Wills.

ARNOLD: Did you hear that, Emmi? David here was born in Hamburg.

EMMI: Yes, I heard.

ARNOLD: I'm sorry about your parents.

(*Uneasy pause*.)

Oh, this is Emmi Straube. She records the interviews. She's been with me a week. She's a good German, aren't you, Emmi? Her father was in the plot against Adolf.

(*Pause*.)

Well, what kind of an intelligence officer are you, David?
You should have asked a question. You should have asked,
'But how do we know she didn't report her father for being
in the plot against Adolf?' Isn't that what he should've asked,
Emmi?
(*No response.*)
Emmi's okay. We've checked her out. You're okay, aren't
you, Emmi?

EMMI: Shall I see if Mr Rode is here? It's after nine.

ARNOLD: When I say so, Emmi, when I say so. (*To* DAVID.) I like
to keep them waiting. Makes them sweat. Which is a
kindness in this weather, wouldn't you say?

EMMI: I expect Mr Rode's here, Major.

ARNOLD: She won't call me Steve, David. She is so correct. And
she likes books and poetry and she's just crazy for
Beethoven, aren't you, Emmi? Do you like Beethoven,
David?

DAVID: Yes.

ARNOLD: Yes. I thought you looked funny when I threatened you
with the old bastard. And I guess you admire musicians.

DAVID: Some.

ARNOLD: Don't.

DAVID: Don't what?

ARNOLD: This is like a criminal investigation, David. Musicians,
morticians, lawyers, butchers, doctors, clerks. They're all
the same. I saw Bergen-Belsen two days after it was
liberated. I know what I'm talking about. I've seen things
with these eyes – do you know what I'm talking about,
David?

DAVID: Yes.

ARNOLD: Think of your parents. Don't think of musicians. We're
after the big guy here, the band leader, that's the one we're
going to nail. You know what I call him, David? I call him a
piece of shit. I call 'em all pieces of shit.

DAVID: Captain Greenwood said hard evidence against him is
difficult to come by.

ARNOLD: Let's talk about it after we get through with this guy
Rode. Here's how we do it. This is my show, I ask the

questions. If you want to ask a question, raise a finger so he can't see. I'll signal yea or nay. Understood?

DAVID: Yes.

ARNOLD: I'll explain my technique. I tell the shitheads why they're here. Then I only ever ask two questions. First, anything that comes to mind. 'How you feeling today?', 'Are you getting enough to eat?', 'You need some cigarettes?' Real friendly. Second, I say, 'I see from your questionnaire that you were never a member of the Party, is that right?' 'Absolutely right, I was never a member of the Party.' And then I wait. I say nothing. I wait. And then they talk. Oh, boy, do they talk. And they'll tell you what a great guy the band leader is, how he defied Adolf and Hermann and Josef. Oh yes, and they always get in the baton story.

DAVID: What's the baton story?

ARNOLD: How many have I questioned, Emmi?

EMMI: Twenty-eight.

ARNOLD: So this guy?

EMMI: Helmuth Rode –

ARNOLD: Rode, he'll be the twenty-ninth. You'll hear the baton story for the first time, I'm going to hear it for the twenty-ninth. Oh yeah, and they always manage to find out Emmi's last name, don't they, Emmi? Straube, they say. Any relation to Joachim Straube? My father, Emmi says. A great man, they say, a great hero. You see, David, what they're trying to do is cover the band leader in roses in the hope they'll come up smelling just as sweet. But it's difficult to smell sweet after you've crawled through raw sewage. I was in insurance before the war, a claims assessor, what were you in?

DAVID: College.

ARNOLD: And when all this is over?

DAVID: I'd like to teach history.

ARNOLD: History. You need a good memory for history, don't you? All those dates and battles. Your memory good?

DAVID: Not bad –

ARNOLD: Me, I've got a terrific memory. I've been examined by psychologists. Because of my memory, nothing else. I've got what they call 'total recall'. I remember everything. But only if I'm interested. It's a curse. (*Suddenly as if briefly invaded by a memory which he shakes off.*) Yeah, a curse, believe me. But I'm bad at names. It's what the shrinks call 'selective'. Tell you the truth, my recall's not total, but it's pretty good. Yeah, insurance. I was trained by a guy called Lou O'Donnell, a kind of Jimmy Cagney type. Pushy, smart, persistent, boy, was that guy persistent. Lou taught me to look out for what he called 'repetitive evidence', because ninety-nine times out of a hundred it covers a conspiracy to defraud. You think a whole orchestra, what, a hundred and twenty or so guys, could be orchestrated?

DAVID: I don't know, I guess it's possible –

ARNOLD: Yeah, me too, I guess it's possible. Okay, Emmi, let's get Mr Rode in.

(EMMI *exits.*)

You sit there.

(DAVID *sits and* ARNOLD *goes to his desk.*)

Remember, I do the talking. Just the two questions, then we wait. You'll see.

(EMMI *re-enters.*)

EMMI: Mr Helmuth Rode.

(RODE *enters, removes his Balaclava, bows to* ARNOLD *and* DAVID. EMMI *sits at her table and takes notes.* RODE *glances nervously round, twists his neck to read the record labels.*)

ARNOLD: Sit down, Helmuth.

(RODE *sits;* ARNOLD *consults a file.*)

I want you to understand why you're here. This is a preliminary investigation into Wilhelm Furtwängler, former Prussian Privy Councillor, who is banned from public life under Control Council Directive No. 24 and who's applied to come before the Tribunal of Artists of the Denazification Commission. We're interested in what he was up to from 1933 to the end of the war, understood?

RODE: Yes.

ARNOLD: I have your questionnaire here. (*Reading.*) Helmuth Alfred Rode. Second violinist, Berlin Philharmonic Orchestra since 1935. What's it mean, second violinist, Helmuth?

RODE: It means I wasn't good enough to be a first violinist.
(*He chuckles, looks round for approval;* ARNOLD *grins encouragingly.*)
Mind you, you have to be pretty good just to be a second violinist in the Berlin Philharmonic. Even though I say so myself.

ARNOLD: And according to your questionnaire, Helmuth, you never joined the Party.

RODE: Me? Never. Never.
(*Long silence;* ARNOLD *just watches him and waits.*)
I hated them. Believe me, please, I know everyone says now they were never Nazis, but in my case it is absolutely one hundred per cent true. I am a Catholic, a convert, it would have been totally against my conscience.
(*Silence.*)
It's difficult to explain what it was like. Terror, that's what you felt from morning till night, even asleep, you felt terror.
(*Brief silence.*)
In the early days, of course, we were much more open in opposition. I'm talking about '33, '34. When I think back on the things I said, I shudder. My God, I used to tell jokes, anti-Hitler jokes, I was well known for my anti-Hitler jokes. For example, this joke, it was very famous around '33, '34. A couple of old Jews. One says to the other, 'I have two bits of news for you, one good, one bad.' 'Tell me the good news first.' 'Hitler's dead.' 'And the bad news?' 'It isn't true.'
(*He chuckles; looks round; nothing from the others.*)
That's the sort of joke I used to tell.
(*Silence; he wipes sweat from his brow.*)
You want to know about Dr Furtwängler? This man is without doubt one of the most courageous people it has been my honour to know. We all acknowledge he is a god among musicians. In my humble, second violinist opinion, the greatest conductor alive. True, I have not played under Arturo Toscanini but I have heard his recordings, and the emotion is not the same. Toscanini is a metronome. Dr Furtwängler is an artist. No, no. Wilhelm Furtwängler is unquestionably a genius, without equal.

(*Silence; he loosens his coat, wipes his brow again.*)
Is it true you're going to interview him today?
(*Silence.*)
Berlin is so full of rumours. I heard –
(*Silence; smiles.*)
You hear things all the time. If rumours were edible we'd all
be well fed. If I may say so, I hope you see to it that he's
properly guarded. There are so many crazy people about.
(*Silence.*)
He gave comfort in terrible times, what man can do more?
(*Silence.*)
Here's something that may interest you. On a famous
occasion, I think it was the second Winter Assistance charity
programme, an all Beethoven concert, this was in '35, it was
suddenly announced that Hitler himself was going to attend.
Well, you can imagine, the Maestro was outraged. You know
how angry he was? He ripped the wooden covering off the
radiator in his dressing room, that's how angry he was.
Because what could he do? He couldn't tell Hitler not to
attend.
(*Chuckles, looks round, silence.*)
You see, the problem was the Nazi salute. He absolutely
refused to give it. Now this I heard him say with my own
ears, I heard him say, 'I don't have to acknowledge him at
all,' over and over again, I heard him say that. But how could
he avoid giving the Devil's salute with Satan actually present
in the audience? You know who came up with a solution?
(*Modestly taps his chest with his thumb.*) I said, 'Maestro, why
not enter with your baton in your right hand? Hitler will be
sitting in the front row. If you give the salute with the baton
in your hand, it'll look like you're going to poke his eyes
out.' (*Chuckles.*) He was really grateful to me for that
suggestion. He came on to the podium, baton in his right
hand which meant he couldn't give the salute. He just bowed
quickly, turned immediately to us, and even while the
audience was still applauding he gave the signal to begin.
(*Smiles fondly at the memory.*) I tell you in confidence, after
the concert, I did something disreputable. I stole that baton.

As a memento of a great act of courage. I still have it. I
should have brought it to show you.

(*Silence.*)

Mind you, it was always a joke in the orchestra. The
Maestro's baton. He has a very eccentric technique. (*Stands
and demonstrates.*) He waves, he sways, he jiggles. God knows
when you're meant to come in. His downbeat was always the
subject of jokes. Other musicians used to ask us, how do you
know when to play the first chord of the 'Eroica'? When his
baton reaches the third stud on his shirt, we'd say. Or, how
do you know when to start the semiquavers at the beginning
of the Ninth? We used to tell them, the moment the Maestro
enters, we all walk round our chairs three times, sit down,
count to ten and play. Or. When we lose patience. (*Chuckles,
sits again; silence.*) Yet he can produce musical sounds like no
other human being alive. (*To* EMMI.) I hope I'm not going
too fast for you, Miss – ?

EMMI: Straube.

RODE: Straube. Any relation to Colonel Joachim Straube?

EMMI: My father.

(RODE *rises.*)

RODE: I am deeply honoured to be in your presence, Miss
Straube. Your father was a true patriot. A man of God.
Requiescat in pacem. (*He crosses himself; sits; silence.*) And all
this nonsense about the Maestro being a Prussian Privy
Councillor. The Fat One – that was our name for Hermann
Göring, The Fat One – he simply *made* the Maestro a Privy
Councillor. The Fat One just conferred the title, by
telegram, just like that. There was nothing to be done about
it.

(*Silence.*)

And the other one, Apollo. That was our name for Josef
Goebbels. Not because he was handsome, God help us, but
because he looked like a Polish Jew. A-Pol – Apoll – (*He
can't make the joke work.*) That's the sort of joke we used to
make. I realize now it's in very bad taste and I apologize.
Anyway, when Goebbels formed the Chamber of Music
which was to control all musical life in this country, he made

Dr Furtwängler Vice-President. It was the same thing. He was simply appointed. But you know who was President? Richard Strauss.

(*Silence.*)

No, no, I want to say categorically that Wilhelm Furtwängler did not serve the regime. None of us who were members of his orchestra served the regime. Forgive me if I make a philosophical observation, but Wilhelm Furtwängler is a symbol to the entire world of all that is great in culture and music and the Nazis needed him. They needed him to make themselves respectable.

(*Silence.*)

(DAVID *raises a discreet finger.*)

ARNOLD: You have a question for Helmuth, David?

DAVID: Yes. There's a photograph, isn't there, Mr Rode, of Dr Furtwängler shaking hands with Hitler. How do you explain that?

RODE: But that's the concert I was talking about, the all Beethoven programme, when he came on with his baton in his right hand to avoid giving the salute. As I said, Hitler was in the front row and at the end of the concert, he suddenly stood up, went to the platform and offered the Maestro his hand. And the Maestro took it, what else could he do? That's all there was to it. I was there. I witnessed it. It was probably a calculated act, not spontaneous at all, because they wanted the Maestro on their side, of course they did, and so they had photographers there, and what could the Maestro do, he simply had to shake Satan's hand? That's all there is to it.

(DAVID *is about to ask another question but* ARNOLD *signals him to wait.*)

And he did not conduct *The Mastersingers* at the Party Congress in Nürnberg in 1935. We played it the evening *before* the Congress. The music was quite separate from the politics. That is the Maestro's creed: politics and art must be kept separate. It's the same with the Devil's birthday. It was the evening before, 19th April, not the 20th. And the Maestro was tricked into it. Usually, when they wanted him to conduct on such occasions, he managed to get his doctors to diagnose spondylitis – inflammation of the vertebrae in the back and neck, common in conductors, and very, very painful. But for Satan's birthday in 1942, Apollo got to the doctors first and that was that. (*Brief pause*.) And don't forget, please, the Maestro had to flee to Switzerland only last year, just before the war ended, because he learned that the Gestapo were about to arrest him. This is an honest, good man we are talking about. And the greatest conductor alive. (*Again* DAVID *raises a finger.* ARNOLD *nods*.)

DAVID: Mr Rode, you only joined the Berlin Philharmonic in 1935. Where were you before that?

RODE: (*Uneasy*) I was a member of another orchestra. In Mannheim. But in 1935, several vacancies arose in Berlin. I auditioned – (*Loses confidence. Becomes agitated*.) Yes, yes, but on the other hand Dr Furtwängler, personally, was very good to Jews. He helped a lot of Jews escape, Jews who were no longer allowed to be members of the orchestra, although he fought to retain them for as long as he could. His secretary, Berta Geissmar, was a Jewess. He relied so much on her. In the end, he had to help her to escape, too. She is now, I believe, in England, secretary to Sir Thomas Beecham. He's also a conductor but he is not Dr Furtwängler.

ARNOLD: Helmuth, do you know Hans Hinkel?

RODE: (*Alarmed*) Do I know Hans Hinkel?

ARNOLD: That's what I asked.

RODE: Do I know Hans Hinkel?

ARNOLD: You seem to understand the question, Helmuth, now how about answering it?

RODE: But how could I know such a man? Hans Hinkel was in the Ministry of Culture, how could I know such a man? (*Silence*.)
I hear he kept this archive, files, records – (*Fishing*.) Do you know what's in the archive, Major?

ARNOLD: I was just going to ask you that, Helmuth.

RODE: Me? How should I know what's in the archive? (*Silence*.)
The only thing I've heard is that there are letters from people

swearing loyalty to the regime, that's all I know.
(*Silence.*)
My personal, second violinist opinion, for what it's worth, is
that Hinkel was in fact a very low level functionary, his
archive won't have anything of interest.
(*Silence.*)

ARNOLD: Okay, you can go now, Helmuth.

RODE: That's it?

ARNOLD: Get out, Helmuth.
(RODE *rises, bows to all three and goes to the double doors. As he
opens them he stops dead, bows deeply to someone in the waiting
room.*)

RODE: (*Awed*) Maestro!
(EMMI *rises involuntarily as* RODE *exits, beaming, closing the
door.*)

EMMI: (*Equally awed, going to the door*) He's here, Major –

ARNOLD: Sit down, Emmi.
(*She sits.*)
We're going to keep him waiting, too. (*To* DAVID.) So now
you know the baton story, David.

DAVID: Yes, but Captain Greenwood is right. When it comes to
hard evidence –

ARNOLD: (*Interrupting*) Get us some coffee, Emmi, will you? And,
Emmi, don't offer coffee to the leader of the band. Don't
even greet him, okay?
(EMMI *goes.*)
Jesus, when are they going to fix the central heating? My
scrotum feels like a shrivelled prune. Probably looks like
one, too.
(*He goes out through the second door.* RODE *hurries across the
rubble.* TAMARA *stops him, questions him, then both disappear,
quickly in opposite directions,* TAMARA, *like a fury, towards the
office. During this* DAVID *looks round, sees the records, flicks
through them.* ARNOLD *returns carrying some wood which he
adds to the stove.*)

ARNOLD: Let me tell you something, David, the evidence, hard
or soft, doesn't matter, because I have the one question he's
going to find it impossible to answer.

DAVID: And what's that, Major?

(*A commotion in the waiting room. A woman's voice shouting.* ARNOLD *goes towards the door but* EMMI *comes rushing in, highly agitated.*)

EMMI: There's a woman attacking Dr Furtwängler, I don't know who she is, she's crazy –

ARNOLD: Emmi, Emmi.

(*She stops but the noise outside continues.*)

Where's our coffee?

(TAMARA *bursts into the room like an avenging angel. She is prematurely grey, intense, driven.*)

TAMARA: This is an outrage, who's in charge, I have to see who's in charge –

(*Overlapping, confused, and at speed.*)

ARNOLD: Get out of here, who the hell –

TAMARA: Do you know who's sitting out there – ?

ARNOLD: Emmi, call the guard –

TAMARA: Wilhelm Furtwängler is sitting out there –

(EMMI *makes for the door but* TAMARA *grabs* EMMI *and starts to shake her.*)

TAMARA: You're crazy, you're all crazy, you don't know what you're doing –

ARNOLD: David, get hold of her –

(DAVID *tries to grab her but she turns on him and starts pounding him with her fists.*)

TAMARA: You can't do this, you can't do this –

(*Just as suddenly she stops, tries to catch her breath, forlorn, distraite.* EMMI *tries not to whimper.*)

I'm sorry. When I saw him, I lost all control. Everything went out of my mind.

ARNOLD: Why don't you sit down for a moment, I'll call a medic –

TAMARA: No, no. I have to talk to you. Are you in charge?

ARNOLD: Who are you?

TAMARA: My name is Tamara Sachs.

ARNOLD: (*To* EMMI) Isn't this the one I'm seeing at two?

(TAMARA *begins to cry.*)

DAVID: Sit down, Miss Sachs.

TAMARA: Mrs Sachs.

DAVID: Emmi, could you find a glass of water for Mrs Sachs?

ARNOLD: Hold it, Emmi. David –

    (*Draws* DAVID *aside; hissed.*)

    I want her out of here, she's crazy, you can see, she's crazy –

TAMARA: I have something of importance to tell you about
    Wilhelm Furtwängler.

    (*Silence.*)

DAVID: Please sit down, Mrs Sachs.

    (TAMARA *sits.*)

ARNOLD: Okay, Emmi, get us all some coffee.

    (EMMI *exits quickly.*)

TAMARA: I told them about it in Wiesbaden. They said I must tell
    you. Then I heard you were interviewing him today. I have
    material evidence to give.

    (ARNOLD *considers for a moment.*)

ARNOLD: Okay. But just wait for my secretary to come back so
    she can take a record.

    (*Silence.*)

TAMARA: You see, I am trying to find some proof that my
    husband, Walter Sachs, existed.

    (*Silence.*)

    Dr Furtwängler may be able to provide that proof. I've
    been waiting since the early hours. Then, when I actually saw
    him – (*She is lost for a moment.*) Could he come in, please?

ARNOLD: No, he can't come in.

DAVID: Was your husband a friend of his?

TAMARA: No. My husband, Walter Sachs, was the most
    promising young pianist of his generation.

DAVID: Were they colleagues, perhaps?

TAMARA: No. That's just the point.

    (EMMI *returns with a tray of coffee and cups, flustered but
    pleased, a little excited.*)

EMMI: Dr Furtwängler spoke to me. He wants to know how long
    he is to be kept waiting.

ARNOLD: Emmi, put the coffee down, then go out there and tell
    him in these words, these exact words, mind, tell him,
    'You'll wait until Major Arnold's ready to see you or until

hell freezes over, whichever takes longer.' You got that, Emmi? And don't say anything else, okay?

TAMARA: Can't he come in, please?

ARNOLD: Go on, Emmi. Then come back and take notes. I'll do the coffee.

(EMMI *goes out*.)

Tamara, how do you take your coffee?

TAMARA: Is there cream and sugar?

ARNOLD: There is in the American Zone.

(*He serves her coffee;* EMMI *returns, sits at her table*.)

Okay, Tamara, let's hear what you have to say. You handle this, David. You and Tamara seem to have a certain – rapport. I'll just sit here and listen.

DAVID: Whatever you say, Mrs Sachs, will be treated as confidential.

TAMARA: But I don't want it treated as confidential. I want the world to know.

DAVID: When I asked if your husband and Dr Furtwängler were colleagues, you said, 'No, that's just the point.' What did you mean exactly?

TAMARA: (*Distraught*) I can't remember what I wanted to say now. It's gone out of my mind. (*She rummages in her handbag*.) I have a list here, why did I bring this list?

DAVID: Perhaps it would help if I asked you questions –

TAMARA: I think Dr Furtwängler is the only man who can give me proof that my husband existed.

DAVID: How could he do that?

TAMARA: I've not been well. For some years now I've not been well. After they took Walter – we were in Paris at the time – I returned to be near my mother. My father was with the army of occupation in Denmark. I shall be thirty-three next birthday, look at my hair – (*She holds out a strand of hair*.) I'm trying to return to France but the French authorities are not helpful. I want to die in Paris. It was the only place we were happy.

ARNOLD: (*Gently*) Tamara, where are you staying? Because I'll have you taken back there and then I can get a doctor to you, and –

TAMARA: (*To* DAVID, *ignoring* ARNOLD) I was a philosophy
  student in 1932, at the University here in Berlin. I was
  eighteen years old. I was taken to a recital in a private house
  to hear a young pianist. The house belonged to Dr Myra
  Samuel, who was a famous piano teacher of the time. The
  young pianist was Walter Sachs, aged seventeen. A year
  younger than me. I fell in love with him just listening to him
  play. He was very beautiful. We were married. He was a
  Jew. I am not. My maiden name was Müller.

ARNOLD: Just tell us how Dr Furtwängler figures in all this.

TAMARA: It's an outrage what you are doing, you know.

ARNOLD: What are we doing?

TAMARA: Behaving like them.

DAVID: What happened to your husband, Mrs Sachs?

TAMARA: He died. In Auschwitz. That's in Poland. I don't know
  the exact date.

DAVID: And Dr Furtwängler?

TAMARA: We were tipped off that my husband was to be arrested
  within the week. We had no money, no influence. We went
  rushing round to Myra Samuel. We asked for help. She said
  she'd see what she could do. That evening she sent a
  message: be at such-and-such an address at midnight. It was
  a cellar, once a nightclub but closed down. We were
  terrified. We knocked. Dr Samuel opened the door and
  admitted us. There was only one other person there. 'This is
  Wilhelm Furtwängler,' she said. 'He will listen to you play.'
  There was an old upright piano, a Bechstein, out of tune.
  Walter sat down and played no more than three minutes of
  the 'Waldstein' Sonata. Dr Furtwängler suddenly stood. He
  said, 'I will try to help,' and left quickly. The very next day
  we received an official permit to leave. We took the train to
  Paris and we were happy again. Walter began to make a
  name for himself. Then. June, 1940. They took Walter
  away. I am not Jewish. My maiden name was Müller – (*She
  suddenly remembers something, becomes agitated*.) Yes, yes, I
  have this list – (*Rummages in her handbag again, produces
  sheets of paper.*) I remember now, these are some of the other
  people he helped, Jews and non-Jews he helped. (*Reading.*)

Ludwig Misch, Felix Lederer, Josef Krips, Arnold Schönberg, dozens and dozens of people he helped. He helped Walter Sachs, my husband, undoubtedly the finest pianist of his generation, I'll find out more, I'll keep asking, I'll write letters, I'll give evidence, because I know what you want to do, you want to destroy him, isn't that true? You want to burn him at the stake –

DAVID: No, we're just trying to find out the truth –

TAMARA: How can you find out the truth? There's no such thing. Who's truth? The victors? The vanquished? The victims? The dead? Whose truth? No, no. You have only one duty. To determine who is good and who is evil. That's all there is to it. To destroy one good man now is to make the future impossible. Don't behave like them, please. I know what I'm talking about, the good are few and far between. You must honour the good, especially if they are few. Like Dr Furtwängler. And the children of the good. Like Miss Straube.

ARNOLD: Gee, Emmi, you're really famous in this city.

TAMARA: I want to see him, please. I want to know if he remembers Walter. I want to know if he remembers that night Walter played the opening of the 'Waldstein' Sonata on an out-of-tune Bechstein upright piano in a Berlin cellar.

(DAVID *looks enquiringly at* ARNOLD.)

ARNOLD: Tamara, not today. We have to talk to your benefactor first, you see?

TAMARA: You're going to set fire to him, aren't you?

ARNOLD: Ah, c'mon, Tamara, I'm only an investigating officer. I don't have the power to set fire to anybody. Even if I wanted to. Which I don't. Believe me. Here's what we'll do. Emmi's going to take you out the back way and she's going to get Sergeant Bonelli to drive you to wherever you want to go. (*Writes on a piece of paper.*) This is my number. I want you to call me if you need anything, I mean anything, food, cigarettes, medicine, anything, okay? How's that sound?

TAMARA: It sounds as if you're going to burn him.

ARNOLD: Emmi, take Tamara out the back way.

(EMMI *starts to take* TAMARA *to the door but* TAMARA *stops*.)

TAMARA: Would you like this list? I have a copy.

ARNOLD: You keep it, Tamara, and the copy. But thanks a lot.

(*She goes quickly followed by* EMMI. ARNOLD *gives a yelp of triumph.*)

Jesus Christ! Are we going to nail him! We're going to nail him good and proper –

(*He stops, noticing* DAVID's *bewildered expression.*)

You don't see it, do you?

DAVID: No, I don't see how a list of people whom he's supposed to have helped –

ARNOLD: (*Interrupting*) You don't? You don't see it? Oh. Tamara, Tamara, I love you. And if I didn't lust after Emmi Straube, I'd lust after you. God bless you, Tamara Sachs!

DAVID: I wish you'd explain –

ARNOLD: David, last month I was in Vienna. I had with me an Austrian driver, Max his name was, he'd done time in the camps. We were looking at these Viennese cleaning up the bomb damage, scavenging for rotting food, butt ends, anything. I said, 'To think, a million of these people came out to welcome Adolf on the day he entered the city, a million of them, and now look at 'em.' And Max said, 'Oh not these people, Major. These people were all at home hiding Jews in their attics.' You get the point, David? The point is they're all full of shit.

DAVID: If I may say so, Major, I think Dr Furtwängler's in a different category. He is, after all, one of the most famous conductors in the world –

ARNOLD: (*Interrupting*) I'm going to tell you another story, David. Before I got this assignment, I was at Ike's headquarters, interrogating prisoners of war. Then they sent for me. They said, 'You ever heard of Wilhelm Furtwängler?' 'No,' I said. 'You heard of Toscanini?' 'Sure,' I said. 'You heard of Stockowski?' 'Yeah,' I said, 'I heard of him, old guy with white hair, looks like Harpo Marx's grandpa.' 'That's the one,' they said, 'and this guy Furtwängler's bigger than both of them.' 'I get it,' I said, 'the guy's a band leader.' They laughed, oh boy, they really laughed. They said, well, he may be more than that, Steve, in this neck of the woods he's probably Bob Hope and Betty Grable rolled into one. 'Jeez,' I said, 'and I never heard of him.' And you know what they said next? They said, 'Steve, that's why you get the job.'

DAVID: Who's 'they', Major?

ARNOLD: Who's they what?

DAVID: Who's the 'they' that sent for you? Who's the 'they' that gave you this assignment?

ARNOLD: There's no 'the they', David. I'm just doing my job. And always remember we're dealing here with degenerates, that's all you got to remember. I seen things with these eyes – (*He shudders.* DAVID *watches him.*)

DAVID: Major –

ARNOLD: Steve, c'mon, please –

DAVID: Don't treat me as if I'm not on your side.

ARNOLD: Well, I do that, David, because I don't yet know what side you're on.

DAVID: I think that's insulting –

ARNOLD: Tough. Hank Greenwood gave me the same feeling. He was interested in justice, evidence, facts. I'm interested in nailing the bastard –

(EMMI *returns.*)

Did Bonelli find her transport?

EMMI: Yes.

ARNOLD: Okay. This is it. Emmi, go get him.

(EMMI *exits.*)

Same rules of engagement. I'll explain why he's here, then I'll ask two questions. And then we'll wait. (*Sits at his desk.*) Oh boy, have I been looking forward to this.

(EMMI *re-appears.*)

EMMI: Dr Wilhelm Furtwängler.

(WILHELM FURTWÄNGLER, *wearing a well-cut but worn overcoat, enters. He is sixty, arrogant and remote but at the moment irritated at having been kept waiting. As he passes her,* EMMI *gives him a small curtsey, no more than a bob.* DAVID *inclines his head, a sort of bow.* FURTWÄNGLER *glances round, sees the visitor's chair and sits in it.* ARNOLD *looks up.*)

ARNOLD: Wilhelm, I didn't hear anyone invite you to sit down.

(FURTWÄNGLER *stands;* ARNOLD *points to the other chair.*)

Sit there.

(FURTWÄNGLER *sits in the witness chair.*)

I'm Steve Arnold. This is David Wills.

(ARNOLD *consults a file.*)

Now, Wilhelm, I want you to understand why you're here. You're automatically banned from public life under Control Council Directive No. 24. We're looking into your case before you appear in front of the Tribunal of Artists of the Denazification Commission. You understand that?

FURTWÄNGLER: I have already been cleared by a denazification tribunal in Austria.

ARNOLD: What they do in Austria doesn't interest me one little bit. Okay? I have your questionnaire here. (*Reading.*) Gustav Heinrich Ernst Martin Wilhelm Furtwängler, born Berlin, January, 1886. Orchestral conductor. And you say here you never joined the Party.

FURTWÄNGLER: That is correct.

(*A very long silence;* ARNOLD *waits; nothing from* FURTWÄNGLER; *when the silence is unbearable* ARNOLD *explodes.*)

ARNOLD: Jesus Christ, aren't you going to tell us about carrying your baton in your right hand so you wouldn't have to salute and poke Adolf's eyes out?

(*Nothing from* FURTWÄNGLER.)

And aren't you going to tell us about being a Prussian Privy Councillor? How did that happen to a non-Party member?

FURTWÄNGLER: I received a telegram from Hermann Göring who was Prime Minister of Prussia, this was in 1933, informing me that he had made me a Privy Councillor. I was not given the opportunity either to accept or to refuse. After the dreadful events of November, '38, the violent attacks against Jews, I stopped using the title.

ARNOLD: Great, great, you stopped using the title, and what about Vice-President of the Chamber of Music, you used that title didn't you, but then I suppose you had no choice there either, because I suppose Josef just sent you a telegram saying, Dear Mr Vice-President.

FURTWÄNGLER: No. I don't think Goebbels sent me a telegram. I

27

was simply told. In a letter, I think. I don't remember exactly –

ARNOLD: You don't remember exactly, okay, but, hell, Hermann and Josef were sure heaping honours on you. One makes you a Privy Councillor, the other makes you Vice-President of the Chamber of Music, and you weren't even a member of the Party, how do you explain that?

FURTWÄNGLER: There was a constant battle between Göring and Goebbels as to which of them would control Nazi culture. People like me, and Richard Strauss, were simply in the middle. We were pawns. Anyway, I resigned from the Chamber of Music at the same time as I resigned as Musical Director of the Berlin Philharmonic Orchestra. In 1934.

DAVID: Why was that? Why did you resign, Dr Furtwängler?

(ARNOLD *shoots* DAVID *a sharp look of annoyance*.)

FURTWÄNGLER: They came to power in January '33. In April, I wrote an open letter to the newspapers condemning what they were doing to music, making these distinctions between Jews and Non-Jews. For my part, the only divide in art is between good and bad. Great artists are rare, I said, and no country can do without them unless it wishes to damage its cultural life irrevocably. I also said that men like Otto Klemperer, Bruno Walter, Max Reinhardt, I may have mentioned others, I don't remember now, must be allowed to serve their art here in this country.

DAVID: And then you resigned?

FURTWÄNGLER: No, not then. Those were early days. No, the matter came to a head when Goebbels decided to ban *Mathis the Painter*, an opera by Paul Hindemith. They called it Jew-infected Bolshevik music, or some such nonsense. Again I wrote to the newspapers. Again I criticized them. Goebbels retaliated with a speech in which he denounced me for what he called 'my disloyalty to the regime'. That's when I resigned. I resigned everything. I simply withdrew from public life and started composing again, which I'd always thought was my true vocation. Eventually, after much toing and froing, I was summoned by Goebbels. He said I could leave the country if I wanted to but under no condition would I ever be allowed to return. That would have been a victory for them. I believe you have to fight from inside not from without. He then demanded I acknowledge Hitler as solely responsible for cultural policy. Well, that was a fact. He was the sole arbiter and it seemed to me pointless to deny it. In return, I demanded I be allowed to stay here, to work, but I would not be obliged to accept any official position. Nor would I have to perform at state functions. I have always held the view that art and politics should have nothing to do with each other.

ARNOLD: Oh, really? Then why did you conduct at one of their Nürnberg rallies?

FURTWÄNGLER: (*Flaring*) I did not conduct at the rally, I conducted on the evening *before* the rally –

ARNOLD: That sounds like the small print in one of our insurance policies, Wilhelm –

FURTWÄNGLER: I had nothing to do with the rally.

ARNOLD: And what about April 19, 1942? The eve of Adolf's fifty-third birthday, the big night, the big celebration, you conducted for Adolf, didn't you? Was that in keeping with your view that art and politics have nothing to do with each other?

FURTWÄNGLER: (*Flustered*) That was a different matter –

ARNOLD: I'll believe that –

FURTWÄNGLER: I was tricked –

ARNOLD: How come?

FURTWÄNGLER: I was in Vienna, rehearsing Beethoven's Ninth with the Viennese Philharmonic when Goebbels called and said I had to conduct at Hitler's birthday. Always, I'd managed to wriggle out of such invitations, pleading previous engagements, illness, and so on. I was also fortunate that Baldur von Schirach, who controlled Vienna, hated Goebbels and would do anything to thwart his wishes. He had often helped me in the past by saying, for example, that he had the prior claim on my services. But on this particular occasion, in 1942, Goebbels got to my doctors before me, they were frightened off, and von Schirach was threatened and bullied and gave in. I had no alternative but

to conduct for Hitler. Believe me, I knew I had
compromised, and I deeply regret it.

ARNOLD: (*Playing with him*) Von Schirach, von Schirach. Is that
the same Baldur von Schirach, the Nazi Youth Leader,
who's now sitting in the dock at Nürnberg, on trial for his
life, charged with crimes against humanity?
(*No response.*)
So that's how you were 'tricked', huh? Doesn't sound much
of a trick to me.

FURTWÄNGLER: To the best of my knowledge that is what
happened. The trick was that pressure was brought to bear
before I was able to manoeuvre. The regime knew as well as I
did that I had not bowed my knee.

ARNOLD: It doesn't sound like that to me. It sounds like you
made a deal —

FURTWÄNGLER: I made no deal. My only concern was preserving
the highest musical standards. That I believe to be my
mission.

ARNOLD: I don't buy that —

FURTWÄNGLER: It's the truth —

ARNOLD: Do you remember a pianist called Walter Sachs?

FURTWÄNGLER: No.

ARNOLD: A young, Jewish pianist?

FURTWÄNGLER: No.

ARNOLD: A pupil of — (*To* EMMI.) What was the teacher's
name?

EMMI: Myra Samuel —

FURTWÄNGLER: I knew Myra Samuel —

ARNOLD: And you don't remember this pupil of hers playing to
you in a cellar, here in Berlin?

FURTWÄNGLER: Vaguely. What was his name?

ARNOLD: Walter Sachs.

FURTWÄNGLER: Sachs, Sachs —

ARNOLD: His widow attacked you a minute ago —

FURTWÄNGLER: No one's attacked me —

ARNOLD: In the waiting-room —

FURTWÄNGLER: But that woman didn't attack me. She was
trying to kiss my hand.

ARNOLD: Right. Right. I guess that was because she's grateful to
you. She wanted to thank you for helping her husband.
You got him a permit to leave for Paris. How did you do
that, Wilhelm?

FURTWÄNGLER: I can't remember. There were so many.

ARNOLD: Yeah, yeah, we've heard about all the folks you
helped. I'm just interested in how you went about it. Did
you call someone you knew?

FURTWÄNGLER: I may have, as I say, I simply don't remember.

ARNOLD: Let me guess then. You picked up the phone and
made a call. (*Mimes a telephone.*) 'Hi, Adolf? Wilhelm
speaking. Listen, old pal, there's a Jew-boy pianist I want
you to help. He needs a permit to get to Paris. Gee, that's
swell of you, Adolf. Shall I have him pick it up or will you
send it round? God bless you, Adolf, and Heil fucking
Hitler!'
(EMMI *sticks her fingers in her ears and shuts her eyes tight.*)
Or maybe you called Hermann or Josef? Because, you see, I
think you made a deal, you shook hands with the Devil and
you became real close to him and his cohorts. You were so
close you were in the same shithouse as them, you could
wipe their asses for them –
(*He suddenly notices* EMMI.)
Emmi, how the hell can you take notes with your goddam
fingers – ? Emmi!
(*She removes her fingers.*)
This is Emmi Straube, Wilhelm. She's a very sensitive girl.
(FURTWÄNGLER *gives her a nod.*)
So, Wilhelm, how many Jews do you think you helped?

FURTWÄNGLER: I have no idea.

ARNOLD: That many, huh?

FURTWÄNGLER: I am not going to defend myself by trumpeting
numbers. May I ask a question?

ARNOLD: Sure.

FURTWÄNGLER: When will my case be heard by the Tribunal?

ARNOLD: Your guess is as good as mine.

FURTWÄNGLER: I recently visited your colleagues in
Wiesbaden, the American Occupation Authorities, those

charged with assisting my defense, they were extremely polite and helpful. They said they –

ARNOLD: This isn't Wiesbaden. And I'm not here to defend you –

FURTWÄNGLER: I need to work. I need to make my living. I have been living off the generosity of friends –

ARNOLD: Tough, but these things take time –

FURTWÄNGLER: (*Growing more and more agitated*) Then why is it, please, that – that – another conductor who was actually a member of the Party, I believe he joined twice, why has he already been cleared and is working again, while I have to wait and wait and wait?

ARNOLD: I don't know who he is, he wasn't my case –

FURTWÄNGLER: And why is it, please, that on good authority I have learned that certain high-ranking Nazi scientists are, even as we speak, being transported to the United States to work on missiles and rocket fuels?

ARNOLD: That's what we call the spoils of war, Wilhelm. Different professions, different rules. Why did you escape to Switzerland in January last year?

FURTWÄNGLER: What?

ARNOLD: Why did you escape to Switzerland last year?

FURTWÄNGLER: Because I learned that the Gestapo were about to arrest me.

ARNOLD: Why were they going to arrest you?

FURTWÄNGLER: I'm not absolutely sure but I believe it was because of another letter I'd written to Goebbels lamenting the decline of musical standards due to racial policies.

ARNOLD: You didn't complain about the racial policies, just about the decline of musical standards, is that right? (*No response.*)
So, how did you learn that the Gestapo was out to get you?

FURTWÄNGLER: During an enforced hour-long interval, because of a power failure, at a concert in the Blüthner Hall, Albert Speer, the Minister of Armaments, said to me, casually, 'You look very tired, Maestro, you should go abroad for a while.' I understood exactly what he meant.

ARNOLD: (*Affecting innocence*) Is that the same Albert Speer who's now sitting beside your other friend, Baldur, in the dock at

Nürnberg, also charged with crimes against humanity?
(*No response.*)
You sure knew a lot of people in high places.

FURTWÄNGLER: It would be truer to say that a lot of people in
high places knew me.

ARNOLD: Don't get smart with me, because your friends seem to
be just a bunch of criminal shitheads. But I know and you
know that you were real close to all of them, to Adolf and
Hermann and Josef and Baldur and now Albert. Make a call,
a Jew is saved. Write a nasty letter, Albert says leave town.
So, let's hear the truth, Wilhelm, let's come clean. What was
your Party number?

FURTWÄNGLER: If you are going to bully me like this, Major,
then you had better do your homework. You obviously have
no idea how stupid and impertinent your remarks are.

ARNOLD: (*Stung*) You remember, David, I said I had a question
for Wilhelm that he wouldn't be able to answer. Well, I'm
going to ask it now. You ready for this, Wilhelm? Take your
time, it's a tough one. Why didn't you get out right at the
start when Adolf came to power in 1933? I have some names
here, people in your line of business, who got out in '33.
Bruno Walter, Otto Klemperer –

FURTWÄNGLER: But they were Jews, they had to leave, they were
right to leave.
(*Brief silence.*)
I love my country and my people. That is a matter of body
and soul. I could not leave my country in her deepest misery.
To have left in '33 or '34 would have been shameful. I
remained here to give comfort, to see that the glorious
musical tradition, of which I believe I am one of the
guardians, remained unbroken, was intact when we woke
from the nightmare. I remained because I believed my place
was with my people.

ARNOLD: See, David? He can't answer the question. I'll ask it
again, Wilhelm, and don't give me any more airy-fairy
bullshit –

FURTWÄNGLER: (*Flaring, at his most arrogant*) I have told you my
reasons, and I only hope, Major, you will be as hard on other

artists who have remained in their countries. Shostakovich,
Prokofiev, Eisenstein, especially Eisenstein with his films
glorifying tyranny, but you could accuse them all of
glorifying tyranny –

ARNOLD: I never heard of them, they're not on my list –

DAVID: No, they're Russians –

ARNOLD: Russians? (*Laughs.*) Yeah, Russians –

(*The telephone rings.*)

EMMI: (*Into telephone*) Major Arnold's office. (*Listens.*) It's Major
Richards for Lieutenant Wills.

DAVID: (*Taking the telephone*) Wills. (*Listens.*) Yes. (*To* ARNOLD.)
Major Richards wants a word. I think you may need to be
private.

ARNOLD: Put it through to the other room, Emmi.

(*He marches off into the small room.* EMMI *cranks a handle,
waits.*)

EMMI: (*Into telephone*) You're through, Major Richards.

(*She replaces the receiver.* FURTWÄNGLER *rises.*)

FURTWÄNGLER: I have had enough of this. I am leaving now.

DAVID: I don't think that would be advisable.

(FURTWÄNGLER *hesitates and doesn't leave. From behind the
closed door, the sound of* ARNOLD *yelping with delight and then
his laughter.* DAVID *summons his courage.*)

DAVID: Dr Furtwängler.

(FURTWÄNGLER *turns to him;* DAVID *feels awkward but takes
the plunge as though he's been preparing a speech.*)

When I was ten, in 1932, my father, he was a publisher,
allowed me to accompany him on a business trip to Berlin.
On the second evening of our visit, he took me to the
Philharmonic. I can't remember the whole programme but I
do remember you conducted both Beethoven's *Egmont*
overture and the Fifth Symphony. I think the concert ended
with the overture to Tannhaüser. You opened a new world to
me –

(*Another yelp and laughter from* ARNOLD; DAVID *falters,
searching now for the words.*)

More than a world. Like waking from sleep. A child of ten.
Waking to a new world. You showed me a place where there

was – an absence of misery. Ever since I first heard you,
music has been central to my life. My chief comfort. And
I've needed comfort. I thank you for that. I thought I could
say this better. I can't. Whatever happens here –
(*He stops, embarrassed, turns away.* FURTWÄNGLER *nods,
smiles sadly.*)

EMMI: I, too. The same. Thank you.
(FURTWÄNGLER *gives her a wonderful smile. She looks away.*)

FURTWÄNGLER: Fräulein – ?

EMMI: Straube.

FURTWÄNGLER: Wann haben *sie* mich zum ersten mal als
dirigent erlebt?

EMMI: (*Mumbling*) Hier. In Berlin.
Neunzehnhundertdreiundvierzig –

FURTWÄNGLER: (*Not having heard; gently*) Wann?
(ARNOLD *re-enters, dangerously pleased with himself, holding a
couple of sheets of paper with notes.*)

ARNOLD: I've got to hand it to the British, David. You know
what those guys are? Decent. Wilhelm, tell me, do you know
Hans Hinkel?

FURTWÄNGLER: Do I know Hans Hinkel?

ARNOLD: Why does everybody repeat my questions?

FURTWÄNGLER: Do I know Hans Hinkel?

ARNOLD: See? There he goes again –

FURTWÄNGLER: Yes, I know him. A despicable human being.
Ask Bruno Walter. It was Hinkel who personally drove him
out. You know what his job was in the Ministry of Culture?
To get rid of Jews in the arts, and since the most talented
artists were inevitably Jewish, he was seldom idle. I could
detail his persecution of my former secretary, Berta
Geissmar, herself a Jewess, but I will not bore you with a
chronicle of cruelty, meanness and mendacity.

ARNOLD: Yup, sounds like the same guy. You know what else
this little creep did? He kept files, close on 250,000 files. And
you know what's in those files?

FURTWÄNGLER: How should I know –

ARNOLD: Oh boy, you're going to love this. Those files contain –
wait for this – the details of every artist working in this

35

country for – guess who? That's right, Wilhelm, your old pals, Adolf and Josef and Hermann. These files are going to tell us when all of you joined the Party, who informed and who was helpful and, what's more, they're full of love letters to your aforementioned pals, swearing everlasting loyalty. Isn't that something? A file on every one of you. Some guy, that Hinkel.

FURTWÄNGLER: I should like to leave now.

ARNOLD: I bet you would, so why don't you? See, we have work to do sifting through those files, and that'll take some time, I guess. So, get out of here. And we'll call you back when we're good and ready.

(FURTWÄNGLER *goes to the door but stops, turns to* EMMI *and gives a curt bow and a smile, then goes.* ARNOLD *hurries to his desk.*)

ARNOLD: We've got him! See how the moment I mentioned Hinkel he wanted out? Boy, oh boy! David, here's what I want you to do. I'm going to give you a list of everybody I interviewed and I want you to check their names against Hinkel's files. This is an Aladdin's cave. Jesus, when you think the Russians had the whole archive in their hands until the city was divided and they didn't know what it was. You know what they'll be doing now? Shitting razor blades. Emmi, give David a list of the witnesses, and get us some more coffee, will you? (*He finds files in his desk drawer.*) These are pretty well verbatims of my interrogations. We'll compare the answers the shitheads gave me with the info in Hinkel's files.

(*He hands some files to* DAVID; *they start to go through them. During this,* EMMI *brings them the list. She is on her way to the door but stops, chooses a record, puts it on and turns up the volume: the opening of Beethoven's Eighth Symphony at full blast.* EMMI *goes quickly.*)

ARNOLD: Hey, turn that off, we can't hear ourselves think. (*Looks up, realizes she's gone.*) David, turn that off.

(DAVID *pretends not to hear.*)

Shit.

(ARNOLD *rises, crosses to the record player and as he takes off the record the music stops abruptly.*
Blackout.)

36

ACT TWO

SCENE ONE

April. 10 p.m. Warm spring evening. Dim light from the desk lamp.
RODE *stands in the double doorway, having just greeted* ARNOLD. *He wears a tattered cardigan over a short-sleeved shirt and slacks.*
ARNOLD *is at his desk which is covered in paper. He is inwardly excited, his mood dangerous.* RODE *carries a slender object wrapped in a cloth.*

RODE: (*Beaming*) Major, you must now guess what I am holding in my hand.

ARNOLD: Your cock.

RODE: No, no, come now, guess. You like guessing games?

ARNOLD: Love 'em. I give up, what you holding in your hand, Helmuth?

RODE: (*Glancing round nervously*) No Miss Straube?

ARNOLD: No. That's because I wanted to see you alone, Helmuth. Off the record. So what you got there?

RODE: You can't guess?
(*He unwraps the object to reveal a well-worn leather case.*)

ARNOLD: Helmuth, I think I know what it is.

RODE: What?

ARNOLD: A telescope. For spying on people. Right?

RODE: (*A little uneasy, a nervous smile*) No, no, no, not at all. (*He opens the case to reveal a conductor's baton.*)

ARNOLD: (*Toying with him*) By Jimminy! A white stick. For the blind!

RODE: No, Major, not a white stick, a baton. A conductor's baton. And not just *a* baton. *The* baton. My guilty secret. The Maestro's baton which I stole.

ARNOLD: The one he kept in his right hand.

RODE: You remember!

ARNOLD: How could I forget? (*Taking the baton.*) Will you look at this? I'm holding the baton he kept in his right hand so he didn't have to salute and poke Adolf's eyes out.
(*Suddenly thrusting it at* RODE.)
Show me, Helmuth.

RODE: Show you?

ARNOLD: Yeah, show me. I want to see you do it. C'mon,
Helmuth, take the baton.

(RODE *reluctantly takes the baton.* ARNOLD *gets out a comb,
flicks a lock of hair over his forehead and holds the comb under
his nose to make a Hitler moustache.*)

Pretend I'm Adolf. You're the Maestro. C'mon. You've got
the baton in your right hand but you give me the salute just
the same.

RODE: No, really, Major, I don't like giving the salute even in –

ARNOLD: (*Sweetly*) Do it, Helmuth.

(RODE *gives a half-hearted salute.*)

Do it right, Helmuth.

(RODE *gives the salute.*)

You look great doing that, Helmuth, and I see what you
mean. You almost poked my eyes out.

RODE: Exactly. (*Puts the baton on Arnold's desk.*) Perhaps you will
do me a favour, Major. If you are seeing the Maestro again,
be so good as to return the baton to him. It is, after all, his
property. But please don't tell him who took it.

ARNOLD: Don't worry, Helmuth, it'll be our secret.

RODE: In the meantime, you can practise conducting. I saw last
time I was here you had some of our records. (*He glances at
the records.*) I am on this one, the Ninth, second fiddle,
difficult to identify me exactly. (*He chuckles.*) You're
working late tonight. You don't usually see people this late –

ARNOLD: All in the cause of humanity, Helmuth. Or should I call
you one–zero–four–nine–three–three–one.

RODE: (*Shaken*) What?

ARNOLD: One–zero–four–nine–three–three–one. Or d'you mind
if I just call you 'one'?

(*An agonizing silence: then* RODE *breaks down and sobs.*)

You know what I say you are, Helmuth? I say you're a piece
of shit.

RODE: (*Through his sobs*) The bastard, the bastard –

ARNOLD: Who's the bastard, Helmuth? Hinkel?

(RODE *nods.*)

Why? Well, why particularly?

RODE: He said – he said there'd be no records – no file –

ARNOLD: He promised to remove your file?

(*No response*.)

And you thought we'd never find out.

(*No response*.)

You thought we'd never find out that you were the Party's man in the orchestra? Hinkel's man.

(RODE *sobs*.)

Oh, don't take on so, Helmuth. You've only got one Party number. A guy called Herbert von Karajan's got two. (*He laughs*.) By the way, why d'you think he joined the Party twice? Once in Austria, once here? Guess he just wanted them to know he cared, huh?

(*No response*.)

So, c'mon, Party member, one–zero–four–nine–three–three–one, talk to me.

RODE: (*Trying to regain his dignity*) I – I – have confessed my sins. I have been given absolution.

ARNOLD: Yeah, but don't you guys have to do penance? What's your penance, Helmuth?

RODE: Living out the rest of my life.

ARNOLD: Hold it, your story moves me deeply, let me wipe away my tears. I'm so choked up, I can't speak.

RODE: (*Burst of anger*) You don't know what it's like to wake up to a power so terrifying, so immense, that all you can think of is you have to be part of it otherwise you will be eaten alive. And here's something else you won't understand. Absolute power offers absolute certainty and absolute hope.

ARNOLD: Doesn't matter if I understand or not, just get it off your chest, Helmuth.

RODE: And you will never have even the slightest inkling of how corrupt the power was, yes, corrupt and corrupting. You have never experienced a Reign of Terror, so there is no way I can make it clear to you. You start by censoring what you say, then you censor what you think, and you end by censoring what you feel. That is the greatest degradation because it means the entire individual will is paralyzed, and all that remains is an obedient husk. In my case – (*He breaks off*.)

ARNOLD: Yeah, go on, Helmuth, in your case?

RODE: It began with a realization.

ARNOLD: And what was that, Helmuth?

RODE: That I am not the best violinist in the world.

ARNOLD: You're not?

RODE: I would never, in my wildest dreams, have been even a second violinist in the Berlin Philharmonic. When they got rid of the – the Jews in the orchestra there were vacancies for people like me. I believed that to be just. I can trace my ancestry back to the thirteenth century.

ARNOLD: I'm told a lot of Jews can go back even further than that.

RODE: (*Suddenly agitated*) I lied about something.

ARNOLD: You surprise me, Helmuth.

RODE: No, no, I have to set the record straight. I told you it was my idea the Maestro should carry the baton in his right hand. Well, it wasn't my idea at all. The idea came from Franz Jastrau. He was the orchestra's handyman.

ARNOLD: Gee, that sure changes the whole picture, Helmuth.

RODE: I don't think the Maestro even knows of my existence. Second violin. A conductor is also a dictator, you know, he is also a terrifying power who gives hope and certainty, and guarantees order. I wanted to be in the Maestro's power, too. The orchestra is a symbol, you see –

ARNOLD: No more philosophy, please, Helmuth, because I want to talk to you about something practical. You ever heard of plea bargaining?

(RODE *shakes his head.*)

Talk about power, I have the power to let you go find work, at least in the American Zone. I could give you a job tomorrow, here, in this building. But I'd have to get something in return. See, Helmuth? That's plea bargaining.

(*Silence.*)

I have to admit, I thought I'd find a great big fat file on the Maestro. I thought, never mind two Party numbers, he'd have three. But his file is just full of letters asking Josef to help this Jew or that Jew.

RODE: Yes, they used to say, there was not a Jew left in Germany whom Furtwängler had not helped.

ARNOLD: Not true, huh?

(*No response.*)

C'mon, Helmuth, I can hand you a letter giving you freedom of movement, freedom to work, freedom, Helmuth. Better than scavenging for food in the ruins. But I need something in return. How's that for penance?

RODE: He is an anti-Semite. Of course.

ARNOLD: (*Gently; wheedling*) Of course. But I need facts, Helmuth, hard facts. You have to tell me where to look.

RODE: Major, we're discussing a man of genius here, I don't want – He's one of the greatest conductors alive, maybe *the* greatest –

ARNOLD: Fuck that, Helmuth. You want to discuss symbols here? This guy was a front man. He was the piper but he played their tune, you get my philosophical meaning? I'm not interested in small fish, I'm after Moby Dick. Come on, Helmuth. At least tell me what to look for and where to look for it. Hard facts.

RODE: You ever heard of Vittorio de Sabata?

ARNOLD: No.

RODE: Italian.

ARNOLD: You're kidding.

RODE: A conductor. Front rank. Furtwängler said something like, 'It's impudent for that Jew Sabata to conduct Brahms.'

ARNOLD: Doesn't knock me out that, Helmuth.

RODE: There's a letter –

ARNOLD: Now I'm hearing music, I like letters –

RODE: It must be in the files somewhere – to Cultural Minister Bernhard Rust, I think – full of – full of the sort of thing you're looking for – about Arnold Schönberg – a Jew – you know who I mean?

(ARNOLD *shakes his head.*)

A composer – modern – atonal.

ARNOLD: What's the date of the letter?

RODE: I'll have to think, early I guess, before the war, but – but there's something else I just remembered –

ARNOLD: Yeah?

RODE: Furtwängler sent Hitler a birthday telegram –

ARNOLD: He did?

RODE: Yes. Oddly enough, I had this from one of your people –

ARNOLD: From one of my people?

RODE: Yes. A Corporal. US Army. A Jew. He said he'd seen the telegram.

ARNOLD: Son-of-a-gun. We'll find the corporal and we'll find the telegram –

RODE: I don't remember his name, but I'll think, it'll come back to me –

ARNOLD: I want you to write all this down, Helmuth.

(*Puts a pad and pen before him.*)

And I want you to think about this. I just know a deal was made, early on. They said, 'Wilhelm, you don't have to join the Party, but just do as we tell you and you won't have to worry about a goddam thing.' And that's why he never left. But I need documentary proof. You know of anything like that?

RODE: No. And if I may say so, Major, I think you're barking up the wrong tree.

ARNOLD: Oh? And what's the right tree, Helmuth?

RODE: Ask him about his private life.

ARNOLD: His private life?

RODE: There's a pattern to his behaviour, you see. Apollo understood. And Hinkel. I can tell you things – There's a rumour – I don't know if it's true or not – but ask him about von der Null.

ARNOLD: Never heard of him, who is he?

RODE: Edwin von der Null. A music critic. He was the one who gave Furtwängler terrible reviews while he raved about Herbert von Karajan, the two-time member of the Party. Called him 'The Miracle Karajan'. Furtwängler was outraged and they say he had von der Null conscripted into the army. The same thing happened to another critic, Walter Steinhauer. He savaged Furtwängler in print for not playing more contemporary music. After that review appeared, he too was conscripted. True or not, it's not such a bad idea. Critics give you bad reviews, you have them sent to the Russian front. (*Chuckles.*) But if you really want to get

Furtwängler, ask him about Herbert von Karajan.

ARNOLD: This Miracle Kid?

RODE: Yes, that, I believe, will prove fruitful. (*He starts to write.*) Yes, ask him about von Karajan. And you may notice, that he cannot even bring himself to utter the name. Furtwängler refers to him as K.

(*And as he continues to write the lights fade to:*
Blackout.)

SCENE TWO

Mid-July. 8.45 a.m. High summer. Intense heat. ARNOLD *is at his desk. He is half-asleep, head lolling. He suddenly wakes and cries out. He becomes aware of his surroundings, stares into space with a distant, forlorn expression.* EMMI *enters carrying a flat brown-paper package. She is glowing.*

EMMI: I've got it, Major.

ARNOLD: Swell.

EMMI: The British were most helpful. They really have a broadcasting station there. And they found it for me. Took no more than ten minutes. Amazing. And I am so pleased you are becoming interested in serious music, Major.

ARNOLD: Don't let one record fool you, Emmi.

EMMI: But Bruckner's Seventh Symphony, that's difficult even for me. Should we play it now? (*She unwraps the parcel which contains a set of records.*)

ARNOLD: No, Emmi, not now. You know what they mean by the Slow Movement?

EMMI: Of course.

ARNOLD: That's the one I want to hear. Put it on ready to play, and I'll tell you when to play it –

EMMI: I never thought you would ask to listen to Bruckner –

ARNOLD: Well, maybe I'm mellowing. Or maybe the heat's getting to me. And, wouldn't you know it? We shiver through a God-awful winter and now the sun's shining the central heating's working. The military, God bless 'em. No sign of the band leader?

EMMI: I wish you'd call him Dr Furtwängler. No, he isn't here but then it's not yet nine o'clock.

(*She peers at him.*)

Are you nervous, Major?

ARNOLD: I wish you'd call me Steve, Emmi. No, I'm not nervous, I'm just not getting enough sleep. Bad dreams. And that's when I'm awake.

(*He smiles; she sits at her desk.*)

Now, Emmi, if you want to be out of the room while I talk to him that's okay by me. What I have to say to him may upset you. And, I guess, working for me, you get upset enough.

EMMI: What are you going to say to him, Major?

ARNOLD: Emmi, go for a walk. It's a lovely day out there. Walk in the Tiergarten, sit under what's left of the linden trees, David can take notes.

EMMI: Major, you upset me when you avoid answering my questions –

(*A knock at the door.*)

ARNOLD: See who it is, Emmi, and if it's the band leader don't let him in yet.

(EMMI *opens the door to* RODE *who is dressed in a janitor's overall and cap that somehow looks like a uniform. He carries a small but bulging canvas sack. He bows.*)

ARNOLD: Attention! Security! Watch out, Emmi, he may want to frisk you.

RODE: Major, a woman left this for you.

ARNOLD: What woman?

RODE: I don't know her name. She talked to Sergeant Adams on the door and he gave me this and said it was for you.

ARNOLD: Did you see her?

RODE: Of course. I was standing here, Sergeant Adams was there, the woman was no more than –

ARNOLD: (*Interrupting*) What she look like?

(RODE *shrugs*.)

Old, young, fat, thin, short, tall?

RODE: No. (RODE *chuckles*.)

ARNOLD: Okay, very funny, so what's in the package?

RODE: I don't know, Major. Sergeant Adams said it was for you –

44

ARNOLD: Jesus Christ, Helmuth, you're supposed to be the security in this building –

RODE: But I was not told to open packages addressed to military personnel –

ARNOLD: Security, Helmuth, use your goddam common sense –

RODE: Sergeant Adams said I must search people, he did not say I must search packages –

ARNOLD: Jesus Christ, no wonder you were a second violinist. I mean, it stands to reason. A woman leaves a package for me, you got to be curious as to what's in it –

RODE: Why should I be curious? It's addressed to you, Major –

ARNOLD: Because it could be a fucking bomb, Helmuth –

RODE: A bomb? You think so?

ARNOLD: Yes, I think so. Open it.

(RODE *hesitates.*)

That's an order, Helmuth. Open it.

(RODE *hesitates.* EMMI *is apprehensive and ducks a little behind her typewriter.* ARNOLD *does not move.*)

RODE: If it's a bomb, Major, shouldn't you take cover?

ARNOLD: Open it.

(*Gingerly,* RODE *opens the sack.*)

Well, feel around inside. Go on, Helmuth, feel around.

(RODE *feels inside the sack.*)

RODE: It just feels like paper, Major.

ARNOLD: Empty it.

(RODE *is about to do so on Arnold's desk.*)

On the floor, Helmuth.

(RODE *empties the sack. Fifty or so envelopes, various sizes and colours, cascade on to the floor.*)

ARNOLD: What the hell's that?

(*All three look at the envelopes, puzzled.*)

RODE: Could be fan mail, Major. I remember with the Maestro –

ARNOLD: Helmuth, who's going to send *me* fan mail for Chrissake? Jesus! Emmi, take a look. Helmuth, get back on duty. The Russians may launch an attack any moment.

(RODE *bows smartly and goes.* EMMI *goes down on her knees and starts to examine the envelopes.*)

ARNOLD: Well, Emmi?

EMMI: They're all addressed to Mrs Tamara Sachs. And they're all open –

ARNOLD: What? I don't get it –

(EMMI *starts to look at the envelopes, then stops.*)

EMMI: Major, can I ask you something?

ARNOLD: The answer's yes, Emmi, I love you, I want you to marry me, and I want you to be the mother of my children, not necessarily in that order.

EMMI: Major!

ARNOLD: What's in those letters, Emmi?

EMMI: No, I want to ask you this. Why have you been so kind to Mr Rode and not so kind to Dr Furtwängler?

ARNOLD: Let's just say I'm a democrat. With a small 'd'. I have more sympathy for the little people. What's in those letters, Emmi?

(DAVID *enters carrying files.*)

DAVID: Good morning –

ARNOLD: Okay, we surrender, the boy scout's here.

DAVID: What's going on?

ARNOLD: Seems like Tamara Sachs's sent me her mail.

DAVID: Why should she do that?

ARNOLD: I don't know exactly. Emmi's trying to come up with an answer.

(DAVID *hands* ARNOLD *the files.*)

DAVID: These are the last of them, Major.

ARNOLD: Anything good?

DAVID: Nothing we didn't know before, but the boys at Wiesbaden have asked me to put some questions to you. And I've found something you're not going to like. I happen to be going through a transcript from the Nürnberg trial –

EMMI: Major?

(ARNOLD *and* DAVID *turn to her.*)

There's one here, unopened. It's addressed, 'To Whom It May Concern'.

ARNOLD: Okay, well, it may concern us, Emmi. Open it. Read it.

(*To* DAVID, *while* EMMI *opens the letter.*)

I said the woman was crazy, didn't I say it? Look at that. Only a crazy woman would send her own mail to whom it may concern.

EMMI: (*Reading*) 'To the American authorities in Wiesbaden and
    Berlin. The good and the not so good. I have been busy.
    Here are more than fifty letters confirming what I have
    already said. Letters, evidence in black and white, from
    survivors, widows, lovers, friends, people now mostly in
    America and England, all testifying that Wilhelm
    Furtwängler was their saviour. Because no one knows when
    Dr Furtwängler's case will come before the tribunal and
    because I have unexpectedly received permission from the
    French authorities to reside in Paris –
    (DAVID *shoots* ARNOLD *a look;* ARNOLD *looks blithely*
    innocent.)
    – I probably will not be here to give evidence on his behalf,
    so I have taken copies of these letters. If you destroy them
    they will still exist.'
    (*Brief silence.* EMMI *continues to sort through the letters.*)
ARNOLD: Son-of-a-gun. Thanks, Tamara, it's a shame they're all
    totally irrelevant.
EMMI: There's one here from Dr Furtwängler. (*Reads.*) 'Dear
    Mrs Sachs, Thank you for your letter. Yes, I remember your
    husband well. As a matter of fact, I was reminded of him
    only the other day. I remembered the Bechstein was out of
    tune. He was indeed a fine pianist. I was deeply distressed to
    hear of his tragic fate.'
    (*Brief silence.*)
ARNOLD: Get them up off the floor, Emmi. (*To* DAVID.) You were
    saying the good guys at Wiesbaden had questions for me?
DAVID: (*Consulting notes; summoning courage*) They – they don't
    think there's a case against Dr Furtwängler and they want to
    know why you're pursuing it.
ARNOLD: Tell them they'll know after they've heard the evidence.
    (*Hands* DAVID *a fat file.*)
    Take a look through that, you'll see what I mean. Next
    question.
DAVID: (*Still tentative*) They think – they think you're being
    ordered to pursue Dr Furtwängler, and they want to know
    who's giving the orders and why?
ARNOLD: Oh, I get it, you've been talking to them, haven't you,

David? You told them about the 'they' who saw me at Ike's
headquarters. I remember you were so interested in who the
'they' were –

DAVID: Yes, I was asked, I –

ARNOLD: Well, you tell the good guys in Wiesbaden to mind their
own goddam business.

DAVID: Are you being ordered, Major?

ARNOLD: What's this about a transcript from Nürnberg?

DAVID: Why, Major? Why Dr Furtwängler? Why him?

ARNOLD: Tell me about Nürnberg.

(*Brief pause.* DAVID *consults one of his own files.*)

DAVID: Yes. A man called Dahlerus, Birger Dahlerus –

ARNOLD: Burger, his name's Burger? What is he, some kind of
short-order cook?

DAVID: A Swede, a businessman, he was called to give evidence in
Göring's defence –

(*The door suddenly bursts open and* FURTWÄNGLER *enters,
highly charged.* RODE *hovers nervously in the doorway as if he's
been advising* FURTWÄNGLER *not to enter.*)

FURTWÄNGLER: It is now nine o'clock precisely. I have prepared
a statement. I do not intend to be kept waiting again.

(*Uneasy, tense silence.*)

ARNOLD: (*Dangerously calm*) Wilhelm, don't talk to me as if I was
a second violinist. Go back into the waiting room, sit down,
and *wait*. Miss Straube will come and get you when I am
ready to see you. If you're not there when she comes to get
you, I'll have you pulled in by the Military Police. Okay,
Wilhelm?

(FURTWÄNGLER *hesitates, loses confidence, turns and marches
off.* RODE *shrugs apologetically and also goes.*)

ARNOLD: (*Incensed, almost losing control*) Jesus God, that prick,
that arrogant prick, who the fuck does he think he is? Who
the fuck? Who the fuck?

(*He paces.* EMMI *watches him, alarmed.*)

DAVID: Major.

(ARNOLD *doesn't seem to hear.*)

Major.

(ARNOLD *stops pacing;* DAVID *again summons courage.*)

I have a favour to ask you.

ARNOLD: (*Suddenly calm*) Okay, I owe you one.

DAVID: When you question him, could I ask you to treat him with more respect?

ARNOLD: With more what? More what?

DAVID: Respect –

ARNOLD: That's what I thought you said. Respect? Are you kidding?

DAVID: He may just be the greatest conductor of this century and that merits respect.

ARNOLD: Yeah, yeah, great conductor, great artist, that's what everybody keeps telling me, and you know what I say to that?

DAVID: I can guess what you say to that, Major –

ARNOLD: You know what I say he is?

DAVID: Yes, I think I can guess that, too –

ARNOLD: David, I just don't understand a thing about you. You're a Jew. Are you a Jew?

DAVID: Yes, I'm a Jew, I'm also a human being –

ARNOLD: A human being, oh, good, I'm relieved, I thought you were going to say you were a music lover. This man, this great artist has made anti-Semitic remarks like you wouldn't believe, I got letters –

DAVID: (*Interrupting*) Major, Major.

(ARNOLD *is still*.)

Show me a non-Jew who hasn't made anti-Semitic remarks and I'll show you the gates of paradise.

ARNOLD: What is it with you? Where are your feelings, David? Where's your hatred, your disgust? Where's your fucking outrage, David? Think of your parents and then think of him conducting 'Happy Birthday, dear Adolf'. I mean, for Chrissake, whose side are you on?

(*Brief pause*.)

So what's this about the Swede in Nürnberg?

DAVID: It doesn't matter now. It's probably irrelevant.

(*Brief pause*.)

ARNOLD: Okay, Emmi. Go get him. Oh, and Emmi. Don't announce him. Just let him come in.

(*She goes. Uneasy silence while they wait.* EMMI *opens the door for* FURTWÄNGLER *who re-enters, angry and resentful.*)

Wilhelm! Nice to see you. How are you? Been keeping well? Not too hot for you? Come in, come in, sit down.

(FURTWÄNGLER, *deeply suspicious, goes for the witness chair.*)

No, no, take this one, it's more comfortable –

(ARNOLD *places the visitor's chair and holds it for* FURTWÄNGLER *who sits.*)

Isn't this heat something else? You want to loosen your tie, take off your jacket? Just relax, because the good news is that this is the last time you'll have to see me.

(FURTWÄNGLER *eyes him suspiciously.*)

But the bad news is that I still have to test the case against you, see if it'll stand up, and if it does, then I hand over to the civil authorities, to your own people, a guy called Alex Vogel, you ever heard of him?

FURTWÄNGLER: Yes, I've heard of him.

ARNOLD: And what have you heard?

FURTWÄNGLER: That he's a Moscow hack, a communist.

ARNOLD: That's the one. Not a nice man. We are not on first name terms. So, today, thank your lucky stars, you've only got me to deal with.

(*Silence;* ARNOLD *waits; nothing from* FURTWÄNGLER.)

Now, let's take it nice and easy. Okay?

(*Still nothing from* FURTWÄNGLER.)

I don't want to go over all the old stuff because I have one or two new things that have come up –

FURTWÄNGLER: (*Interrupting*) I wish to say something.

ARNOLD: Go ahead, be my guest.

FURTWÄNGLER: (*Takes out a piece of paper*) When I last saw you, I was unprepared, I did not know what to expect. In the past weeks, I have been thinking more carefully and making some notes.

(*Glances at notes; more to* DAVID.)

You have to understand who I am and what I am. I am a musician and I believe in music. I am an artist and I believe in art. You could say that art is my religion. Art in general, and music, of course, in particular, has for me mystical powers which nurture man's spiritual needs. I must confess, however, to being extremely naïve. I insisted for many years, until quite recently in fact, on the absolute separation of art and politics. I truly had no interest in politics, I hardly read newspapers, my entire life was devoted to music because, and this is very important, I believed that I could, through music, create something practical.

ARNOLD: And what was that?

FURTWÄNGLER: The maintenance of liberty, humanity and justice.

ARNOLD: Gee, Wilhelm, that's a thing of beauty, honest to God, a thing of beauty. I'm going to try to remember that. How's it go? Liberty, humanity and justice. Beautiful. But you used the word 'naïve'. Are you now saying you think you were wrong? That art and politics can't be separated?

FURTWÄNGLER: I believe they must be kept separate, but that they weren't kept separate I learned to my cost.

ARNOLD: And when did you first learn that? When you sent the telegram? Was that the surrender signal, the waving of the white flag?

FURTWÄNGLER: What telegram?

ARNOLD: 'Happy Birthday, dear Adolf, love Wilhelm.' Or words to that effect. That sounds to me like you were dropping on your knees and saying, 'Okay, Adolf, you win. You're top dog in everything, so let's be pals. Have a swell party.' Is that when you decided you couldn't keep art and politics separate, when you sent the telegram?

FURTWÄNGLER: I have no idea what you're talking about.

ARNOLD: I'm talking about the birthday greetings to your old pal, Adolf.

FURTWÄNGLER: I never sent him birthday greetings or any other kind of greetings.

ARNOLD: Think carefully, Wilhelm –

FURTWÄNGLER: I don't have to think carefully. This is utterly ridiculous. I never sent him a telegram.

(DAVID, *who has been consulting the file* ARNOLD *gave him, raises a discreet finger.*)

ARNOLD: Yes, David?

DAVID: (*Apparently innocently*) Why not show Dr Furtwängler the evidence? It may refresh his memory.

(ARNOLD *shoots* DAVID *a sharp, furious look.*)

I can't seem to find it here, Emmi, perhaps you have the telegram in your files –

EMMI: No, I have never seen such a telegram –

DAVID: Major, if you tell me where the telegram is –

FURTWÄNGLER: You won't find it because no such telegram exists.

(*Ominous silence. Then,* ARNOLD *forces a boisterous laugh.*)

ARNOLD: Well, I tried, you got to admit, I tried. I thought I might just trap you there, Wilhelm, but David here was a little too quick for me. Smart move, David. Smart move. No, I don't have the telegram, but I know it exists. And I just want to tell you. Wilhelm, we're going to keep looking for it because I happen to believe you sent it.

FURTWÄNGLER: Then you are wrong.

(ARNOLD *is not pleased.*)

ARNOLD: Art and politics, yeah, art and politics. Are you saying that touring abroad, conducting the Berlin Philharmonic Orchestra in foreign lands from 1933 on wasn't a commercial for Adolf and all he stood for?

FURTWÄNGLER: We never, never officially represented the regime when we played abroad. We always played as a private ensemble. As I think I already told you, I was a freelance conductor –

ARNOLD: You know something? You should've written our policies for us because you got more exclusion clauses than Double Indemnity. Don't give me fine print again, I'm an expert when it comes to fine print. What d'you imagine people thought? The Berlin Philharmonic's taken over by Josef's Propaganda Ministry but Wilhelm's a freelance, so music and politics are now entirely separate? Is that what you believed ordinary people thought?

FURTWÄNGLER: I have no idea what ordinary people thought –

ARNOLD: No –

FURTWÄNGLER: – because I had only one intention, from 1933 onwards. Whatever I did, and this is also the real reason I did not leave my country, I had only one intention and that was to prove that art means more than politics.

ARNOLD: Did that include Herbert von Karajan?

FURTWÄNGLER: (*Flustered*) What – what – I don't know what you mean –

ARNOLD: Tell me about von der Nüll.

FURTWÄNGLER: (*Taken off guard*) Von der Nüll?

ARNOLD: Yes, von der Nüll –

FURTWÄNGLER: Von der Nüll –

ARNOLD: How long's this going to go on, Wilhelm? I say von der Nüll, you say von der Nüll, I say von der Nüll, you say von der Nüll, we could go on all day. You know who von der Nüll is, don't you? Edwin von der Nüll, music critic –

FURTWÄNGLER: Yes, I know who he is –

ARNOLD: Isn't it true that because he gave you bad reviews and praised this young guy, von Karajan, called him a goddam miracle, said he was better than you, you had von der Nüll conscripted into the army and nobody's heard from him since?

FURTWÄNGLER: That's an outrageous lie!

ARNOLD: You sure you didn't call one of your close buddies and say, God in heaven, did you see what that guy von der Nüll wrote about me? I want him out the way. And the same with that other critic, Steinhauer. He had the nerve to accuse me, the greatest conductor on earth, of not playing enough modern music. Send him to Stalingrad. Isn't that what you did? You don't like criticism, do you? You certainly didn't like them saying there was another conductor who was better than you –

(FURTWÄNGLER *rises angrily*.)

FURTWÄNGLER: (*Exploding; pacing*) Please stop playing these games with me. You seem to take pleasure in teasing and baiting and hectoring me. Have some regard for my intelligence. We are dealing here with matters concerning my entire existence, my career, my life. Why you should introduce the name of – of another conductor is beyond my understanding.

ARNOLD: I'll tell you why. You remember we talked about you

53

playing for Adolf's birthday? And you told me that Josef got
to your doctors first, that you were tricked, outflanked?

FURTWÄNGLER: Yes, and that's what happened –

ARNOLD: I have a different story to tell. I don't believe you were
tricked. Not in the way you describe. I believe something
else happened. I've looked at the Hinkel Archive, made a
few enquiries, I've seen records of phone calls, and putting it
all together, this is what I think happened. I think Josef said,
'Wilhelm, if you won't conduct for Adolf's birthday, we'll
get the Miracle Kid, the guy that critic von der Null thinks is
the greatest conductor in the world, the guy you call K. He's
not just willing to conduct for Adolf, he's offered to sing
"Happy Birthday" as a solo.'

(*Silence.*)

Come on now, Wilhelm, admit it. K worried you, didn't he?
He always worried you. In 1942, he's thirty-four years old,
you're already fifty-six. He's the Young Pretender, the
comet, yeah, the miracle. He's tilting at your throne. Your
position's in danger. And Josef and Hermann keep saying to
you, 'If you don't do it, little K will.' Never mind art and
politics and symbols and airy-fairy bullshit about liberty,
humanity and justice. You were tricked all right, because
they got you where you were most vulnerable. Youth was
knocking on the door, and I don't care how great you are,
how noble, how fantastic with your little white stick, because
it's the oldest story in the book. The ageing Romeo jealous of
the young buck, the Heavyweight Champion of the World
frightened of the Young Contender. And the great maestro
terrified of the new boy on the podium. Wasn't that how they
got you, Wilhelm, time after time? Admit it. The real reason
you didn't leave the country when you knew you should have
was that you were frightened. You were frightened that,
once you were out of the way, you'd be supplanted by the
Miracle Kid, the Party's boy twice over, flashy, talented little
K.

FURTWÄNGLER: This is absolute nonsense –

DAVID: (*Overlapping*) Major, wait a moment, where is this
leading? This isn't establishing –

ARNOLD: (*Turning on him, cutting him off*) Not now, David, I
haven't finished with him. As a matter of fact, I've hardly
begun. I'm only just developing my theme. Isn't that what
you call it in classical music, developing a theme? Okay,
Wilhelm, so they played on your insecurity. That's human,
understandable, nothing to be ashamed of. After all, it's
pretty well agreed that little K's got what it takes, and nearly
everyone in the Party loved him. Jesus, he's a member twice
over, he's one of theirs. But, take note of what I said. I said
nearly everyone in the Party because there's one exception.
One guy doesn't like little K as much as he likes you, there's
one guy who thinks little K is not fit to brush your coat tails,
and that guy just happens to be – yeah, the number one man,
your old pal, Adolf. He thinks you're the greatest and when
he says, I want Wilhelm for my birthday party, boy, they
better go get Wilhelm. So, Josef calls and threatens you with
little K. And you said to hell with the Ninth in Vienna, I'll
give it to Adolf as a birthday present in Berlin. That's the
trick they played, they got you by the balls and they
squeezed. Hard.

DAVID: Major, I simply can't see how this line of questioning –

ARNOLD: (*Turning on him*) David, what is this? What are you all
of a sudden, Counsel for the Defense? What you want me to
say? Objection overruled? Objection sustained? My line of
questioning is establishing motive, Counsellor, plain,
ordinary human motive. Why did he stay? Why did he play
for them? Why was he the flag carrier for the regime? Why
was he their servant? Not art or culture or music and its
mystical power, but good old-fashioned insecurity, fear and
jealousy. And that was only part of his reason for staying –

FURTWÄNGLER: (*Suddenly interrupting, blurting out*) Of course
there was a conspiracy against me, a campaign –
(*He stops. Silence.* DAVID *is about to say something but* ARNOLD
points a finger at him to stop him speaking.)
They controlled the press. Every word that was written,
every word that was published. When I resigned from the
Philharmonic, when I refused to take part in a film they
made about the orchestra, oh, countless things of that kind,

55

refusing to co-operate in one way or another, they were determined to keep me in my place. You mentioned the critic, Edwin von der Null. His praise of – of – that man may have been genuine, I have no idea. But his remarks were encouraged and guided, and then seized on. They wanted another 'star', as they called it, to take my place. They had their own concert agency under a man called Rudolf Vedder, a human being beneath contempt. He was determined to foist K on the public. I'm not going to recount the difficulties I had with that man but if I tell you that his chief ally in this was Ludolf von Alvensleben, personal adjutant to Heinrich Himmler, and when that particular individual did not get his way he threatened only one sanction: death. They controlled every aspect of our lives. They manipulated, bullied and imposed their monstrous will. When they finally understood that I would do everything in my power to prevent art from being directed and supervised, they determined to undermine me. They regarded any action of dissent, however small, as a criticism of the state, tantamount to high treason.

ARNOLD: And you didn't have von der Null conscripted because of that review he wrote?

FURTWÄNGLER: (*Blazing*) I've told you, it's absolute nonsense. How could I have managed such a thing? He was in their power, not mine. It's a total lie. And I have never in my life tried or even wanted to silence my critics, never. I believe serious criticism to be an essential part of cultural life.

(*Turning to* DAVID; *becoming excited.*)

And the reason you have detected a certain distaste I have for K is not because I was jealous or insecure but because I have serious criticism to make of him. In my opinion, he is an intellectual conductor. He does not experience the piece afresh each time. He conducts only what he knows and wants, in other words the nuances, which is why the nuances are all exaggerated. The slow tempi are too slow, the fast ones too fast. The whole effect is somewhat hysterical – (*He falls silent.*)

ARNOLD: Wilhelm, I'm trying to understand you, I really am,

believe me. You see, when you talk about cultural life, I'm
lost. Because I am, to put it at its best, totally uncultured. So
when I look at you, I don't see the great artist, the greatest
conductor alive, I see a man, an ordinary guy, like a million
other ordinary guys. And I ask myself, what keeps him in a
situation which he says he did everything in his power to
resist, except get the hell out of it? What keeps him here, I
ask myself? Not being a cultured guy, I don't buy all this
stuff about music creating liberty, justice and humanity. I
look for ordinary reasons, reasons I can understand, reasons
my buddies can understand. So, if I said to my buddies,
imagine you love your wife – well, maybe I'm stretching
reality here – no, stay with me – I say to them, imagine you
love your wife and they tell you you're being sent overseas.
But they exempt some young guy who it's possible could
take your wife's fancy. What would you do? Like a man
they'd say, Steve, we'd do everything we could to stay put.
See, Wilhelm, I'm talking about ordinary, everyday motives.
Which is why I want to discuss your private life.

DAVID: Oh, come along, Major, this can't be right –

ARNOLD: (*Quietly*) Objection overruled, Counsellor. I'm
establishing motive.

(*To* FURTWÄNGLER.)

How many illegitimate children do you have?

DAVID: Major, this is outrageous, what has this to do with
anything at all?

ARNOLD: You'll see. Wilhelm, did you hear the question?

FURTWÄNGLER: (*Barely audible*) I have illegitimate children –

ARNOLD: What?

FURTWÄNGLER: I said I have illegitimate children. I don't know
how many.

ARNOLD: No, I bet you don't. Four, five, six?

(*No response.*)

You like the ladies, don't you, Wilhelm?

(*No response.*)

Isn't it true that before every concert you got a woman in
your dressing room and gave her the old conductor's baton,
isn't that true?

DAVID: Major, this is deeply offensive and repugnant –

ARNOLD: You bet –

DAVID: – and totally irrelevant.

ARNOLD: Not so, Counsellor. The women threw themselves at you, didn't they, Wilhelm? That secretary of yours, Berta Geissmar, who's now working for *Sir* Thomas Beecham, she wasn't only your secretary, she was your procuress, wasn't she? She procured women for you, didn't she, as many and as often as you wanted –

FURTWÄNGLER: Stop this, please, stop this –

ARNOLD: No, I'm not going to stop it, because if I said to my buddies, you're living in a whorehouse where you get the whores free, you going to leave? See, Wilhelm, I think you stayed because you were in paradise here. Adolf himself offered you a beautiful house and a special bomb shelter –

FURTWÄNGLER: I absolutely refused the house and the bomb shelter –

ARNOLD: But you see what I'm getting at? You didn't leave because you felt an affinity with your people, or because you wanted to preserve the traditions of which, I think you said, you were a guardian, or because you believed that art and music and culture were above politics. See, if I said to my buddies, you're top dog in your profession, favourite of the number one man in the country, you get all the women you lust after, you're highly paid, you get a gorgeous house and a personal, private bomb shelter if you want it, what you going to do, leave or stay? One voice comes back at me: *stay!*

DAVID: That's not a good argument, Major. If Dr Furtwängler did indeed enjoy all these – these privileges, he enjoyed them because of who he is and what he is –

ARNOLD: Now we're back to the great artist –

DAVID: Right. His position would have guaranteed him anything he wanted wherever he chose to live and work. That's true of any leading artist in any country in the world. They're rare specimens, Major, and that sets them apart –

ARNOLD: Okay, but it doesn't make them saints. They still have to get up and piss in the middle of the night, don't they?

And they can be envious and vindictive and mean just like you and me. Well, just like me. Can't they?

(*No response.*)

See, Wilhelm, everybody says what a great benefactor you were to the Jews, but what about that Italian conductor –

FURTWÄNGLER: I don't understand what you're talking about, but if you're now referring to Arturo Toscanini, he is not a Jew, of course, but he is greatly loved by you Americans –

ARNOLD: No, I was thinking of another Italian –

FURTWÄNGLER: (*Not hearing* ARNOLD; *again addressing* DAVID, *rather over-excitedly*) – and to my taste, he is too disciplined, his tempi are too strict. If he were a greater artist, if he had deeper insights, a livelier imagination, greater warmth and devotion to the work, he would not have become so disciplined. This is why his success is disastrous. Inspiration and understanding in art are more important than discipline and autocratic behaviour –

ARNOLD: (*Interrupting*) But otherwise you like the guy. (*He chuckles.*) I'm beginning to get the picture. You're not crazy about any of your rivals, are you? I guess it was the same with this other Italian, the one I was thinking of, de Sabata –

FURTWÄNGLER: De Sabata?

ARNOLD: Vittorio de Sabata. I have a letter here, written in 1939, which states: (*Reading.*) 'What should I do when Dr Furtwängler said to me that it was a piece of impudence for that Jew de Sabata to conduct Brahms. Since the day when de Sabata performed *Tristan* in Bayreuth, Furtwängler speaks only of "Jew Sabata".'

FURTWÄNGLER: Who wrote that letter?

ARNOLD: I'm not at liberty to tell you that. But it's a genuine letter. David, you have a copy in the file, it's a genuine letter.

FURTWÄNGLER: There's only one thing I can say. I have never said anything that goes counter to my convictions and simply cannot have said anything that did. Of course there were instances when I was speaking to specific Party members. I had to use their language, one had to say Heil Hitler, for example, but quite apart from these instances, I did not make any compromises by saying things other than I

believed. And I have always been frank in my attitude
towards the Jews –

ARNOLD: I believe that. But just answer the question, don't give
me explanations –

FURTWÄNGLER: But I have to explain. An attitude must exist in
one to make such an outburst possible. And this is what I
deny. I know that even in the greatest anger I couldn't have
said such a thing. De Sabata was my friend, one of my few
close friends. I invited him to conduct my orchestra. We
discussed his programme, we discussed everything –

ARNOLD: Okay, so, here's another letter, July 4, 1933, written by
you to the Minister of Culture, Bernhard Rust. It's about
this modern composer, a Jew, Arnold Schönberg who was
about to be suspended. There's a copy of this one, too, in
your file, David. This is what you wrote, Wilhelm.
(*Reading*.) 'Arnold Schönberg is considered by the Jewish
International as the most significant musician of the present.
It must be recommended that he not be made a martyr.'
What do you say to that?

FURTWÄNGLER: I say exactly what I said before. You have to use
their language –

DAVID: And you didn't finish the letter, Major. (*Reading*.) 'And if
he is suspended now – and I would not indeed consider this
right – the question of indemnity should be treated with
generosity.' He's pleading for the man, not condemning
him –

ARNOLD: Then what about these things he said? 'Jewish pen-
pushers should be removed from the Jewish press', 'Jewish
musicians lack a genuine affinity with *our* music', and
'Jewish musicians are good businessmen with few scruples,
lacking roots.' You deny you said these things?

FURTWÄNGLER: But it depends on the circumstances, to whom
one was speaking, these attitudes simply don't exist in me, I
used their language, of course I did, everyone did.

DAVID: Major, you have to balance those things – if indeed he said
them – against his assistance to his Jewish colleagues. Listen
to this, Major, from the transcript of the proceedings at
Nürnberg –

ARNOLD: (*Enjoying this*) Okay, Counsellor, here we go, it's your day in court. But be careful, there's nothing I enjoy more than a guy putting his own neck in the noose.

DAVID: A Swedish businessman, Birger Dahlerus, testified in cross-examination that he had several meetings with Hermann Göring. 'I first saw Göring', Dahlerus testified, 'embroiled in a stormy interview with Wilhelm Furtwängler, the famous conductor of the Berlin Philharmonic, who was vainly seeking permission to keep his Jewish concert master.'

FURTWÄNGLER: Yes, I remember well, I was pleading for Szymon Goldberg, a wonderful musician and a wonderful man, the youngest concert master the orchestra ever had. Thank God he escaped, and I pray that he is safe now –

ARNOLD: Why is it, Wilhelm, that everything you say touches me so deeply?

DAVID: (*Flaring*) Emmi, read some of those letters to Mrs Sachs. Pick any two, read them –
(EMMI, *uncertain, looks at* ARNOLD, *who, indifferent, gestures for her to do as she's been told. She selects a letter at random.*)

EMMI: (*Reading*) From Heinrich Wollheim. 'I am half Jewish and a former member of the Berlin State Opera Orchestra. I lived near the Swiss border and so was easily able to help friends and colleagues to escape. When the Gestapo finally caught up with me, I was sent to the concentration camp at Dachau. My wife contacted Dr Furtwängler who interceded on my behalf with Himmler and Goebbels and arranged for me to be his copyist. I believe Himmler said to him, "Well, Privy Councillor, we know you like to help criminals." I remained in Dachau but received better treatment than most of the other inmates. If Dr Furtwängler had not stood by me so steadfastly during my imprisonment, I certainly would not have come out of it with my life. I certainly would have been consigned to a "commando" unit, which would not have done my health any good.'

DAVID: Go on, Emmi, read another.

EMMI: I can't decipher this signature, but – (*Reading.*) 'Please remember that helping Jews was a capital offence. People were being publicly hanged on mere suspicion of such

activities but Dr Furtwängler helped anyone who asked him.
I personally testify to having seen literally hundreds of
people lined up outside his dressing room after concerts to
ask for his help. He never turned anyone away. He gave me
money because I was unable to feed myself or my family and
then he helped me to escape to Sweden. He helped countless
people in similar ways.'

DAVID: Doesn't sound like much of an anti-Semite to me, Major.
These were acts of enormous courage –

ARNOLD: (*Smiling*) You don't listen to what I say, David. How
many times have I got to tell you I was in insurance? You
think I can't smell a phoney policy when it's shoved under
my nose? Sure, he helped Jews but that was just insurance,
his cover, because the whole time he was maestro of all he
surveyed. (*Turning on* FURTWÄNGLER.) See, Wilhelm, I
think you're cunning, devious, dealing off the bottom of the
pack. You were their boy, their creature. That's the case
against you, old pal. You were like an advertising slogan for
them. This is what we produce, the greatest conductor in the
world. And you went along with it. You may not have been a
member of the Party because the truth is, Wilhelm, you
didn't need to be.

(*Suddenly, to* EMMI.)

Emmi, put that record on –

(EMMI *puts on the record of the Adagio from Bruckner's Seventh
Symphony*.)

ARNOLD: You know what that is?

FURTWÄNGLER: Of course I know what that is –

ARNOLD: Okay, so what is it?

FURTWÄNGLER: Bruckner's Seventh. The Adagio.

ARNOLD: Who's conducting?

FURTWÄNGLER: I am.

ARNOLD: You know the last time it was played on these air
waves?

FURTWÄNGLER: How should I know such a thing?

ARNOLD: Well then, I'll tell you. The last time this music was
played on these air waves was after they announced that your
pal Adolf had blown his brains out. Listen to it.

(*They listen.*)

Did they pick little K's recording? Did they pick some other band leader? No, they picked you and why? Because you and nobody else represented them so beautifully. When the Devil died they wanted his band leader to play the funeral march. You were *everything* to them.

(*The music plays.*)

FURTWÄNGLER: (*Near to breakdown but struggling for control*) I have always tried – I have tried to analyze myself closely. You are right, Major. I am no better than anybody else. But I must always say what my instincts are. In staying here, I believed – I thought – I walked a tightrope between exile and the gallows. You seem to be blaming me for not having allowed myself to be hanged.

(DAVID *takes the record off.*)

I tried to defend the intellectual life of my people against an evil ideology. I did not directly oppose the Party because, I told myself, this was not my job. I would have benefitted no one by active resistance. But I never hid my opinions. As an artist I was determined that music, at least, would remain untouched, untainted. If I had taken any active part in politics I couldn't have remained here. Please understand me correctly: an artist cannot be entirely apolitical. He must have some political convictions because he is, after all, a human being. As a citizen, it is an artist's duty to express these convictions. But as a musician, I am more than a citizen. I am a citizen of this country in that eternal sense to which the genius of great music testifies. I know that a single performance of a great masterpiece was a stronger and more vital negation of the spirit of Buchenwald and Auschwitz than words. Human beings are free wherever Wagner and Beethoven are played. Music transported them to regions where the torturers and murderers could do them no harm.

(ARNOLD *reacts as if a volcano is about to erupt inside him. A great, uncontrollable surge of anger wells up in him, causing him to pace alarmingly. He grabs the baton from his desk, stands trembling before* FURTWÄNGLER, *and snaps it in half. He pushes his face close to* FURTWÄNGLER *who recoils, terrified.*

DAVID *half stands, ready to intervene physically. During this*
EMMI *puts her fingers in her ears.*)

ARNOLD: (*His rage erupting with quiet, terrifying menace*) Have you
ever smelled burning flesh? I smelt it four miles away. Four
miles away, I smelt it. I smell it now, I smell it at night
because I can't sleep any more with the stench of it in my
nostrils. I'll smell it for the rest of my life. Have you seen the
crematoria and the gas ovens? Have you seen the mounds of
rotting corpses being shovelled into gigantic craters by the
men and women who murdered them? I saw these things
with my own eyes. And I've seen it every night since, night
after night, and I wake screaming seeing it. I know I won't
sleep undisturbed ever again. You talk to me about culture
and art and music? You putting that in the scales, Wilhelm?
You setting culture and art and music against the millions
put to death by your pals? The pals you could call to save a
couple of Jews when thousands, millions of them, were being
annihilated? Is that what you're putting on the scales? Yes, I
blame you for not getting hanged, I blame you for your
cowardice. You strutted and swaggered, king-pin in a
shithouse. You talk to me of walking a tightrope between
exile and the gallows, and I say to you, lies –

FURTWÄNGLER: (*Breaking down*) I love my country, I believe in
art, what was I to do?

ARNOLD: Act courageously. Just think of real courage, think of
what men like Emmi's father did, risking their lives, not
their careers –

(*He sees* EMMI *has her fingers in her ears, yells at her.*)

For Chrissake, Emmi, take your goddam fingers out of your
ears –

(*She does so, tense, strained.*)

I'm talking about your father, I'm talking about real
courage, I'm talking about him risking his fucking life –

(*She screams, the chilling sound of one who can take no more.*
RODE *comes to the door and looks in. All stare at her, shocked.*)

EMMI: My father only joined the plot when he realized we could
not win the war.

(*She cries quietly.*)

ARNOLD: Get out, Helmuth, you revolt me.

(RODE *goes.*)

FURTWÄNGLER: (*Desperate*) Major, what kind of a world do you want? What kind of world are you going to make? Don't you honestly understand the power of art to communicate beauty and pain and triumph? Even if you can't admit it, don't you believe that music especially transcends language and national barriers and speaks directly to the human spirit? If you honestly believe the only reality is the material world, you will have nothing left but feculence more foul-smelling than that which pervades your nights – (*Near to breakdown.*) This isn't just, this isn't fair. How was I to know what they were capable of? No one knew. No one knew they were gangsters, atrocious, depraved. (*He breaks down, buries his face in his hands.*) Oh God, I don't want to stay in this country. Yes, yes, it would have been better if I'd left in 1934, it would have been better if I'd left – (*Suddenly retching.*) I'm going to be sick –

(*He stands, a hand to his mouth.* EMMI *goes to him.*)

ARNOLD: (*Yelling*) Helmuth!

(RODE *comes to the door.*)

Show your friend to the toilet and then tell him to get the hell out of here.

(RODE *and* EMMI *help* FURTWÄNGLER.

Emmi, Helmuth can manage –

(EMMI *ignores him and exits with* RODE *and* FURTWÄNGLER. ARNOLD *stares into space as if bereft.* DAVID *seems drained.*)

DAVID: We'll never understand. Only tyrannies understand the power of art. I wonder how I would have behaved in his position? I'm not certain I'd have 'acted courageously'. And what about you, Major? I have a feeling we might just have followed orders.

ARNOLD: I'm only a claims assessor. Who cares about me? But everyone kept telling me your man was something special. And you know what? He's not special at all.

DAVID: You know what I say he is, Major?

ARNOLD: No, what do you say he is, David?

DAVID: I say he's like a fallen priest –

ARNOLD: And what would you know about priests, Lieutenant Vile?

DAVID: (*A smile*) Only what I read in books.

ARNOLD: Yeah, and what did you read?

DAVID: That they can be inadequate human beings. They can lie, they can fornicate, they can drink, they can deceive. But they can still put God into the mouths of the faithful. If you believe in that sort of thing.

ARNOLD: You know what I say *you* are, David?

DAVID: I know what you say I am, Major.

ARNOLD: Yeah, but you're worse. You're a liberal piece of shit. You don't know right from wrong.

(EMMI *returns, slightly dazed, holding a visitor's card.* ARNOLD *goes to his desk, lifts the telephone and dials.*)

ARNOLD: (*Into the telephone*) Give me Alex Vogel. Major Arnold.

(DAVID *turns to the records near Emmi's desk, starts to sort through until he finds what he's looking for.*)

EMMI (*To* DAVID; *quietly*) He thanked me and gave me his visiting card. He asked me to have dinner with him.

(DAVID *half smiles, then removes the Bruckner and puts another record on the turntable.*)

ARNOLD: (*Into the telephone*) Vogel? Major Arnold. I don't know if we've got a case that'll stand up, but we can sure as hell give him a hard time –

(*At full volume the sound of the subdued opening of Beethoven's Ninth Symphony.*)

ARNOLD: (*To* DAVID) Hey, turn that off, can't you see I'm on the phone? (*Into the telephone.*) Yeah, yeah, but it makes no – never mind, we got a tame journalist who'll write what we'll tell him. (*Listens.*) Yeah, a guy called Delbert Clark, *New York Times* –

(*The great chords sound.*)

ARNOLD: Jesus Christ, what the hell are you doing? Turn that goddam thing down –

(*But* DAVID *ignores him, sits, implacable, listening.* RODE *opens the door a crack, stands listening with a sickly smile.*

FURTWÄNGLER *stumbles into the bomb rubble, as if a broken man struggling to regain his composure.*)

ARNOLD: Turn if off!

(ARNOLD *rises carrying the telephone, goes to the door of the back
room but the flex won't reach. He stands in the doorway, talking
and listening, his back to the others who sit, expressionless,
listening.*
In the rubble, FURTWÄNGLER *hears the music but he cannot
identify its source. His left hand trembles but it is only his way of
sensing the tempo.*
After a while the music and the lights begin to fade to Blackout.)

POISON PEN

For
Judy Daish

O I am very sick and sorrowful,
O brown halo in the sky near the moon, drooping upon the sea.
O troubled reflection in the sea!
O throat! O throbbing heart!
And I sing uselessly, uselessly all the night.
O past! O happy life! O songs of joy!

In the air, in the woods, over fields,
Loved! loved! loved! loved! loved!
But my mate no more, no more with me!
      We two together no more!

from *Out of the Cradle Endlessly Rocking* by Walt Whitman,
set to music by Frederick Delius as *Sea Drift*

AUTHOR'S NOTE

This play is inspired by the events surrounding the death of the music critic, Philip Heseltine, in December 1930. A coroner's jury returned an open verdict.

The author wishes to acknowledge a memoir of Philip Heseltine by Cecil Gray, published by Jonathan Cape, 1934.

CHARACTERS

ERIC WELLS, a music critic, aged between 35 and 45
LARRY RIDER, 25ish, a dancer
RUPERT GRACE, 40ish, a music publisher
JULIETTE SMITH, a student of music, aged between 25 and 30
PEANUT COE, 45ish, one of Eric's drinking companions
CONRAD LEARY, 40ish, another drinking companion
A LONDON POLICEMAN
A COUNTRY POLICEMAN

The action takes place between Saturday 27 and Tuesday 30 December 1930, simultaneously in a basement flat in Tite Street, Chelsea, and a country cottage in Eynsford, Kent.

SET

The stage is divided in two, but not necessarily in half or on the same level.

One set is the main room of a basement flat in Tite Street, Chelsea. Through a barred window at the back, steps can be seen leading down from the street. There are two doors: one to the bedroom, the other to a narrow hallway and the front door. One corner of the room is hidden by a screen which conceals a gas cooker and a sink. Gas and electric meters are visible above the screen. There is an upright piano, a table, chairs and a desk. There is also a telephone and a gramophone. Christmas cards here and there, and a small Christmas tree brightly decorated. Flowers. A gas fire. Although there are many books and musical scores, it is meticulously tidy.

The other set is the small front room on the ground floor of a country cottage in Kent, somewhat in disrepair. Through leaded windows greenery can be seen. The cottage is neglected, the garden wild and encroaching. There is one door to a back kitchen and upstairs. There is an upright piano with a metronome on it, a divan, a couple of chairs. There is a sad little Christmas tree in a corner, decorated with a single strand of tinsel. A fire in a grate. The room is strewn with music manuscript, empty bottles and is a mess.

NOTE: The switch of focus from one set to another is, for the sake of clarity, indicated as if the moments are precisely marked. In performance, these moments should overlap when appropriate.

Poison Pen was first presented at the Royal Exchange Theatre, Manchester, on 13 May 1993 with the following cast:

ERIC WELLS	Tom Courtenay
LARRY RIDER	Rhys Ifans
RUPERT GRACE	Michael Simkins
JULIETTE SMITH	Emma Amos
PEANUT COE	Polly James
CONRAD LEARY	Sean Barrett
LONDON POLICEMAN	John Capps
COUNTRY POLICEMAN	Tim Lambert
Directed by	Ronald Harwood
Design by	Johanna Bryant
Lighting by	Robert Bryan
Music by	Alexândra Harwood

ACT ONE

SCENE ONE

Just before 7 p.m. on Saturday 27 December 1930.

In the cottage: JULIETTE SMITH *lies on the divan, near the fire. She wears a dressing-gown. She stares into space. She is in her late twenties. She is extremely beautiful, but fragile, withdrawn and, at present, almost lifeless. She wears no make-up. The metronome on the piano is beating out a slow, adagio rhythm.*

In the basement flat: ERIC WELLS, *distraught, is pacing furiously as though in torment, almost demented. While striding to and fro, he holds on to his head as if trying to keep it on his shoulders. He is bearded, neat. In calmer mood he is precise, gentle, kind but can also be prissy and sharp.*

LARRY RIDER, *twenty-five, enters from the bedroom. He is in the middle of dressing and wears the trousers of a grey, pinstripe suit. He is struggling to fix the front stud of his shirt collar. He is pretty, pale, highly nervous. Alarmed by* ERIC's *mood, he tries to stand in his way or keep pace with him.*

LARRY: (*Gently*) Eric, stop it, stop it, please, stop it, he'll be here any moment, please calm down, please, sweetie, sweetie, please –
(*But* ERIC *continues to pace for a moment and then, turning, stops dead as if suddenly aware of* LARRY's *presence. Silence. Then:*)

ERIC: What time is it?

LARRY: Almost seven. He's due any minute. (*Watches him carefully.*) Are you all right?

ERIC: Yes.

LARRY: I wish you wouldn't pace like that, Eric –

ERIC: I just wish all this was behind us. God knows we don't deserve any of it, you and I, Larry. I'm sorry. I know the pacing frightens you.
(ERIC *sinks into a chair.*)

LARRY: Don't apologize, I understand, I understand only too well.

ERIC: The whole business is so dispiriting –

LARRY: Don't be cross with me now, but I do wish you'd see a
doctor –

ERIC: No, thank you –

LARRY: But why not? These days they can give you pills for
nerves –

ERIC: I'm not suffering from nerves, dear, I'm suffering from
terror which in turn makes me depressed. And I have never
seen a doctor in all my life, and I'm not going to start now.
No, that's not entirely accurate. I was, of course, examined
for my army medical –

LARRY: Yes, but that's just 'Let's see your privates and cough',
isn't it? I mean a real doctor –

ERIC: When we get this business settled one way or another, my
spirits will rise. I promise you.

LARRY: All right, have it your own way. I'll tell you what will
make your spirits rise. After we've heard what this Mr Grace
has to say, we'll pop down to the pub, keep our date with
Peanut and Conrad, and glad-eye the Grenadier Guards. All
of them. That'll cheer us up, won't it?
(ERIC *manages a laugh.*)
There, never mind your spirits rising, they're fluttering
heavenwards.
(ERIC *suddenly has a lost look now.* LARRY *watches him
anxiously, then exits into the bedroom.*
In the cottage: JULIETTE *snaps to, crosses to the metronome and
stops it ticking. She goes to the windows and looks out.*
In the basement flat: ERIC *leans back in the chair, eyes closed,
calm.* LARRY *returns from the bedroom. He has put on his tie and
jacket. He goes to* ERIC, *stands behind him and gently massages
his temples.*
In the cottage: JULIETTE *suddenly exits.*
In the basement flat:)

LARRY: Better now?

ERIC: Much. Thank you, Larry.

LARRY: I'm nervous, too. As a matter of fact, I'm also frightened
out of my wits.

ERIC: I don't see why you should be. It's my life that's being
threatened, not yours.

LARRY: But this man we're expecting, this Mr Grace, he may be a hired assassin –

ERIC: Oh, don't be ridiculous. Godwin hasn't the money to hire an assassin –

LARRY: Well, it could be a friend of his, someone who'd do it as a favour –

ERIC: Do what as a favour?

LARRY: Kill us, Eric, kill us!

ERIC: (*Amused*) Why should he want to kill you? It's me he's threatened, dear –

LARRY: I'd be a witness, wouldn't I, I mean, if he murdered you and I saw him do it, he'd want me out the way, wouldn't he?

ERIC: Larry, you really must stop reading Edgar Wallace. (*Rising.*) Thank you, dear, you do that beautifully. (*He turns and looks at* LARRY.) What are you wearing?

LARRY: A suit. You said I had to look manly.

ERIC: Yes, dear, manly, not boring.

LARRY: Same thing, isn't it? I thought I looked very BBC.

ERIC: Precisely. Where did you get it?

(ERIC *goes to a mirror, tidies his appearance, combing his hair, smoothing his beard, straightening his bow tie.* LARRY *starts to tidy the already tidy room.*)

LARRY: From Mavis Parr. She was the wardrobe mistress on *No, No, Nanette!*, she's on *Show Boat* now, she'll do anything for me, she's a terrible slut, I said, 'Mavis, I need your help, I'm going to a fancy dress party tomorrow,' – I didn't want to tell her the real reason, of course – and she said, 'Fancy dress, oh, lovely, what d'you want to go as?' I said, 'Normal.' 'Ooh,' she said, 'that'll take some doing,' and produced this. Cheeky tart.

(ERIC *goes to a cupboard, finds a bottle of Scotch, a soda siphon, three glasses and arranges them on a tray.*)

ERIC: We mustn't drink too much tonight. We have to keep our wits about us.

LARRY: You shouldn't have invited him here, Eric. We should have met him on neutral ground, in broad daylight, in Piccadilly Circus –

(*He continues to tidy needlessly and obsessively.* ERIC *crosses to the gramophone, finds a record, puts it on the lid in readiness. He turns to the upright piano and opens the lid. From a shelf he takes the printed copy of a song and as he places it on the piano there is the sound of footsteps descending the stone stairs into the basement area.*)

LARRY: (*Freezing*) He's here! Oh Christ, Eric, let's have a drink before he –

(*The doorbell rings.*)

ERIC: Good idea. You have a little one, mind –

LARRY: No need to be personal –

(ERIC *laughs as* LARRY *quickly pours them both a Scotch which they drink. The doorbell rings again.*)

LARRY: (*A whisper*) Shall I go – ?

ERIC: No. And remember, say as little as possible.

(LARRY *pours another Scotch for himself.*)

Just lurk. We'll listen to what he has to say. Then I'll do the talking. You keep as quiet as possible. And be menacing.

LARRY: Menacing? Me? Now I know what they mean by a character part. Should we search him for concealed weapons?

ERIC: Larry, dear, don't be such a bloody fool –

LARRY: Could be fun –

(*He drinks. The doorbell rings again.*)

LARRY: Ooh, she's an impatient one.

(ERIC *steadies himself, goes out into the hall and is heard opening the door.*)

ERIC'S VOICE: Mr Grace? Come in.

(ERIC *returns followed by* RUPERT GRACE, *thirty-nine, fine looking in the Rupert Brooke mould. He carries a briefcase. He is tense and watchful. The atmosphere is awkward, uneasy.*)

ERIC: May I introduce Laurence Rider?

(RUPERT *and* LARRY, *both wary, nod to each other.*)

He's my bodyguard. Scotch?

RUPERT: Thank you.

ERIC: Soda?

RUPERT: A splash.

ERIC: You won't mind if I don't join you. I hardly touch the stuff. Help yourself, Larry.

LARRY: I already have.

    (ERIC *pours the drink which he hands to* RUPERT. LARRY *helps himself to another. Throughout,* LARRY *drinks almost continuously,* ERIC *hardly at all.*)

ERIC and LARRY: (*Toasting* RUPERT) Merry Christmas.

RUPERT: And to you. (*He sips his drink.*) I had hoped this would be a private meeting.

ERIC: These days I see no one alone.

    (*A brief silence.*)

RUPERT: I suspect you know why I'm here.

ERIC: (*Tight smile*) I suspect I don't.

LARRY: Before you begin, can you say you are who you prove – ? (*Breaks off.*) You know what I mean – I mean –

ERIC: Do be quiet, Larry, there's a good boy. (*To* RUPERT; *another squeezed smile.*) He's very fastidious.

    (RUPERT *produces a business card and hands it to* LARRY *who scrutinizes it.*)

LARRY: Anyone could have a business card printed.

RUPERT: I haven't come here to play games, Mr Wells. You know very well who I am. I'm a director of Williams and Hawker and we publish the music of Peter Godwin.

ERIC: I apologize if we seem rude, but we cannot be too careful. I have received threatening letters from Godwin and must take every precaution.

RUPERT: Peter's threatened you?

ERIC: You didn't know?

RUPERT: No –

ERIC: When I say threaten I put it mildly. And he has already taken steps to carry out his threats. My life is in danger, Mr Grace. I live in daily terror. Hence, Mr Rider here.

RUPERT: What do you mean, he has already taken steps?

ERIC: (*Ignoring the question*) Would you like to begin this 'meeting'? Your word, I think. You said you wanted a 'meeting'. Shall we begin? Do sit.

    (ERIC *sits at the table.* RUPERT *sits opposite, takes out a file from his briefcase.* LARRY *produces a notebook.*)

LARRY: Should I take notes, Eric? Is that a good idea?

ERIC: If it keeps you quiet, a very good idea. Let us hear the reason for your visit, Mr Grace.

(LARRY *remains standing, drinks steadily, watches. He becomes tipsy quickly.*)

RUPERT: Williams and Hawker have published the music of Peter Godwin since 1922, so we are well aware of how important your reviews and your articles have been. All of them, I believe, in the monthly publication, *The Sackbut.*

ERIC: And also in *The Musical Times.* And in foreign publications. I have written extensively about Peter Godwin's music. I say this in all modesty, Mr Grace, I made Peter Godwin. I don't think that should be forgotten. I discovered Peter Godwin. I brought his name to the notice of the musical world. Yes, mostly in *The Sackbut.* I think it fair to say he would have no career, no reputation, without me.

RUPERT: There's no dispute about that, although I'm bound to point out that if you hadn't discovered him, someone else would have. He is a brilliant composer, as you yourself have said on many occasions –

ERIC: *Was* a brilliant composer. There is very little you can tell me about Peter Godwin. I've known him all my life, well, nearly all my life. We were at school together, Sedbergh, in Yorkshire. We met again at Oxford. He wasn't up at the University but lived in the town, off the Cowley Road, I remember. We lost touch a bit after that but then, of course, we were both conscientious objectors –

LARRY: I was too young to fight –

ERIC: (*Sweetly*) Larry, do be quiet, there's a dear, or go to the pub and tell Peanut and Conrad we shall be with them shortly –

LARRY: I only said –

ERIC: (*Flaring with disproportionate rage*) Shut up, keep your mouth tight shut.

(*Brief embarrassed silence.*)

LARRY: (*To* RUPERT) I do find it a laugh, don't you, that pacifists are always more violent than your average Tommy? I've known both sorts so you take my word for it, ducky –

ERIC: When I first heard Godwin's music, fourteen or fifteen years ago, I knew instantly I was listening to a magical and

original sound. I was just beginning my career as a critic but
I was lavish with my praise. Young critics usually start by
giving anything new bad reviews. That's because they're
cautious and because bad reviews are so much easier to write.
But I threw caution to the winds and said that, after Delius,
Peter Godwin was probably the most gifted composer of our
time. He wrote to thank me. Of course, artists are always
prone to think that the critics who praise them have the finest
minds. He was very – grateful and complimentary. We met.
We dined. We drank. We discussed trivia, such as music and
art and life. We had so much in common. School, our
sojourn in Oxford, our shared pacifist views. I like to think
we became friends. He took my advice on matters musical –
a tonality here, a harmony there. More importantly, we
discussed standards of excellence, aspirations in art. And, I
believe this to be indisputable, it was entirely due to me that
he became greatly respected.

RUPERT: As I've said, that's not in dispute, Mr Wells –

ERIC: However, in recent months, oh, it's well over a year now,
there is no doubt in my mind that his music has deteriorated
alarmingly. Before publishing any adverse criticism I wrote
to him personally, on more than one occasion, warning him
of my misgivings. I suggested we meet. I thought I might be
of some help. We had, I believed, a civilized, agreeable
relationship, unusual between a critic and a creative artist. I
received no reply.

LARRY: There's gratitude for you –

ERIC: I'm sorry to sound arrogant but my integrity as a critic and
as a musicologist had to be protected. I had no alternative
but to make the matter public. Last year, yes, exactly a year
ago, after a recital of his gruesome carols and drinking songs
at the Wigmore Hall, I expressed my opinions in print.

RUPERT: That was the review in which you asserted that his work
had become – (*Consults the file.*) 'lightweight, superficial, not
to say meretricious'.

ERIC: Finish the quotation, Mr Grace. I believe I went on to say
that he was now giving the public what he thought they
wanted to hear, which is the mark of a truly second-rate

artist. I believe I also said that the only conclusion to be drawn is that Mr Godwin, whom I had long thought was touched with genius, had decided to betray his unearthly gifts.

RUPERT: You are entitled to your opinions –

ERIC: Thank you, how kind –

RUPERT: And since, as far as I know, we never thanked you for the good reviews, I have no intention now of complaining about the bad ones.

LARRY: What a balanced view of life you must have.

RUPERT: You are, I believe, now not only the chief critic of *The Sackbut* but also have recently become its editor.

ERIC: That's correct. I have edited the magazine for almost a year.

RUPERT: Then your legal advisers will no doubt have made you aware of the dangers that arise out of your latest attack on Godwin in this month's edition.

ERIC: We may be an influential publication, Mr Grace, but we are very small. We can't afford legal advisers.

RUPERT: I suspected that might be the case. So, allow me to explain your legal position.

LARRY: I'm taking notes of this, Eric –

RUPERT: In this month's edition of your magazine, published last week, you accused Peter Godwin of plagiarism.

ERIC: Just so.

RUPERT: That is a very serious charge.

ERIC: Yes.

RUPERT: You accused him of plagiarizing *Sea Drift* by Frederick Delius.

ERIC: And the words by Walt Whitman which Delius had set so magnificently. Godwin has shamelessly copied both the music and the poem.

RUPERT: I have to tell you, Mr Wells, that, in my opinion, you have made a ridiculous accusation that will not hold up in a court of law.

(ERIC *rises, suddenly agitated*.)

ERIC: Oh, really? And what are your qualifications for reaching such a conclusion? You call yourself a music publisher. Well,

are you a musician or a publisher? An artist or a man of
business? I should like to know your credentials.

LARRY: Don't worry, Eric, I'm taking a note of this, too. (*To*
RUPERT; *pouring himself another drink, too*.) Your credentials,
if you please, dear sir. I'm poised and ready.

RUPERT: After the war, I read music at Balliol –

ERIC: Oh dear, how very impressive. Are you a precocious
instrumentalist then, a dab hand on the pianoforte, or do you
sing? Perhaps you're a counter tenor, or what is popularly
known in the trade as a castrato?

RUPERT: (*Not allowing himself to be provoked*) I play the organ.

LARRY: Same thing, really.

RUPERT: Actually, I'm a not very good organist.

LARRY: Oh, what a shame –

ERIC: Larry –

RUPERT: Mr Wells, I have brought with me a document which I
am going to ask you to sign.
(*He searches in the file.*)

LARRY: Oh God, never sign anything, Eric, without a solicitor
present. You remember what happened to poor old Johnny
Fielding? And never put anything in writing, that's what a
vicar told me when I was quite young –

RUPERT: (*Offers the document*) By signing this, you will agree to
withdraw your charge of plagiarism against Peter Godwin.
You will print a retraction on the front page of your
magazine. You will say you were mistaken and that –
(ERIC *marches to the desk, pulls open a drawer, produces a
bundle of letters which he waves in* RUPERT's *face*.)

ERIC: What about these, then? Will you guarantee that these are
no longer sent to me?

RUPERT: I don't know what you're talking about –

ERIC: These letters – (*Reading from the letters at random*.) 'Judas!
Judas! If you persist you will die like Judas, I will see to it
personally that you die like Judas!' Yes, yes, yes, and what
about this? 'Why do you crucify me? Why do you drive the
nails into my hands and feet and pierce my heart with your
knife? Know that I will take my revenge!' And here, oh yes,
here, 'Watch each step you take with particular care. I'll get

you when you least expect it. I shall choke the life out of you.
You are a dead man, Eric Wells.' And this –

LARRY: Please don't go on, sweetie, I can't bear it –
(*Silence.*)

RUPERT: (*Subdued*) May I see?
(ERIC *hands the letters to him. While* RUPERT *reads,* ERIC *pours himself another drink. So does* LARRY.)

ERIC: Wonderful, isn't it, all that violence gushing out of an
avowed pacifist. And he, like me, was a conscientious
objector –

LARRY: You've said that before, Eric –

ERIC: Did you serve in the late conflict, Mr Grace?

RUPERT: Yes.

LARRY: Navy, were you? Or Guards?

ERIC: Were you bombed and shelled and did you watch young
men die in agony? Or did you have what they call a good
war? Perhaps you served in an office or perhaps you played
marching songs on the organ?

RUPERT: I was a Military Policeman.

LARRY: Oh Gawd –

RUPERT: My job was to arrest deserters, interrogate them and
then hand them over for trial. No. It was not a particularly
good war.
(*Brief silence.*)

ERIC: I'm sorry. I'm sorry. My outburst was uncalled for. I'm in
a particularly –
(*He falls silent, lost.* RUPERT *continues to read, looks up.*)

RUPERT: I'm bound to say I'm shocked by these letters.

ERIC: I'm shocked, too.

LARRY: There you are, Eric, he's shocked, you're shocked, we're
all shocked. That's the reason I'm here, Mr Grace.
Protection. I can be a demon when roused. And how can we
know when he'll strike?

ERIC: When I said he's already taken steps, I have to tell you that
he has been following me. Two days ago, at Sloane Square
Tube Station, someone nudged me just as the train was
coming in. I nearly fell on the rails.

LARRY: The Circle Line.

(*Silence.* LARRY *sips his drink.* RUPERT *looks through the letters again. Then:*)

ERIC: Believe me, Mr Grace, no one regrets this turn of events more than I. Peter Godwin and I were friends, dare I say it, collaborators. (*As if in a dream.*) He was everything I was not. Creative. Extrovert. Wild. Insensitive in an attractive, amusing sort of way. Resilient. (*Snapping out of it.*) Yet we had at least one important thing in common. I remember once a wonderful conversation with Godwin. I said I'd never been able to understand patriotism, the love of empire, my country right or wrong. They always seemed to me such empty and intangible ideas, so supremely unimportant when one considers the things that really matter – the common heritage of humanity without distinction of race or colour or creed. He agreed absolutely and said – I remember this so clearly – he said that holding such views made one's position extremely difficult, because unless one follows the line of least resistance and becomes a hypocrite, one is cut off from at least nine-tenths of one's fellow beings. I am determined, he said, not to live a lie. That is my creed also.

LARRY: Cut off, yes, but then who isn't?

(RUPERT *finishes reading. He looks up.*)

RUPERT: These letters are appalling, I had no idea –

ERIC: No.

RUPERT: Have you gone to the police?

(*Incredulous silence.*)

LARRY: Are you out of your tiny Chinese mind, dear?

(*He and* ERIC *laugh quietly.* RUPERT *re-reads a couple of passages.*

In the cottage: JULIETTE *returns carrying an oil lamp, a mirror and a small make-up tray. She is now dressed, wearing the clothes of a cheap whore: hair loose, low-cut blouse, tight skirt with a split, high-heeled shoes, black fishnet stockings. She goes to the window, places the oil lamp so as to get as much light as possible for making up her face. Eventually, when she is finished, she powders but doesn't remove the powder so that she looks like a white-faced clown. She sits facing the door, waiting.*

In the basement flat: At the appropriate moment.)

RUPERT: May I ask what was the sequence of events?

ERIC: What do you mean?

RUPERT: Did these letters arrive after your bad reviews of Godwin's music? Or did you receive the letters and then decide to write what you did?

ERIC: (*Very quiet*) I deeply resent the implication of that remark. Of course those letters came in response to his bad notices. I would never allow personal feelings to tarnish my professional judgement. How dare you. I myself lead too precarious a life to permit such folly. Peter Godwin has sullied his gift. But had he kept it pure and beautiful, I would have said so loudly and with pride. He did not protect what he'd been given. And I said so. In print. (*Starting to pace again.*) And don't think I don't know the kind of life he leads –

LARRY: (*Concerned*) Calmly, sweetie –

RUPERT: But that's irrelevant, isn't it? His private life has nothing to do with you as a critic, don't you agree? You're a musicologist not a moralist. In my view, an artist's private life has nothing to do with his art. If it did, what would we make of Beethoven or Schubert or Wagner? If you've allowed some innate disapproval of Godwin's moral character to influence your appreciation of his music, I would say that was unworthy, unjust and – and vindictive. (LARRY *becomes anxious.*)

ERIC: Let me try to explain something, Mr Grace. In art, be it music or poetry or painting, the artist has constantly to make choices. Not whether he will employ one harmony or another, use one word instead of two, prefer magenta to crimson. No, although I've no doubt those choices have to be made every minute, every hour, what really matters is the moral choice: what will his work of art express? And how is that choice to be made? The great artist, in my opinion, has to listen to his inner voice, the one that dictates the nature of his creation. Just as in life, we make moral decisions daily. The few really good people I know, those who do others no deliberate harm, hear an inner voice which forbids them to act unworthily. Others hear the voice but ignore it most of

the time. Yet others hear no voice at all. Peter Godwin now
belongs to the last category –

RUPERT: Is that fair? You said he was a pacifist. Isn't that because
he listened to some voice that forbade him to go to war?
Wasn't that a moral choice?

ERIC: Listen to what I've said –

RUPERT: I'm sorry –

ERIC: He belongs to that category *now*. He has lost what little – for
want of a better word – conscience he may once have had.
Music has always poured out of him, good music, bad,
indifferent music and sometimes great music. And until fairly
recently he relied on me – this is not a boast but a statement of
fact – he relied on me to guide him. His inner voice, it was
never any more than a whisper, has fallen silent. He will write
anything and everything. He has no voice to tell him right
from wrong, good from evil. Herein, as I'm sure you've
grasped, lies the role of the critic. If the voice is not a force
within the artist, then it had better be provided by a force
outside.

RUPERT: That is bestowing upon the critic more than perhaps he
deserves. And what of critics who use their so-called critical
objectivity as a shield to hide their animosity, personal
prejudices, and their deep envy of the creative artist?

ERIC: I didn't say all critics. As in everything, there are good critics
and bad critics –

RUPERT: But how is one to know the difference?

ERIC: You can always tell a bad critic. He reviews the programme
notes instead of the music.

LARRY: Tell him your theory, Eric. You'll like this, Mr Grace, it's
ever so interesting.

ERIC: All right. Let's try it on him. This is only a theory, Mr Grace.
It's a way of trying to understand artists, just as some people
use astrology as a way of trying to classify the human
personality. I believe that all creative artists come into this
world with two elements: a gift, be it to compose or write or
paint. And a talent, the two elements being entirely different.
The gift is the gift. But talent is what he makes of it. When the
two are equally disposed you get genius. And it is very rare.

(RUPERT *is about to say something*.)

Don't bother to argue, I will not defend it reasonably. It is, as I said, only a theory. The talent has to nurture the gift which is a secret, arcane thing, a mystery, sometimes even to the artist himself. The gift has to be tended, disciplined, trained, exposed to the world, and at all times, the gift has to be kept alive. Talent, in my theory, is the inner voice that restrains, encourages, understands, is the innate arbiter of taste, and sometimes a ruthless exploiter, especially if the gift is small. I believe Godwin was born with a great gift but almost no talent. And now, for reasons known or unknown to him, his gift has degenerated, like a once respectable woman whoring on the streets, hoping to take the fancy of the first customer who passes. In my review I used the word meretricious. Let me remind you that it means 'befitting a harlot'.

LARRY: Does it? Befitting a harlot? Fancy that, Hedda Gabler, fancy that –

RUPERT: But what about the critic's talent, his inner world, Mr Wells? What if that befits a harlot?

(LARRY *pours himself a drink*.)

ERIC: Criticism is not the same as creation. At the highest level it is an objective endeavour. I am not talking about journalists in the popular press –

LARRY: Don't mention them to me, what they did to poor dear Ivor, crucifixion isn't the word, I remember him saying to me –

ERIC: (*Vehement*) Larry, get out! You're as pissed as a judge in chambers. Get out!

LARRY: Pissed? Me?

ERIC: I don't know why I bother with you. What good would you be if Godwin stuck a knife in my back?

LARRY: I'd pluck it out, that's what I'd do, I'd pluck it out –

ERIC: Oh, pluck off!

(*They laugh joyously*. LARRY *pours drinks*. RUPERT *refuses one*.)

RUPERT: What about the artist as a man in all this, Mr Wells? The creator, battling against himself, the world, his talent at odds with his gift, to use your image, struggling to make a living –

ERIC: Oh dear, you're a romantic. Godwin doesn't battle. Godwin doesn't struggle. He's ruthless and tough and unscrupulous. Like all artists. He has facility and that's a trivial thing. Like his ability to make up rather bad limericks on the spur of the moment. Meaningless. He's always needed an exterior censor, guide, mentor, because he is both morally and critically deficient within. I have true and profound feeling for Peter Godwin. I want him to climb the heights, not grovel in the gutter.

RUPERT: Then please, please, leave him in peace to attempt that climb in his own way and in his own time. I've had two conversations with him in the last week. He is extremely distressed and I think you are now seriously threatening his sanity and his ability to compose.

ERIC: (*Sudden agitation*) I'm threatening *his* sanity? What about me? What about me?

LARRY: Quietly now, Eric, quietly –

ERIC: (*Driven, overlapping*) He is going to kill me. He has said so and I believe him. I'm going to die at his hands –

LARRY: Oh please don't say that, I can't bear it.

ERIC: (*He downs a drink*) I'm living in a state of terror at the moment, terror of my life –

LARRY: Don't be frightened, Eric, I'm here, I'm here –
(ERIC *is still, staring into space, his back to the others.* LARRY *takes this opportunity of scuttling to* RUPERT.)

LARRY: (*Mouthing, whispered*) I must talk to you alone. It's terribly important –

ERIC: (*Turning suddenly*) As sure as I stand here, I know with absolute certainty that Peter Godwin means to put an end to my existence.
(*He squeezes a smile. Silence.*)

RUPERT: Mr Wells, will you allow me to try to lower the temperature? If you sign this document agreeing to retract your charges, I'll give you my word that I will personally see Godwin, and get him to stop making these threats.

ERIC: You obviously don't know him very well. How often have you met him?

RUPERT: The truth is I've never met him. I'm new to the firm. I've only spoken to him on the telephone.

ERIC: Oh, he's got a telephone now, has he?

RUPERT: No, he telephones me from a public call box. And we correspond, of course.

ERIC: Yes, he's always been secretive has Godwin.

RUPERT: I don't even know what he looks like. There were no photographs of him in the files.

(ERIC *hesitates a moment, then goes to a drawer, rummages in it, finds a photograph and hands it to* RUPERT.)

RUPERT: Which one is he?

ERIC: Second from the left. Given time and the life he leads, I daresay he's changed.

RUPERT: I daresay. (*Handing back the photograph.*) One of you has to take the first step towards reconciliation. Why not you? Stop persecuting him.

ERIC: I am not persecuting him. And I hope you realize, Mr Grace, that you are publishing a composer who is a plagiarist. I am not as certain of the law as you seem to be but I suspect, in the circumstances, you are as guilty as he. Like a fence. Selling stolen property knowing it to be stolen.

RUPERT: Rubbish.

LARRY: Take care now, Eric –

ERIC: Do you dismiss the charge of plagiarism? Or are you denying your own culpability?

RUPERT: Both.

ERIC: Very well. Let's settle this once and for all. (*Goes to the gramophone.*) Kindly listen. *Sea Drift* by Frederick Delius, words by Walt Whitman.

(*While* ERIC *winds up the gramophone:*)

LARRY: (*To* RUPERT) I'm a dancer myself, but resting at the moment. (*Then again urgent, whispered.*) We must talk. There's something you have to know –

(ERIC *puts the arm on the record.*)

BARITONE: (*On the record*) 'In the air, in the woods, over fields,
　　Loved! loved! loved! loved! loved!
　　But my mate no more, no more with me!
　　We two together no more!'

(ERIC *lifts the arm, then goes to the piano.*)

ERIC: And now, this, *Shanty for a Dead Love* by Peter Godwin.

You must forgive me, I'm not a very good pianist. Although at
school my nickname was 'Pianoplayer'.

(LARRY *reacts sharply;* ERIC *sings and plays.*)

'Let us sail the sea the two of us,
The two of us,
But you no more with me,
No more.'

(*He turns to* RUPERT.)

Surely, even you, on your own admission a not very good
organist, can detect, what shall I call it, the similarity?

RUPERT: No. Frankly, I can't.

LARRY: Wishy-washy sort of stuff, isn't it? Not my glass of Scotch,
dear. Couldn't dance to that, no tune, I like a tune, don't you?

RUPERT: I hear two or three words the same –

ERIC: Two or three words? Listen to them, listen to them.
Whitman: 'But my mate no more, no more with me!/We two
together no more.' Godwin: 'Let us sail the sea the two of us,
the two of us, but you no more with me, no more.' Bad enough
stealing from Delius, but cribbing Whitman as well. What did
he think? That I wouldn't notice, that he'd fool me, me of all
people? Issue your summons. Take me to court. I am armed.

LARRY: Careful, Eric, it'll cost you a wig and a gown, dear –

ERIC: (*Pacing again*) I deplore self-destruction. Godwin has
destroyed a gift that was of a sublime dimension. And now
he means to destroy me because I have found him out.

RUPERT: I'm going to make one more try. Please sign this
document and withdraw the accusation. And one further
thing. This is a request from Peter himself. I ask you, well,
I'll beg you if you like, not to review his concert next
Tuesday.

ERIC: He asked you to say that, did he?

RUPERT: Yes.

ERIC: Why won't he come and say it to me, face to face? What's
he afraid of?

RUPERT: He's not afraid. He chooses to live in a quiet village in
Kent and work.

LARRY: (*Alarmed*) For God's sake, Eric, stop pacing like that,
you'll die of exhaustion and then what will Godwin do with

himself? He'll have no one to kill – (*To* RUPERT.) I don't know what gets into him – (*And again the mouthed, urgent whisper.*) We must talk.

(ERIC *stops. Silence.*)

ERIC: He meant so much to me.

RUPERT: Then leave him in peace. Do you want my honest opinion, Mr Wells?

ERIC: You'll give it whether I say yea or nay.

LARRY: That's the truth –

RUPERT: Without knowing all the details, I'd say that both of you, you and Godwin, have allowed your private feelings for each other to interfere with your professional lives. I've now listened to both of you, and I think both of you are in the grip of a – of a – of an unnatural obsession with each other –

LARRY: Unnatural? Is he implying something untoward?

ERIC: You're wrong, Mr Grace. I am only interested in the quality of his music. Or, as is now the case, the lack of quality.

RUPERT: You remind me of one of my schoolmasters. His name was Taylor. He was obsessed with one of the boys, a rather plain, dumpy little chap, but Taylor was absolutely beastly to him, gave him dreadful punishments, picked on him in class for no rhyme or reason all in the name of 'could do better'. And then – well, it was all very unfortunate – one night Mr Taylor came into our dorm stark naked, said he loved the boy and tried to get into his bed. You remind me of Mr Taylor.

LARRY: What school was that?

(*The telephone rings.* ERIC *and* LARRY *freeze.* ERIC *nods to* LARRY, *who answers it.*)

LARRY: (*Nervously*) Sloane 2496. (*Relaxing.*) Peanut! Merry Christmas! Oh, ducky, I'm sorry, but we've been in a meeting. (*Covering the mouthpiece.*) It's Peanut, she's furious – (*Into telephone.*) No, dear, not a public meeting, no, with a publisher, a business meeting. Well, of course we're coming, dear, it's just that we'll be a little late –

(RUPERT *starts to pack his papers.*)

Five minutes. Promise. Ta-ta. (*He replaces the receiver.*) She says you said seven.

ERIC: I didn't, I said eight –

LARRY: She's fuming, and pissed as Lady Godiva.

RUPERT: Mr Wells, please sign this document. Print a retraction and undertake not to review Godwin's Wigmore Hall concert on Tuesday. In return I promise to talk to Godwin and ensure that these threats against your life –

ERIC: Come, Larry, we'll be late.

(*Brief silence.*)

LARRY: (*Quickly*) I'll see Mr Grace to the door.

(RUPERT *hesitates a moment, then goes, followed by* LARRY. *Alone,* ERIC *breathes deeply in an effort to control his alarm. He drains what is left of the Scotch, drinking from the bottle. He sways a little.*

In the cottage: JULIETTE, *now white-faced, goes to the door, opens it.*)

JULIETTE: Peter, is that you?

(*Silence. She shuts the door, stands, lost, a little frightened. She sits again, lights a cigarette, watches the door.*

In the basement flat: The sound of RUPERT *ascending the steps outside.* LARRY *returns. He is nervous.*)

LARRY: Perhaps you should have signed, Eric.

ERIC: No. I cannot recant. I know what I've written is the truth. I will not recant.

LARRY: (*A sad smile*) You sound like Joan of Arc.

ERIC: Godwin is a charlatan, a fraud, and has to be exposed.

LARRY: But is it worth risking your life?

ERIC: Yes. If one betrays one's own standards one may as well be dead.

(*Silence.*)

LARRY: (*Edgy*) Mustn't keep Peanut waiting. She'll throw a fit. You go on, sweetie, I'm going to change. I daren't go into the pub like this, I'd get laughs.

(ERIC *doesn't move, is lost in thought.*)

Go on, sweetie, it's only across the road. Don't be frightened. No harm will befall you.

(ERIC *is about to go, stops –*)

ERIC: (*Near to tears*) I don't know what I'd do without you, Larry, I do love you so –

(*He hugs him and then goes quickly.* LARRY *goes to the window, draws the curtain an inch and watches Eric ascend the steps. Nervous now, he exits.*

In the cottage: JULIETTE *stands, looks at her watch. She goes to the door again, opens it:*)

JULIETTE: Peter, I know you're there! (*No response; shouting.*) Bastard!

(*She shuts the door. She looks at her watch again, then takes off her shoes and throws them across the room. She stomps out of the room.*

In the basement flat: LARRY *returns. He is doing up a sporty shirt but isn't wearing trousers. He goes to the window and looks out carefully. He is terribly anxious. He goes back into the bedroom.*

In the cottage: JULIETTE *re-enters in her underwear. She searches for something, but cannot find it which enrages her. She exits.*

In the basement flat: Sound of footsteps down the stone steps.

LARRY *emerges from the bedroom now wearing casual clothes. A soft knock on the front door.* LARRY *goes out into the hall. Sound of the door opening.* LARRY *leads in* RUPERT.)

LARRY: Thank you for coming back.

RUPERT: I haven't very long, Mr Rider.

LARRY: Larry, please. Can't bear formality. Want a drink?

RUPERT: No, thank you –

LARRY: (*At the bottle*) Just as well, there isn't any left. I've probably had enough anyway. But I needed a little courage –

RUPERT: What is it that's so important?

LARRY: (*Nervous, uncertain*) I don't know if I should be telling you this. I don't want to be disloyal. I'm a very faithful sort of person. I'm not flighty, though I know I sometimes give that impression. But, please believe me, I don't want Eric to be hurt physically or – or in any other way. I certainly don't want him to die. But when you talked about unnatural obsessions and the artist's personal life and all that sort of thing, I had to bite my tongue. You were on to something. Whatever he may say, I'm afraid Eric has allowed personal feelings to affect his judgement. (*Brief silence.*) There's a woman, you see. (*Brief silence.*) Her name's Juliette. She lives with Godwin in the country. In Eynsford, Kent. She's

Godwin's mistress. (*Brief silence*.) I think Eric's in love with her. (*Brief silence*.) It means he's 'bi', you see. Do you know what 'bi' means? (*No response*.) Bisexual. Well, it widens the field, I always say. Eric, it seems, is ambisextrous. (*No response*.) I'm not. (*No response*.) I – I didn't know he played for the other team, if you see what I mean. We've only been together nine months and it's been ever so happy. Not that he's very demanding, far from it, but it's been – well – it's been all right. (*He hesitates*.) I shouldn't be telling you this –

RUPERT: Please go on.

(LARRY *takes a deep breath*.)

LARRY: Four months ago, at the end of August, I discovered a letter when I was tidying. I'm out of work, have been for months, and there's nothing much else to do. Eric goes into his office and I'm alone. The address at the top of the letter was simply, Eynsford, Kent. It said, 'Pianoplayer! Where have you been? It's hell without you. I want you body and soul. I want to taste you. I want to dig my nails into your back.' There was no signature. Just an initial. J. (*Brief silence*.) I must have read that letter a million times. I was in torment. You see, Eric's away a lot, visiting his old father in Abingdon, or he's at the printers, or he's just wanting to be alone to write. He was off yesterday, as a matter of fact, to Abingdon. Or so he said. Well, it was Boxing Day, wasn't it, so one may as well give him the benefit of the doubt. (*Brief silence*.) What I'm going to tell you now does not reflect well on me. The next time he said he was off to visit his father, I followed him. Instead of going to Paddington, he went to Charing Cross. I saw what train he took and caught the next one. (*Brief silence*.) Eynsford's a pretty little village. I went into a pub. Ever such a nice barman. Tony his name was. We talked. I said, 'Any celebrities living here, Tony?' Casually, you know, as if I was a star gazer. 'Oh yes,' he said. 'Peter Godwin.' 'The composer,' I said. 'Never!' He told me he was a bit of a boozer, played the piano in the pub for a sing-song, he's a wonderful pianist, Tony said. Has he a girlfriend, I asked?

Yes, he said, a tart. And he said he thought she was totally barmy. He also said there was talk she played around with another man on the side. Very uncomfortable on the side, I said. Then I asked where they lived. (*Brief silence.*) Talk about isolated. The middle of nowhere. Must be bleak in winter. But it was a lovely day, probably the last hot day we had. The cottage sits high on a sort of wooded hill. It was easy to get near without being seen. I watched from the trees, I looked right over into the garden. I couldn't have been more than, oh, from here to the door, I was that close. There was a girl in the garden sunbathing. Half naked. Awfully pretty. No sign of Eric. But then I heard her call. I hope I'm not going to offend you, Mr Grace, please forgive me, but this is exactly what she said. 'Pianoplayer,' she said, 'let's make music, let's fuck.' And then I heard him laugh. I heard Eric laugh. (*Brief silence.*) You can imagine my feelings. No. Perhaps you can't. I was devastated. Utterly devastated. I ran into the woods and – I don't mind admitting it, I – I wept. (*Brief silence.*) I don't know if you'll understand this, but it'd be easier for me if it was Peter Godwin he was seeing. Another man would be more bearable. I don't know how long it's been going on but now I suspect it's what the vendetta's all about. (*Silence.*) You're the only person I've told. It's a weight off my chest. (*Brief silence.*)

RUPERT: I realize how difficult it's been for you. But thank you for telling me. It explains much.

LARRY: I didn't confront Eric with it, although I wanted to. But, one is not without experience. I came straight back to London, got very drunk, but I was sober by the time Eric returned. And I asked myself, 'Do you want to go on living with him or not?' The answer was yes. So, I said nothing. I just have to learn to be accommodating. I mean, even marriages have ups and downs, don't they? Are you married?

RUPERT: Yes.

LARRY: Children?

RUPERT: No. We can't.

LARRY: Shame. Oh, that's a shame. I'm sorry. (*No response.*) I wanted you to know the facts. You see, I thought Eric was getting at Godwin because Godwin said he no longer needed him. But now I know the real reason is that Eric wants the girl to himself. Is that clear? I think the girl's the reason for Eric's attacks, not personal pique, not music, not art or gift or talent –

RUPERT: No –

LARRY: (*Near to breakdown*) And Godwin's jealous, that's obvious. If murder's here, can sex be far behind? (*Trying not to cry.*) Go and see her. Please. Tell her to give Eric up. Please. Will you?

(*Silence.*)

RUPERT: Yes. I will.

LARRY: (*With enormous dignity*) Thank you. Thank you very much.

(*Silence.*

In the cottage: JULIETTE *re-enters. She is wearing a see-through chiffon négligé now. She goes to a drawer and finds nail polish. She sits on the floor, in front of the fire, begins to paint her toe nails.*

In the basement flat: LARRY *pulls himself together.*)

LARRY: You better go now –

(*A rumpus outside. Clattering footsteps descend the stone steps.* ERIC *enters, followed by* PEANUT COE, *forty-five, and* CONRAD LEARY, *forty-ish, who are drunk.* PEANUT *wears black, is heavily made-up and has a bright, brittle manner.* CONRAD *is a nervy, sinewy individual. Both are heavy drinkers. They have brought bottles which* CONRAD *puts out on the table.*)

CONRAD: Merry Christmas, one and all!

(ERIC *sees* RUPERT.)

ERIC: I thought you'd gone –

LARRY: He had to come back. He forgot his briefcase –

(ERIC *stands staring dangerously at* RUPERT.)

PEANUT: (*Seeing* RUPERT) Oh! I say! Merry Christmas, there he is! Eric's told me all about you. My dear, let me introduce myself because no one else will. They call me Peanut. My real name's Monica which is frightfully common, but Peanut has a certain chic, don't you think? You're not a pansy, are you? All the most attractive men are pansies. Or married. Or both. It's the tragedy *de nos jours* –

CONRAD: Peanut, for God's sake, not straight off, you've hardly met the fellow –

PEANUT: Eric tells me you play the organ. I should love to hear you. Do you have your own organ and, if so, may I see it?

CONRAD: Shut up, Peanut, you're embarrassing.

PEANUT: Have you met Mr Leary? Conrad Leary, formerly Sergeant Leary of the Irish Fusileers, MM and bar, the bar being the one in The Man in the Moon at World's End.

CONRAD: She's been at the bottle since God created woman.

PEANUT: (*To* RUPERT) What is your name, beloved?

RUPERT: Rupert Grace, I'm just off –

PEANUT: Rupert Grace, now that's poetry, pure iambic pentameter. Rupert Grace, oh yes, that's the name for an organ-grinder if ever I've heard one –

LARRY: What sort of Christmas did you have, ducky?

PEANUT: The usual. I burned the turkey –

CONRAD: Nonsense, it was fine, Peanut, just fine –

PEANUT: He was so pissed, dear, he wouldn't have noticed if the turkey was burned or buggered.
(*They laugh.*)

CONRAD: Jesu, she's a foul-mouthed thing, God wot.

ERIC: Good presents? Larry gave me these – (*Shows cuff-links.*) Doesn't he have wonderful taste?

PEANUT: Conrad gave me soap. I always think soap the rudest present you can give. It always seems to me that the giver is trying to tell you something –
(*More laughter.*)

CONRAD: She gave me soap, too.

PEANUT: But I was trying to tell you something –
(*More laughter.*)

CONRAD: And what did you get, Laurence Rider of Tite Street?

LARRY: Eric was lavish this year –

ERIC: You deserve it –

LARRY: Bath salts, a silk shirt and this –
(*He is about to go to a drawer.*)

ERIC: No, no, no, don't, Larry. I've got them one, too –

LARRY: I was forgetting, fancy that, Hedda Gabler, fancy that –
   (ERIC *takes from his desk a gift-wrapped box and gives it to*
   PEANUT.)

ERIC: It's for both of you. (*To* RUPERT.) I always give a little
   something to special friends –
   (PEANUT *tears open the package and takes out a toy: a
   clockwork monkey with cymbals.*)

LARRY: (*Going to the drawer*) Wind it up, wind it up, I adore toys,
   don't you?
   (PEANUT *winds it up. The monkey bangs its cymbals.* LARRY
   *produces an identical monkey and winds it up, too. The two
   monkeys bang their cymbals. All, except* RUPERT, *laugh and
   make appropriate noises of approval and delight.*)

PEANUT: They remind me of those two queens who serve behind
   the bar at the Lord Nelson.

LARRY: Yes, I see what you mean –
   (*The toys run down. The laughter runs dry. They stand staring at
   the toys.*)

CONRAD: It's not what I call a useful present, is it? Drink, Mr
   Grace?

RUPERT: Thank you, no, I have to be going –

PEANUT: Nonsense, nonsense, give him a drink –

RUPERT: Really not, thank you –

PEANUT: (*Suddenly belligerent*) Why are you refusing to drink
   with me? Are you too stuck up? Don't you like the company
   of women?

CONRAD: Shut up, Peanut, you get under my armpits. (*To*
   RUPERT; *confidentially.*) Just have one, it won't harm –

PEANUT: If there's one thing I hate, it's a man who refuses to
   drink with me – like that willowy queen you were talking to
   in the pub, Eric –

LARRY: (*Sharp*) Who was that, Eric?

PEANUT: A dreadful little quiddity, a broad-stroked bitch in deep
   cerise if she was a day. Flatulently refused to drink with me.
   And why did you give her five shillings, Eric? I saw the
   money pass hands. Do we live in pleasurable anticipation of
   homotherapy?

ERIC: He'd lent Larry money –

LARRY: Oh, that one. She's a guardsman by day, God knows what she does at night –

ERIC: Someone had to pay her back.

LARRY: But she only lent me half a crown –

PEANUT: (*Mischievous*) Then Eric paid her back double, I wonder why?

ERIC: I did not, Peanut, I gave her one half-crown.

PEANUT: I distinctly saw you –

CONRAD: Shut it, Peanut, you wouldn't know a half-crown from a six-pound note.

ERIC: (*To* LARRY; *sharp*) And have you and Mr Grace been talking intimately?

LARRY: He came back for his briefcase, leave off, Eric –

PEANUT: God, if there's one thing I hate it's a man who refuses to drink with me –

ERIC: (*To* RUPERT; *cheerful*) These, as Addison said of the Spectator Club, are my ordinary companions. (*To the others.*) Rupert is good and straight, a Balliol man, and he says he can deal with Godwin.

RUPERT: I don't think I said that exactly. I said I'd try –

CONRAD: (*Giving* RUPERT *a drink*) Between you, me and the man in the moon, the one in the sky, not the public house, I'm sick of Godwin. Eric talks of no one else. (*Raising his glass.*) Down the hatch.
(*They drink.*)

PEANUT: (*To* RUPERT, *still in aggressive mood*) I'll tell you another thing, my ex-husband, the Honourable Francis Coe –

LARRY: Here we go –

PEANUT: My ex-husband was caught *in flagrante delicto* by a private investigator called appropriately, Prior, in a Brighton hotel with guess what? (*No response; angry.*) I said guess what? Well, guess.

RUPERT: I've really no idea –

CONRAD: Oh, leave him be, Peanut. He was found in bed with a boy, so what? If I hear it again, I'll strangle you with my own bare feet.

PEANUT: (*Near to tears*) You've spoiled it, you swine, you've spoiled it, you always spoil everything –

CONRAD: You know what I think?

ERIC: No, what do you think, Conrad?

CONRAD: I think I should get some of my old army mates together, we should go down and see Conshie Godwin and frighten the life out of him, wave my shooter in his face, dust him up, smack him about, kick him and shove him, give him a melancholy evening.

(*He punches and kicks the air.*)

ERIC: You have to find him first.

CONRAD: My boys will find him, don't you worry. Yes, kick him and shove him and smack him about –

ERIC: (*To* RUPERT) Pay no attention, Mr Grace. He means no harm. Poor Conrad here is a shoe salesman in Oxford Street.

CONRAD: True. It's all I could get after the war to end wars.

PEANUT: And he can't raise an eyebrow let alone a private army. (*Going close to* RUPERT.) I, beloved, work in the twisted wire department of Peter Jones in Sloane Square. If you need your wire twisted, I'm your girl –

CONRAD: Peanut, where's your modesty?

PEANUT: Taken from me by the lady Francis who left me destitute and unsatisfied. Do you like the company of pansies, Mr Grace?

LARRY: I shall ask you to leave, Peanut, if you go on like this.

CONRAD: Did you serve in the war, Mr Grace?

LARRY: He was a Military Policeman, weren't you dear?

ERIC: Interrogated deserters and had them tried.

CONRAD: Oh Jesu, Jesu, the Rat Catchers, oh, Jesu –

RUPERT: I really must go now, Mr Wells. I shall leave a copy of this document. If you decide to sign it, so much the better. Otherwise we will take legal action. In the meantime, I shall certainly try to see Godwin and –

ERIC: (*Suddenly belligerent*) What have you and Larry been talking about? You didn't forget your briefcase, I saw you take it, what's going on?

PEANUT: Oh dear, we have upset our hostess. (*To* RUPERT.) What did you do to cause the frissant, Robert dear?

CONRAD: Not Robert. Rupert. Rupert the organ-grinder –

PEANUT: Whatever. What did you do?

ERIC: Larry, I want an explanation as to why Mr Grace –

    (*A clatter of footsteps outside. All freeze. Sound of letter box.*
    Footsteps run off, fade away. Silence.)

CONRAD: Oh Jesu.

ERIC: Larry, go and see what it is.

LARRY: I daren't –

ERIC: Conrad?

CONRAD: Comes the hour, comes the man.

    (*He exits unsteadily.*)

PEANUT: It's probably an invitation to the pansies' ball –

ERIC: Shut up, Peanut –

    (CONRAD *returns with a letter.*)

CONRAD: It's addressed to you –

    (*He hands the letter to* ERIC *who slowly opens it. He reads.*
    In the cottage: JULIETTE *rises, starts the metronome ticking its*
    slow adagio tempo. She lies down on the divan.
    In the basement flat: ERIC *looks up from the letter.*)

ERIC: It's from Godwin. In his own hand. What price
reconciliation now, Mr Grace? (*Reads.*) 'Wells, your time is
up. You have a putrescent soul which I shall take pleasure in
personally sending to hell. You have very few days left to
live.'

    (ERIC *hands the letter to* RUPERT *who reads.* PEANUT *begins to*
    weep quietly. CONRAD *sways uneasily.* ERIC *stares into space.*
    LARRY *goes to him and puts a hand on his arm. The ticking of*
    the metronome.
    Blackout.)

SCENE TWO

5 p.m. on Monday 29 December 1930.

    In the basement flat: Empty. Dark.

    In the cottage: Also empty and dark. A sudden knocking on the
front door. Silence. The knocking again, louder. After a moment,
JULIETTE *enters carrying an oil lamp. She wears her dressing-gown*
over her chiffon négligé. Her hair is wild, her make-up smudged, but

*she wears high-heeled, ankle-strap shoes. She looks sluttish. She opens
the door.* RUPERT *stands there with a bunch of flowers.*

JULIETTE: (*Alarmed*) Yes?

RUPERT: I'm Rupert Grace. I've come to see Peter Godwin.

JULIETTE: He's not here.

>   (*She tries to close the door.* RUPERT *stops her.*)

RUPERT: He's expecting me.

JULIETTE: No, he's not.

RUPERT: I sent a telegram saying I was coming down this
afternoon unless I heard to the contrary. I didn't hear to the
contrary. Are you sure he's not here?

JULIETTE: He's not in this room, is he? And there's only one
room upstairs, the bedroom, and he's not there either. So,
my conclusion is, he's not here. What's your conclusion?

RUPERT: Did he receive the telegram?

JULIETTE: Yes, he received the telegram, he read it, he tore it up
and left last night –

>   (*She tries to shut the door again.*)

RUPERT: (*Using his weight to resist*) When will he be back?

JULIETTE: I've no idea. He never tells me.

RUPERT: But you are expecting him?

JULIETTE: I'm always expecting him, but I never know when –

RUPERT: (*Pushing a little harder*) It's rather chilly. Can't I come
inside?

>   (*She hesitates, nervous and uncertain. In that moment,* RUPERT
>   *steps inside. Awkward silence.*)

RUPERT: (*Offering her the flowers*) These are for you.
(*Embarrassed.*) Merry Christmas. Happy New Year.
(*She doesn't take them at first.*)

JULIETTE: How did you know I'd be here? Peter didn't tell you,
did he?

RUPERT: I – no – yes, I think he did –

JULIETTE: (*Accepting them*) Thank you.
(*She puts them higgledy-piggledy in a vase.*)

RUPERT: Do you mind if I wait?

JULIETTE: Yes, I do mind. It's not very convenient at the
moment.

RUPERT: I've come all the way from London.

JULIETTE: That's not my fault, is it?

RUPERT: I'll give him half an hour, is that all right?

JULIETTE: Oh, give him what you like. Only, if you're coming in, shut the door. It's cold enough in here as it is.

(*He looks round for somewhere to sit. She notices and leans over to clear a space on the divan. Her dressing-gown opens, partially revealing her nakedness.* RUPERT *is embarrassed, turns away.*)

RUPERT: I'll – just – I'll – just – (*He sits.*) – sit and – and wait. Please, carry on as if I weren't here, don't let me disturb you, Miss –

JULIETTE: Smith. Juliette Smith.

(*Silence.*)

RUPERT: Would you like a cigarette?

(*He rises, offers her a cigarette. She takes one. Her hand trembles. He lights it. She gently holds his hand, eyeing him all the while. He lights his own cigarette. He sits again. Abruptly she sweeps a pile of music manuscript from a chair and sits opposite him. She crosses her legs. The dressing-gown parts, revealing her négligé and her legs.* RUPERT *is made deeply uncomfortable. She doesn't take her eyes off him. He keeps his eyes averted.*)

RUPERT: Do you know where Mr Godwin might be?

JULIETTE: No.

RUPERT: In the village perhaps?

JULIETTE: Perhaps.

RUPERT: Or up in London?

JULIETTE: Possibly. By the way, I'm not his wife, I'm his whore.

(*Silence.*)

RUPERT: Does Peter go up to London often?

JULIETTE: Not often, but often enough.

RUPERT: But he never attends the performances of his own music, does he?

JULIETTE: No. I do that for him. I report back. In detail.

RUPERT: Odd that he doesn't go himself, isn't it?

JULIETTE: He has a nervous disposition. He hates music critics. He can't bear to see them, scribbling their notes in venom. He's not too keen on musicians either.

RUPERT: (*Fishing*) But he admires Frederick Delius, doesn't he?

JULIETTE: I said musicians, not gods.
 (*Silence.*)

RUPERT: Do you know why I'm here? (*No response.*) I want to talk to Peter about Eric Wells. (*No response.*) Do you know him? (*No response.*) He's the editor of *The Sackbut*. A critic and musicologist.

JULIETTE: I should find another subject to talk to Peter about if I were you.

RUPERT: Why?

JULIETTE: 'There once was a critic called Wells,
  Whose religion was all bells and smells,
  As a saint he was known
  To pee eau-de-Cologne
  But of his orgasms nobody tells.'

That's one of Peter's limericks, you know. He makes them up. Just like that. On the spur of the moment. He hates Eric Wells. Tread carefully.

RUPERT: Do you know him?

JULIETTE: Who?

RUPERT: Eric Wells.

JULIETTE: Is that a joke?

RUPERT: No, I –

JULIETTE: Peter made up a limerick about you.

RUPERT: Did he.

JULIETTE: Just the other day.
  'There once was a fellow called Grace,
  Who thought a composer was base,
  He called him a skunk
  'Cos he drank like a drunk,
  And they've never yet met face to face.'
 (*She laughs a little out of control.*)

RUPERT: (*Smiles*) Strange. I didn't know he drank –

JULIETTE: You should have seen him on Boxing Day.

RUPERT: What about Christmas?

JULIETTE: He wasn't here for Christmas.

RUPERT: Did you spend the day alone?

JULIETTE: No. (*Amused.*) Peter left me here with a friend.
 (*She rises, crosses to the Christmas tree, scrabbles among the mess*

and produces the monkey toy which she proceeds to wind up. She lets it play. The cymbals clash. RUPERT *barely moves.*)

RUPERT: Peter gave you that?

JULIETTE: Yes. And soap. What did you get for Christmas?

RUPERT: The usual. Socks. Handkerchiefs. This tie.

JULIETTE: That's what I gave Peter. Socks.

RUPERT: I wish I could meet Peter. He refuses to come into the office. Do you know why? (*No response.*) We've talked on the telephone, of course. And we've corresponded. But we've never met.

JULIETTE: And you've sent him telegrams, haven't you?

RUPERT: Yes – (*Casual.*) What sort of man is he?

JULIETTE: Drunk or sober?

RUPERT: (*More of a smile*) Sober.

JULIETTE: Oh, sober, he's a frightful bore. Morose. (*Silence.*)

RUPERT: And drunk?

JULIETTE: Looser after one or two. After three or four, rowdy, bawdy, fun. After five or six, or seven or eight, not to be lived with.

RUPERT: But you live with him. (*No response.*) How long have you known him?

JULIETTE: Long enough.

RUPERT: How did you meet?

JULIETTE: Has anyone ever told you that you ask too many questions? I can't take much more of this, honest injun. I was brought up to believe that asking questions was rude.

RUPERT: Yes, it's bad manners, I know, but I acquired the habit against my will. I'm interested. We publish him. I only joined the firm a few months ago, I – how did you meet?

JULIETTE: I wrote to him. I admired his music. I too am a composer but only a beginner. I sent him some of my scores. And a photograph. He invited me down. He offered to teach me.

RUPERT: You're a musician, then.

JULIETTE: Obviously.

RUPERT: I'm a musician. Was. Sort of. I read music at Oxford. Organ.

JULIETTE: (*Amused*) Do you like making music?

RUPERT: I used to. Not any more. Not since the war. I don't know why.
(*She loosens her dressing-gown a little so that the see-through négligé is visible. She leans forward and eyes him intensely. He is again made uneasy.*)

RUPERT: And you?

JULIETTE: And me what?

RUPERT: You said you compose. Do you play an instrument?

JULIETTE: Clarinet. I love making music.

RUPERT: I tried the clarinet when I was about twelve but I never quite got the hang of it.

JULIETTE: Your *embouchure* was probably inadequate. My *embouchure* is thought to be good. *Embouchure* is the disposition of the tongue, you know.

RUPERT: Yes, I know.

JULIETTE: Do you still have your clarinet?

RUPERT: No.

JULIETTE: Oh, what a pity, I could have played it for you. You'd have seen my *embouchure* for yourself. It's all to do with the tongue. Like so much in life. You have to like the taste of an instrument, too. I'm sure I'd have liked the taste of your clarinet. I expect you play the piano –

RUPERT: A little –

JULIETTE: Peter's a very fine pianist. He likes the taste of the piano. He has a wonderful touch, from one end to the other, a gentle, delicate touch. He knows what keys to press, to cajole, to tickle, to stroke. His fortissimo is equally impressive. He has very long fingers.
(RUPERT *rises, moves away.*)

RUPERT: Shall I tell you why I'm here?

JULIETTE: You already have.

RUPERT: (*Cautiously*) I'm here to try to diffuse a serious and potentially disastrous situation.

JULIETTE: Oh, and what's that?
(*Silence for a moment, then* RUPERT *turns on her.*)

RUPERT: I don't think you've told me the truth. (*No response.*)
Peter Godwin has threatened to kill Eric Wells. Wells

maintains it's because he wrote scathing reviews of Godwin's music. But I've been led to believe the real cause of the dispute is – is you. (*No response.*) You know Eric Wells, don't you?

JULIETTE: Are you quite well? Do you know what you're saying? I have never set eyes on Eric Wells, and I have no wish to do so. (*Suddenly.*) I'm cold. I'm going to put on something warm. I'll leave you the light.

(*She exits quickly.*

In the basement flat: Sound of footsteps descending and door being unlocked. LARRY *enters with a shopping bag. He turns on the light, but as he crosses the room the lights go out.*)

LARRY: Knickers.

(*He disappears behind the screen. The sound of coins being shaken from a mug. Now, his head appears above the screen – he's standing on a chair – and he puts the coins in the electricity meter. The lights come on again. He emerges, stops, considers for a moment, then goes to the telephone and dials.*)

LARRY: (*Into telephone*) Violet? Hello, ducky, it's Larry. And Happy New Year to you, dear. Is Eric there? What d'you mean he popped out? Is he in the loo? Oh. Did he say when he'd be back? Oh, good. Well, please ask him to phone the moment he returns and certainly before he leaves the office. Why are you going early? Lucky you. Then just put a message on his desk, dear. You can write, can't you, ducky? Leave him a message on his desk. All right? No, ducky, it's just that I want to know what he wants for dinner. Yesterday's stew or today's rissoles. Rissoles, dear, rissoles. Cheeky monkey. Don't forget. Bless you. Bye.

(*He switches off the light and exits, singing 'The Man I Love'. In the cottage:* JULIETTE *returns. She has a shawl round her shoulders and wears a pair of men's woollen socks. Her manner, her persona, seems a little different. Superficially she is more polite, friendly, social, but the strain is still severe and, therefore, apparent.*)

JULIETTE: Take off your coat.

RUPERT: (*Taken off-guard*) No, no – I'm fine I –

(*She resumes her seat.*)

JULIETTE: What were you saying? Something about Eric Wells threatening the life of Peter Godwin? Or was it the other way round?

RUPERT: Yes. Godwin is threatening Wells.

JULIETTE: I didn't know that it had gone that far.

RUPERT: Peter Godwin and Eric Wells are locked in what I've come to believe is mortal combat. I have a feeling you know more about it than you'll let on –

JULIETTE: Peter Godwin is among the four or five most gifted composers in England. Frederick Delius said he believed Peter had genius. I believe that, too. Composing came easily to him, his music poured out, unfettered. Eric Wells, who is influential and was, I believe, Peter's friend, after years of praising him, suddenly took it into his head to condemn him in the most abhorrent and repulsive way. He accused Peter, in print, of plagiarism –

RUPERT: Yes, I know –

JULIETTE: You may know but you don't understand. Peter is in despair. Unable to write a note. I am myself acquainted with despair so I don't use the word lightly. He has been in despair for almost a month. That's all I know.

RUPERT: And Eric Wells has never come down here to visit you?

JULIETTE: (*Losing control*) For Christ's sake, will you stop that? Spread lies like that and he'll turn on me. Have you ever said anything like that to Peter?

RUPERT: No –

JULIETTE: Don't ever, promise me. Never. Do you know how deep his hatred is for Eric Wells? He's obsessed by him –

RUPERT: Yes –

JULIETTE: Obsessed, obsessed, obsessed. Put something like that into Peter's head – (*She stops; then suddenly light, casual.*) Have you ever been terrified out of your wits, Mr Grace? Literally. Out of your wits?

RUPERT: (*A smile*) Often. But not for some time.

JULIETTE: (*Inquisitive*) How did you rid yourself of fear?

RUPERT: The war ended.

(*Silence.*)

JULIETTE: (*A smile*) Frightened is such an inadequate adjective, don't you think?
(*She begins to cry, silently at first, but then her whole body trembles and she sobs.* RUPERT *rises, but stands watching her helplessly.*)

RUPERT: What is it – can I – ?

JULIETTE: (*Through her sobs*) One wrong word – God knows – it's a knife edge – a tightrope – I'm not a strong person – I had a – a sort of breakdown when I was eighteen – when Daddy died – he was a Judge in Ceylon – my mother died years ago, giving birth to me –
(*Her voice trails off. Brief silence.*)

RUPERT: Talk to me. I want to help. I want to help Peter, too. I want to stop him from –

JULIETTE: (*Without warning*) Do you think I'm beautiful?

RUPERT: (*Off-guard*) What – ?

JULIETTE: Good-looking, beautiful, attractive, pretty? Beautiful – it's a common word, I believe, a very common word. Do you think I'm beautiful?

RUPERT: Yes, I do – I –

JULIETTE: (*A sad smile*) Good. Thank you. But I must warn you. It's only skin deep. *In corpore ipso quid forma est, cuticula bene colorata?* Which means 'In the body itself what is beauty save a little skin, well coloured?' I'm sorry, I'm not showing off, I have a compulsion to test my memory –
(*He is about to interrupt.*)
No, don't speak. I know what you're going to say. It's the brothel question, isn't it? What's a nice girl like you doing in a place like this? (*Suddenly.*) Have you ever had a breakdown?

RUPERT: No.

JULIETTE: I've had several. But not for a year. Not since I met Peter. He's a giver of life, is Peter. This is better than a brothel, not that I have any experience of brothels. Have you? (*No response.*) I don't want anything to happen to him.

RUPERT: What was wrong with you?

JULIETTE: Life. (*She laughs, goes to the metronome and sets it going prestissimo.*) I was studying for a medical degree but I couldn't remember all the symptoms. I went rigid with fear. It's called catatonia. I was catatonic. They put you in lovely warm baths. It doesn't do any good. Only time and Peter do any good. And music.

(*She smiles. Brief silence.* RUPERT *crosses to the metronome and stops it.*)

RUPERT: How did you happen to study music?

JULIETTE: It came naturally to me. (*She laughs quietly, then:*) Have you ever heard of *folie à deux*?

(*He responds vaguely.*)

It is, I believe, the only mental disease that's catching. There was a girl, her name was Trotty. She suffered from *folie à deux. Folie à deux* is a mental disorder first identified by a couple of Frogs, Lasègue and Falret. In 1877. There's my memory test again. The illness works like this: a person suffers from mental delusions. He or she may then communicate those delusions to another person with whom he or she's associated, usually for years, but not necessarily. In Trotty's case, it was her husband. Trotty's husband was the dominant individual and suffered from what the Frog doctors called the primary psychosis. He believed that Trotty's mother was a German agent who was trying to poison him. And he infected Trotty with his delusions. She was weak was Trotty, weak and submissive and particularly susceptible. One night, she and her husband tried to strangle Trotty's mother. But here's the interesting thing. They were arrested and taken to separate institutions. The moment they were apart, Trotty's symptoms, her delusions, began to disappear. Her husband's, on the other hand, worsened. This gave the doctors the clue. Trotty's quite well now. Living with her mother. She sends me postcards from time to time. Her husband is in Broadmoor, I believe. You get the picture, do you, Mr Grace? The husband, the stronger individual, infected Trotty with his delusions. But the moment they were apart, Trotty was cured. It's fascinating how deviants seem always to find the partner they need.

(*Silence.*)

RUPERT: (*Gently; smiling*) Are you trying to tell me something about yourself?

JULIETTE: It doesn't matter. Nothing matters.
(*Silence.*)

RUPERT: You sound as if you're crying out for help.

JULIETTE: Everything I do and say is a cry for help.
(*She smiles. Brief silence.*)

RUPERT: If you trust me –

JULIETTE: *Déjà vu.* I know what you're going to say next. This has happened before.

RUPERT: (*Smiling*) Then you know the story I'm going to tell you.
(*She watches him expectantly.*)
I had a rotten posting during the war. I was in France, in charge of a small detachment of Military Policemen whose job it was to catch deserters. We were called Rat Catchers, of course. The deserters were charged with desertion in the face of the enemy. It was a capital offence. There was a lot of it about, more than most people know or care to admit. The curious thing is these men were so terrified that they made a run for it but all the time knowing the consequences if they were caught. Their terror got the better of them, their terror took precedence over loyalty to King, country and their fellow soldiers. And here's an even more curious thing. In the majority of cases, the moment they were caught, the terror vanished. They stopped being frightened. So, my advice, in answer to your earlier question, is if you want to stop being frightened – stop being loyal, allow yourself to be caught.

JULIETTE: (*Smiles*) Easier said than done, Mr Grace. All this is now new. I don't know any more what's going to happen or what you're going to say. You better leave now. Peter's not going to come tonight.

RUPERT: Do you think he's capable of killing Eric Wells?
(*Silence.*)

JULIETTE: Yes. Go now.
(*Brief silence.*)

RUPERT: Please trust me. I need to see Peter. I think he needs

help. I think I could be successful as a go-between. I've seen
Eric Wells and I think if I could sit down and talk to Peter –
(*Stops.*) We're running out of time – (*No response; urgent.*)
You're playing a very dangerous game.

JULIETTE: Yes, it's a game all right. You either know the rules or
you don't. And if you don't you can't play it.

RUPERT: Stop seeing Eric Wells, I beg you –

JULIETTE: (*Almost a scream*) I am not seeing him! I've never
clapped eyes on him. And he's a queer, isn't he? What would
he be doing with me? Peter says he's a queer who picks up
men in cottages. Cottages is their word for public lavatories,
did you know that? He's vile and hateful and I don't know
him –

RUPERT: You're not telling me the truth –
(*Silence.*)

JULIETTE: (*Quiet, inward*) I don't think you know what terror is.
He can make me do anything he wants. And I never know
what's expected of me. I don't know who I am from one
moment to the next. I am a person of no fixed identity. Do
you know who you are and, if so, can you prove it?

RUPERT: I want to help you. Please let me. If you don't,
something terrible's going to happen. To Eric Wells, to Peter
himself and, perhaps, to you –

JULIETTE: No. It's already happened to me.

RUPERT: Confide in me. I believe we can prevent a real tragedy
from occurring –
(*Silence.*
In the basement flat: LARRY *enters, switches on the light, crosses
to the telephone and dials.*
In the cottage:)

RUPERT: Let me help.

JULIETTE: Go now.

RUPERT: God, do you realize how dangerous this is? The recital's
tomorrow night. I am going to try to stop Eric Wells from
attending. If he publishes yet another bad review of Peter's
music, God knows what the consequences will be. If you see
Peter, say I said he's not to write or utter another threatening
word –

JULIETTE: Please, please go.
    (RUPERT *hesitates*.)
    For my sake. Please.
    (*In the basement flat:* LARRY *listens but no one answers.*
    In the cottage:)
JULIETTE: I hope to see you at the concert tomorrow.
    (RUPERT *turns abruptly and goes.*
    In the basement flat: LARRY *slowly replaces the receiver on its*
    cradle. He stands staring into space.
    In the cottage: JULIETTE *rises, goes to the door, opens it.*)
JULIETTE: (*Calling up the stairs*) He fell for it. He's gone –
    (*As she exits, the sound from upstairs of a record being played on*
    a gramophone: 'Sea Drift' by Delius.
    Blackout.)

ACT TWO

SCENE ONE

4.30 p.m. on Tuesday 30 December 1930.

In the cottage: Empty. Dark. A sudden gust of wind rattles the windows.

In the basement flat: LARRY *is tying Eric's bow tie.* LARRY *is in casual clothes, but* ERIC *needs only a dinner jacket to complete his evening wear. After a moment:*

ERIC: Larry, I have to tell you something.

LARRY: I don't want to hear, thank you ever so much. I've had things told to me before in that tone of voice and they always end in tears.

ERIC: This won't –

LARRY: What you do is your business, Eric. Change the subject. Why do you think Mr Grace is coming here this afternoon? Do you think he's seen Godwin and made him – ?

ERIC: (*Interrupting*) I don't know why Mr Grace is coming here and I don't really care. It'll alter nothing. Just shut up and listen to me –

LARRY: (*Finishing the tie; admiring him, singing*) 'Ain't she sweet, see her walking down the street –'

ERIC: Larry!

(LARRY *falls silent and turns away, nervous.*)

LARRY: Can't I have just one little drinkie?

ERIC: No. No drink tonight. Not until after the recital.

(LARRY *sits, hugs his knees, closes his eyes, fearful.*)

This morning I went to the bank. I have a little money my mother left me. I've never touched a penny of it. (*He goes to the desk and finds an envelope.*) I drew out a thousand pounds. Here. (*He holds it out to* LARRY *who looks up at him.*) I thought that if I were to die violently –

LARRY: Stop it, Eric, you're going to make me cry –

ERIC: If I were to die violently, and you were, for example, named as a beneficiary in my will, all sorts of questions would be asked. You know what the police are like. I wanted to spare you as much pain as possible. Anyway, it's a tidy sum, use it to go abroad, far, far away, buy a place in the sun, and live out your life – flamboyantly.

(LARRY *is crying*.)

LARRY: I don't want your money. Nothing's going to happen. It'll all be all right –

ERIC: I doubt it. I am consumed with a feeling of impending disaster.

(*He ruffles* LARRY's *hair and starts towards the bedroom door*.)

LARRY: I've always wondered why they say 'Happy as Larry'.

(ERIC *smiles sadly, goes quickly into the bedroom*. LARRY *sits, hugging his knees, weeping quietly.*

In the cottage: JULIETTE, *wearing a coat and beret, and carrying a small overnight case, enters, looks for and finds a pair of gloves and then goes to the front door and opens it. The wind buffets her a little. She goes out and is heard locking the door. The sound of the wind dies away.*

In the basement flat: The doorbell rings. LARRY *wipes his eyes and hurries out to the front door. He returns with* RUPERT, *who is wearing a dinner jacket.* LARRY *hovers, wanting to question him but not knowing how to.*)

LARRY: I'll tell him you're here. He's just dressing –

RUPERT: Thank you.

(LARRY *crosses towards the bedroom door, but stops.*)

LARRY: (*Urgent, hurried*) I have to ask, I have to know, did you see Godwin?

RUPERT: No.

LARRY: Did you see the girl?

RUPERT: Yes.

LARRY: Her name's Juliette, isn't it?

RUPERT: Yes –

LARRY: Oh, God. And was I right? Are she and Eric – ?

RUPERT: I don't know for certain but –

ERIC'S VOICE: (*Calling from the bedroom*) Larry? Is Mr Grace here?

LARRY: (*Calling back*) Yes –

ERIC'S VOICE: (*Calling*) I'm just coming –

LARRY: (*To* RUPERT) I don't wish to pry, but it does concern me after all, may I ask what you're going to say to Eric now?

RUPERT: I'm going to try to find out the truth, Mr Rider.

LARRY: All I ask is that you don't make it too difficult for me. Don't tell him I followed him. Please. Don't tell him I told you what I told you, please, please –

RUPERT: I won't. I promise.

LARRY: Thank you. It's difficult enough for me –

(ERIC *enters, dressed now;* LARRY *continues without pause.*)

– sitting through Mozart let alone a whole evening of Peter Godwin's music. No offence, but you know what I mean. However, Peanut and Conrad are going to keep Eric company and he's taking them to a little supper beforehand at the Café Royal, aren't you, Eric?

ERIC: Mr Grace.

LARRY: Yes, a New Year supper. May 1931 bring us all that we desire. In confidence, I desire a drink, and so will Peanut and Conrad, but Eric absolutely forbids it until after the recital, don't you, Eric? For what he calls security reasons. (*Awkward silence.*)

RUPERT: I'd like to see Mr Wells alone, please.

ERIC: I'd prefer Mr Rider to stay. (*Another awkward silence.*) I'm sorry about not offering you a drink –

RUPERT: I don't want one –

ERIC: But I never drink before I work. And this evening I have work to do. At the Wigmore Hall. I shall also have to keep my wits about me. And so will my friends. I attend the recital tonight in the belief that there is safety in sober numbers. Well, Mr Grace?

RUPERT: Have you signed that document I left, promising to print a retraction?

ERIC: Certainly not. I will not retract the truth. Won't you sit down?

(*They both sit.* LARRY *hovers in the background.*)

RUPERT: What I have to say is extremely – delicate. I want to talk about Juliette Smith.

ERIC: Who?

RUPERT: Juliette Smith.

ERIC: (*Genuinely puzzled*) Who is Juliette Smith? (*Brief silence.*)

RUPERT: Yesterday, I went down to Eynsford in Kent. I was hoping to see Peter Godwin. He wasn't there –

ERIC: Forgive me for saying this, but I told you so –

RUPERT: A young lady answered the door. She said her name was Juliette Smith –

ERIC: Is she a friend of Godwin?

RUPERT: She lives with him. But then, of course, you know that.

ERIC: I've never heard her name before this moment. Have you, Larry?

(*A vague response from* LARRY.)

RUPERT: I'm bound to admit I found it hard to believe anything she told me. She is, in my opinion, mentally unwell and in need of treatment, but there were certain –

ERIC: You didn't see Godwin, that's the long and the short of it. I have no interest in Miss Smith, whoever she may be. There is nothing more to be said. You failed in your mission to get Godwin to leave me in peace. As I knew you would. This meeting is ended. My friends will be here shortly. We are going to have a light supper before making our way to the Wigmore Hall. Perhaps we shall see you later at the recital. Larry, please show Mr Grace out. Good afternoon.

RUPERT: Mr Wells, when I was here the other day, you insisted that your adverse criticism of Peter Godwin's music was objective and detached. You had, I think you said, no other interest but to preserve the highest standards as you perceived them –

ERIC: (*Rising*) Not as I perceive them but as I know them to be. Objectively. I judge by the standards with which, all my life, I have informed my ear and mind.

RUPERT: (*Summoning his courage*) You're lying, Mr Wells. I think your motives are of another kind. I think you're having an affair with Juliette Smith. Godwin's mistress.

(ERIC *stops dead still. He looks at* RUPERT *with total amazement.*)

ERIC: (*Quietly*) I beg your pardon?

RUPERT: You heard what I said.

ERIC: Are you serious? Or is this some sort of joke, a trick, a trap – ?

RUPERT: I believe the reason for your attacks on Peter Godwin are entirely personal. I think the real cause of your dispute is not music, not plagiarism, not Frederick Delius, but this girl, Juliette Smith.

ERIC: Larry, do you hear what he's saying?

LARRY: Yes –

ERIC: I'm trying to keep calm, Mr Grace. I want you to leave now –

RUPERT: No. I'm going to finish what I've come to say –

ERIC: (*Pacing again*) I don't want to hear your fantasies. This is what war does to people, Larry. Not only cripples and maims their bodies, but also their minds –

RUPERT: (*With some force*) Listen to me.

(ERIC *stops*.)

I received information, reliable information, I'm not going to reveal the source, that you were – friendly with this girl –

ERIC: It's simply not true, I've never heard of her, to the best of my knowledge I've never clapped eyes on her, and I've certainly never met her –

RUPERT: I've been told you were there. In Godwin's cottage. With the girl.

ERIC: (*Cracks appearing in his calm*) I've never visited Godwin in his cottage. I've never been to Eynsford. Who told you these things? (*No response.*) Did you get this from Godwin? (*No response.*) Who then?

RUPERT: I am not at liberty to say.

ERIC: And you expect me to take seriously the accusation of someone whose name you won't reveal? Are you a journalist? (*He laughs a little out of control.*) What if I say to you you're making it all up, that it's all part of Godwin's strategy to discredit me?

RUPERT: It comes from an unimpeachable source, believe me –

ERIC: Believe you? Why should I believe you? Your source, Mr Grace, if he or she really exists, is a liar and a calumniator. This is a deliberate attempt to undermine me. Godwin's behind this, isn't he, go on, admit it –

RUPERT: No, he has nothing to do with it –

ERIC: (*Holding on to his head*) Larry, this is a nightmare. This isn't happening. Christ, I think my head's going to come off my body –

LARRY: Calmly, Eric, hear him out –

RUPERT: This woman –

ERIC: (*Turning on him*) This woman? This woman? Are you blind? Are you so naïve? Are you entirely and utterly insensitive? Do you not understand about Larry and me? I have no interest in women –

RUPERT: All I was going to say was that this woman, Juliette Smith, also denies the affair –

ERIC: I should damn well hope so. So, what it amounts to is that this entire business is based on information received from an unknown source, real or unreal, and you expect me to –

RUPERT: (*Interrupting*) No, there are other things –

ERIC: What other things?

RUPERT: The woman herself. I was not convinced by her denials. She's not well. She's not reliable –

ERIC: (*Icy*) But she'd know whom she was fucking, wouldn't she?

LARRY: (*Pained*) Eric. Please. Let's keep our dignity.
(*Brief silence.*)

RUPERT: And there's the matter of a Christmas present.

ERIC: A what?

RUPERT: A present –

ERIC: A present?

RUPERT: She says Godwin gave her a present. A toy. But it's straining coincidence too far for me to believe that both you and he would choose the same present to give to –

ERIC: The monkey!

RUPERT: (*Thrown*) Yes –
(*Momentary silence, then* ERIC *begins to laugh.*)

ERIC: I sent one to Godwin.

RUPERT: You sent Godwin a Christmas present?

ERIC: Anonymously. A joke. I sent one to several friends. You were here when I gave one to Peanut and Conrad, don't you remember?

LARRY: You didn't tell me you'd sent Godwin one –

ERIC: I knew it was a mistake. I couldn't help myself. It just amused me to do so. But you can ask my secretary, Violet, if you don't believe me. She wrote out the address and posted the package. So you see, Mr Grace, it's all typically Godwin. He receives a Christmas present from me and then gives it to his harlot. It reveals much about him. I want this interview to end now, I want you –

(*The doorbell rings.* LARRY *goes to answer it; after a moment.*) I believe this is what is called an impasse.

(LARRY *returns with* PEANUT *and* CONRAD. CONRAD *wears a shabby dinner jacket.* PEANUT *is in a long evening dress, muted in colour but not without style. They are sober.*)

ERIC: Ah! My Praetorian Guard.

(RUPERT *nods to them. Surreptitiously,* CONRAD *takes a small brown paper bag from his jacket and slips it to* ERIC, *who pockets it quickly. During this:*)

PEANUT: (*To* RUPERT; *a nervous smile and holding out a hand*) Have we met? My name's Monica Coe. My friends call me Peanut.

LARRY: Ducky, you met Mr Grace the other night.

PEANUT: Did we? I'm so sorry. My memory's – (*She trails off.*)

CONRAD: Have we interrupted something?

LARRY: (*Laughs*) I'll say.

RUPERT: (*To* ERIC) Could I be so rude as to ask your friends to wait in another room until we have finished our conversation?

ERIC: We have finished our conversation.

RUPERT: I haven't.

ERIC: Larry, show Mr Grace out.

RUPERT: Don't bother, I'm going. But I have one more thing to say and I shall say it in front of these witnesses –

ERIC: Please leave my house.

RUPERT: If you insist on reviewing Peter Godwin's music tonight, I shall see to it that my suspicions about you and Juliette Smith are made public.

ERIC: (*A smile*) Ah. Good. Blackmail.

LARRY: Aren't you going to say it's an ugly word, Eric?

RUPERT: Peter Godwin is the victim in this and I shall do everything in my power to protect him.

(*He goes.*)

ERIC: (*Explodes*) God, have you ever heard anything so monstrous?

PEANUT: Difficult to say, angel, since we didn't hear it.
(*Silence.* ERIC *calms down, takes out a comb and neatens his hair and beard.*)

CONRAD: Who's Juliette Smith?

ERIC: Peter Godwin's whore.

CONRAD: Anything known?

ERIC: Not by me. I don't wish to discuss her or anything else to do with Godwin –
(LARRY *is gazing at* ERIC.)
Larry, stop looking at me like that.

LARRY: I'm upset, that's all, of course I'm upset, wouldn't you be?

ERIC: He's lying, he's desperate, he'll do anything to protect Godwin, can't you see that?
(*Silence.* LARRY *turns away.*)

PEANUT: I would make a comment if I had the slightest inkling of what you were talking about. But don't row, I hate rows. Kiss and make up. Please.

LARRY: Yes, yes, yes, yes, let's forget the whole thing –

ERIC: I'm really astonished, Larry, that you should allow what that man said to upset you in any way whatsoever –

LARRY: It's over, I've said it's over and forgotten. Go to supper.

PEANUT: Can't we have just one little one for the road?

ERIC: No. You must stay sober until it's over. You mustn't leave my side, not for a moment. We will creep into the hall just as the recital begins and remain at the back so that we can see the entire audience.

CONRAD: I shouldn't have listened to you, Eric. I should have got the boys together, they'd have done a better job of guarding you than Peanut and me –

ERIC: Sweet of you. But I can trust you. Your boys, Conrad, could be got at. You don't know just how cunning Peter Godwin is.

LARRY: Go on, off you go, off you go –

ERIC: Larry, don't let anyone in until I return safe and sound. When I do we'll get as pissed as Chloe.

CONRAD: Three cheers for Chloe.

(ERIC *collects up his notebook and pencil.*)

ERIC: Yes, let the condemned man eat a hearty supper –

LARRY: Eric, if I didn't know better, I'd say you were hoping for the worst –

ERIC: No. I want us to go out to supper, and then to the recital. I want us to tell sad stories of the death of kings, how some have been deposed, some slain in war, some haunted by the ghosts they have deposed, some poisoned by their wives, some sleeping killed. All murdered.

(*Silence.*)

CONRAD: And to think that only a week or two ago, Members of Parliament recommended that we abolish the death penalty. Idjits. Well, I, for one, hope they never do. Hang the bastard, that's what I say. Take Godwin to a place of execution and hang him by the neck until he's dead.

LARRY: He hasn't done anything yet.

(PEANUT *laughs softly.*)

ERIC: Shall we go?

(PEANUT *and* CONRAD *leave.* ERIC *kisses* LARRY *on both cheeks, then hugs him hard.*)

LARRY: Got your keys?

ERIC: Yes –

(*He leaves quickly.* LARRY *goes to the window, watches them ascend the stairs, waves.*)

LARRY: (*Calling*) Looks like a fog. Take care –

(*He draws the curtains. He stands lost for a moment, then struggles unsuccessfully to control his tears. He takes out a full bottle of Scotch, pours a drink, and downs it. The lights fade to blackout.*

In the darkness: A tenor sings to a piano accompaniment 'Quia Amore Langueo', a fourteenth-century anonymous poem, set to music by Peter Godwin.)

TENOR: (*Singing*) 'In a valley of this restless mind
　　　　I sought in mountain and in mead,
　　　　Trusting a true love to find.
　　　　Upon a hill then took I heed;
　　　　A voice I heard (and near I yede)

In great dolour complaining tho:
See, dear soul, how my sides bleed
   Quia amore langueo.

Upon this hill I found a tree,
Under a tree a man sitting;
From head to foot wounded was he;
His hearte blood I saw bleeding:
A seemly man to be a king,
A gracious face to look unto.
I askéd why he had paining:
   Quia amore langueo.

I am true love that false was never;
My sister, man's soul –

ERIC'S VOICE: (*A great cry*) Godwin, have you no shame? That's
   Delius again, note for bloody note! Thief! Vandal! Plagiarist!
   (*Sound of audience's shocked reaction. And then a scream,*
   JULIETTE's, *long and harrowing.*)

SCENE TWO

9.30 p.m. on Tuesday 30 December 1930.
   In the basement flat: LARRY *is asleep, his head resting on the table.*
He wears an eye-mask. A glass and the bottle of Scotch, now half-
empty, beside him. Sound of a taxi coming to a stop. Then the taxi
door banging to. The taxi going. LARRY *wakes, doesn't know quite*
where he is, stands, stumbles, removes the eye-shade, listens, hears the
sound of footsteps on the stairs outside and then JULIETTE's *muffled*
cries. LARRY *hurries out of the room to the front door which is being*
thumped on and rattled. Confused, overlapping:
LARRY'S VOICE: Who's there?
JULIETTE'S VOICE: Please let us in –
LARRY'S VOICE: Who are you?
JULIETTE'S VOICE: Open the door –
LARRY'S VOICE: Go away –
ERIC'S VOICE: Open the bloody door –
LARRY'S VOICE: Eric, is that you?

JULIETTE'S VOICE: Please let us in –
LARRY'S VOICE: Eric, are you all right?
JULIETTE'S VOICE: Peter, stop it –
LARRY'S VOICE: Who are you, go away, for God's sake, go away!
JULIETTE'S VOICE: Stop it, Peter, you're hurting me –
ERIC'S VOICE: Christ! Of course, I've got his keys –
LARRY'S VOICE: Eric, Eric? Who is it?
JULIETTE'S VOICE: Peter! Let go –
(*Sound of keys in the lock.*)
LARRY'S VOICE: Don't come in, please don't come in –
JULIETTE'S VOICE: Peter! Let go of me! Peter!
(*Sound of the front door being pushed open.*)
LARRY'S VOICE: Stop it, get out, help! Help!
(*Sound of a scuffle,* JULIETTE *crying near to hysteria, a groan from* LARRY, *the door being banged to and locked. Then, in the clear:*)
JULIETTE'S VOICE: (*Terrified*) Peter! Peter!
(ERIC *bursts into the room, wild, driven, his tie and collar loose, hair and beard unruly. He is in the throes of a severe attack of acute disassociation, a dual personality disorder. His entire persona is transformed at this moment into his second being,* PETER GODWIN.)
[NOTE: *Because* ERIC WELLS *and* PETER GODWIN *are one and the same person, and because the switch from one persona to another occurs without warning, the character in which he speaks is designated by that name.*]
GODWIN: (*Hoarse, intense*) Where is he, the little bastard? Where is he?
(JULIETTE *comes stumbling into the room, distraught, one shoe off, followed a moment later by* LARRY, *nursing a bleeding nose.*)
LARRY: Eric – !
GODWIN: (*Turning on* LARRY, *grabbing him*) Keep your mouth tight shut, you little ponce! (*He throws him aside; then to* JULIETTE:) And you. I don't want to hear from you either. Slut! (*Desperate.*) Where is he? Where is Eric Wells?
(*He disappears behind the screen, reappears, then opens the*

bedroom door and looks in. He removes the key from the inside of the bedroom door and locks it from the outside. LARRY *makes a dash for it.* GODWIN *spins round, grabs him, pulls him back, throws him so that he ends up near* JULIETTE. GODWIN *rips the telephone wire from its socket.*)

GODWIN: We're going to wait for Eric Wells.

(*He stares at them, breathing hard, but as though unseeing. They stand together terrified.* GODWIN *closes his eyes, begins to sway.*)

GODWIN: (*Softly*) Where is he? Where is he?

(*He begins to cry, quietly at first, then painful sobs and moans. He sinks down on a chair, rocks back and forth.*)

LARRY: (*Almost inaudible*) I can't – I don't know what's –

GODWIN: (*Suddenly swinging round*) Stop whispering! (*He rises, advances on* LARRY *who cowers.*)

Who are you? What are you doing here?

(LARRY *cannot speak.*)

Are you his catamite? (*Still no response.*) Where is he? (*Silence.*) Juliette, do you know this man?

JULIETTE: No –

(*Suddenly,* GODWIN *doubles up, as if in pain, holds on to his head.* LARRY *watches, terrified.* JULIETTE *trembles alarmingly.*)

ERIC: Oh, Larry, Larry, it's out of my hands, our world is coming apart at the seams –

LARRY: (*Fearful, tentative*) Eric?

(ERIC *weeps.*)

JULIETTE: (*A whisper*) We've got to get out of here, he'll kill us, I know about these things, how did they deal with these things, what did they do, what did they say, I can't remember, I can't remember –

(*Silence.* ERIC *looks up.*)

ERIC: Larry?

(LARRY *takes a tentative step towards him.* JULIETTE *watches as though she is about to witness an accident.*)

ERIC: Larry, I did something dreadful tonight. At the recital. The second item. '*Quia Amore Langueo*'. I couldn't restrain myself. It was so blatant. He'd done it again. Stolen from the Master. I shouted out. 'Plagiarist, vandal, thief!' There was uproar. I ran out into the night, dark, cold, unfriendly. The worlds collided. An explosion so mighty it blew the shadows into a hundred thousand particles. After that, there was the fog, the yellow of absinthe, the taste of a mustard pea-souper. I remember nothing but entering the fog. Now he'll find me and kill me. He won't put up with me any more. Why should he? It's either him or me. And he's the stronger.

(LARRY *kneels beside him, takes his hand*.)

LARRY: (*Gently*) Eric, listen to me, sweetie. You've been taken ill. I want you to come with me now to get some help. There's a thick fog outside, all very Sherlock Holmes. So, we'll feel our way in the fog and go to St Stephen's in the Fulham Road. They'll know what to do, he won't find you there –

(ERIC *looks at* JULIETTE. *Agonizing pause*.)

ERIC: Who is this young lady?

(LARRY *looks at* JULIETTE *helplessly*.)

JULIETTE: I'm – I'm Juliette. Juliette Smith.

ERIC: Please forgive my rudeness, but what are you doing here? Larry, I told you not to let anyone in –

JULIETTE: I – I – after the – I recognized you – that's when I understood –

ERIC: I think I've seen you before. At Peter's concerts. I always creep in late, sit at the back when it's dark, and I think I've seen you there. Tell me what happened tonight.

JULIETTE: I saw you – that you were – I saw you –

ERIC: (*Gently*) Do try to be a little more coherent, my dear, it would be such a help –

JULIETTE: I saw you were – distressed – and in need of assistance – I helped you into a taxi – and brought you back – I –

(*He suddenly stands, begins to pace. He disappears behind the screen for a moment, then reappears*.)

GODWIN: You lying bitch. You ran out screaming. I grabbed you, you were about to give the game away, you lying bitch –

(*Again he storms off behind the screen*.)

JULIETTE: No, no, no, Peter, I want to help you –

(*Agonized silence. He reappears*.)

ERIC: Did I introduce myself? My name is Eric Wells. I'm a
music critic. Not unknown. I don't remember, you see, after
shouting out – (*Breaks off.*) Were you at the recital at the
Wigmore Hall?

JULIETTE: Yes.

ERIC: Was it me who shouted out, or him?

(*He starts to sway again, and to hyperventilate.* LARRY *backs
away. They watch him, nervously.*)

ERIC: Larry, you must go away, the money I gave you, pack your
things, if he finds me, tomorrow morning when the banks
open, lose yourself, book into a cheap hotel near Victoria
Station, you know what the police are like, tonight, tonight,
he's hated me all my life, take the train to Paris, I gave birth
to him, you've got your passport, he's in the shadows, use
the money, because he's near –

(*He becomes rigid, trembling, struggling inwardly. Then:*)

GODWIN: (*A great cry*) Jesus Christ! It was nothing like. Listen for
yourself – (*He goes to the piano, plays and sings.*)

   'In a valley of this restless mind
   I sought in mountain and in mead
   Trusting a true love to find.
   Upon a hill then I took heed – '

(*He breaks off.*)

It's entirely mine! It's entirely original! I don't need you or
anyone else as a critic. I am my own critic!

ERIC: (*Without pause, the change of voice and demeanour instant*)
But that's always been the problem hasn't it, Peter? You
lacked talent. I was your talent. I was the critic within you.
You have no taste, Peter. No standards. Listen – (*He plays a
phrase on the piano with one finger.*) Delius. (*He plays another
phrase.*) Godwin. You see? You simply regurgitate the last
sounds you hear. You need me, Peter, because you yourself
are inadequate to the task.

(GODWIN *thumps out a dissonant chord.*)

GODWIN: (*Sings*) 'Let us sail the sea the two of us,
   The two of us,
   But you no more with me,
   No more.'

(*Breaks off.*)

No one's written that before. I plucked it out of the air, out of my mind, I set it down, note after note, the act of creation about which you know nothing, absolutely nothing, and then, envious and resentful, you, you parasite, you set out to destroy my life source – Christ, he's gone again. Ugly, slimy, grimy – (*He swings round.*) Juliette! Juliette!

(*He holds out his arm to her; she goes slowly to him.*)

Find him. Tell him he's a criminal, a destroyer of talent, a betrayer –

(*She reaches him; he grabs her fiercely.*)

Get me a drink, I want a drink. Get it for me. Jesus, you little whore, what have you been up to, you and Wells, making the beast with two backs, haven't you? Haven't you?

JULIETTE: (*To* LARRY; *in pain*) Get him a drink –

(LARRY *starts towards the cupboard when* GODWIN *draws a small automatic pistol.* LARRY *screams with fright.*)

GODWIN: Don't try anything clever. Because I'll shoot, believe me, I have nothing more to lose – (*He cannot hold the gun still. His hand is trembling alarmingly.*)

ERIC: Put the gun away, Peter. It's very melodramatic, even for you. Let's see if we can sort this out like reasonable human beings. (*Puts the gun in his trouser pocket; to* JULIETTE, *very matter-of-fact.*) May I explain something, my dear? I came first into this world. I came first. Larry, I've never told you this but my mother died giving birth to me –

JULIETTE: (*Involuntarily*) No, you never told me that –

ERIC: My dear, I was talking to Larry. My mother died forcing me into this world.

JULIETTE: So did mine.

ERIC: Did she? (*A sweet smile.*) I knew we shared something. It's an odd thing to have in common. A dead, unknown mother. Odd, but lovely in a way, don't you think? I'm sure we're going to be friends, Juliette. I believe Larry likes you, too, otherwise he wouldn't have let you in. And that's a great comfort to me. I set great store by what Larry thinks. Could I have just a little nip of something, Larry?

(LARRY *pours* ERIC *and himself a drink.*)

And Miss Smith. Where are your manners, Larry?

(LARRY *pours* JULIETTE *a drink*.)

My father, Septimus Wells KC, married again. My
stepmother was kind and loving and treated me as her own.
But it's not the same thing, is it, you understand that, don't
you, Juliette? I remember as if it were yesterday the moment
I learned my real mother was dead. I still spend long hours at
her grave. In Abingdon. Rest in peace.

(*Shudders;* LARRY *gives him another drink*.)

My father, Septimus Wells, KC, had been to Sedbergh. He
was forever saying his time there was the unhappiest of his
life. Yet he sent me down the same road. Aren't fathers
whimsical? Sedbergh was misery. My only solace was music
and the kindness of my music master. His report to my
father put the cat among the crotchets. He wrote that he
thought me 'arresting, something apart, something
strikingly different. Not that he shows musical or pianistic
precocity', he went on, 'no, it is his approach, his attitude
that differs'. Wasn't that charming? My father read it and
said at once I should go into the army, toughen up, be a man,
my son, and all that sort of thing. But it was about that time I
first heard the music of Frederick Delius and that released in
my head a torrent of musical sound. That's when I met Peter
Godwin.

(*He takes* JULIETTE's *hand*.)

You see, Juliette dear, I never stood on my own feet, never
woke up to life beyond the nursery and my stepmother's
apron strings. But when I met Peter, oh, that was an
awakening. He was everything I was not. We became such
good, close friends. I went up to Oxford – I read Classics –
but my entire life was devoted to learning about music. Peter
came with me but said he didn't need to study anything. All
he wanted to do was compose. We took a small room for him
off the Cowley Road, and that's what he did, every moment
of the living day, hear the sounds in his head and put them
down, demonic, demented. And after every day's work he'd
ask my opinion of what he had written. That was the
loveliest time. Beginnings and endings are best. It's what

goes on in between that gives pain. No one knew. It was our secret. If he hadn't been with me, God knows what hell I would have endured. Sedbergh was misery, Oxford torment. But Peter Godwin and I, together –

(*A clatter of footsteps outside. Then a banging on the door.* ERIC *freezes.*)

LARRY: Thank God –

PEANUT'S VOICE: Eric? Larry? Guess who!

(LARRY *goes towards the door.*)

GODWIN: Stop! (*He draws the gun, paces, swinging the gun wildly this way and that.*)

LARRY: (*Trying to remain calm and be cheerful*) Eric, please, I must let them in, we can all help, Juliette, Peanut, Conrad and me, we'll all be able to help you, you'd like that wouldn't you, sweetie?

GODWIN: Just shut up, nancy boy! Where did he find you? In a cottage off Leicester Square?

(*Rattling of the door.*)

CONRAD'S VOICE: Jesu, it's locked, I'll break it down, that's what I'll do, I'll break it down –

(*Tapping on the window.*)

PEANUT'S VOICE: Eric? Larry?

JULIETTE: (*To* LARRY) Let them in, quickly –

(*But* GODWIN *gets to the door before him, holds him away with the gun. The rattling of the door and the tapping on the window continues.*)

GODWIN: Just let me give you this warning. If either of you try anything or say anything out of hand, I'll shoot. I'll kill the lot of us. (*Directly to* LARRY.) And you'll be first –

(*He exits and is heard unlocking and opening the front door.*)

LARRY: (*Breaking down*) Oh Jesus, dear Jesus, dear loving Jesus –
(*Holding a handkerchief to his nose.*) I wish I could stop this bleeding –

CONRAD'S VOICE: (*Coming into the hall*) Thank God, you're safe, Eric –

(*The sound of the door being locked again.*)

CONRAD'S VOICE: That's right, Eric, lock the door, you can't be too careful –

JULIETTE: (*Overlapping; staccato*) We must find a way, humour him, Jesus Christ, we're done for –

(GODWIN *returns with* PEANUT *and* CONRAD, *who are hopelessly drunk.* GODWIN, *gun now in his jacket pocket, stands behind* LARRY, *threatening him silently.*)

CONRAD: Sorry we're late. The fog, you know. Oh God, what a pea-souper! Slow going. And we stopped off for a spot of warmth at The Bricklayer's Arms –

PEANUT: But not a bricklayer in sight. More's the pity. No bricklayers. It's the tragedy *de nos jours*.

(*She helps herself to Scotch, pours one for* CONRAD. *They drink steadily and continually.* CONRAD *sidles up to* GODWIN.)

CONRAD: (*A loud whisper*) Have you still got the shooter? Better give it back to me now –

PEANUT: (*To* JULIETTE) Oh, good evening. They call me Peanut. My real name's Monica, which is frightfully common, but Peanut has a certain chic, don't you think? What's your name?

JULIETTE: Juliette.

PEANUT: And who's your Romeo? Eric or Larry? (*She laughs.*) Are you friends of these two gentle gentlemen? (*No response.*) Tell me, in confidence, are you a queer's dear? (*No response.*) I am. Queers adore me, so much so that one of them married me.

CONRAD: Oh, Jesus, Peanut, you're a cracked record, that's what you are –

PEANUT: That's Mr Conrad Leary with whom I co-habit. And I co-habit with him because the only other men I know are all screamers. Mr Leary is not. But he lives in the past and the past is not a good place for a holiday.

GODWIN: Get out, the pair of you.

CONRAD: That's a welcome, isn't it? Oh Jesus, just let us have a few drinks, we've been dry all the long night through –

GODWIN: Get out, scum!

PEANUT: Oh! The queen's turned vicious. They're all vicious, you know. They've all got a vicious streak. If there's one thing I hate it's a vicious queen and as they're all vicious I hate them all. Come on, Conrad, we're not wanted –

JULIETTE: (*Desperate*) No, don't go –

LARRY: (*At speed*) No, no, don't go. Is that Mr Grace going to call round, do you know? Did you see him? Is he going to come?

PEANUT: Oh, I do hope so. I do hope he's going to join us. What a beauty! And he's in possession of a very fine organ, I believe. I shall twist some wire round it, given half the chance. I should love to see him again. If he gets here, of course. No taxis, no trams. We saw you getting into your cab, it must have been the last one running in London. The fog worsens every minute. It's as thick as a bricklayer's arms.

CONRAD: (*To* GODWIN) Tell me something, was that shouting out you did, was that all part of the music? Was it all part of the song? This modern business. No tune but what a furore!

PEANUT: (*To* JULIETTE) Did you know, my dear, you've lost a shoe?

(GODWIN *bars the way, draws the gun.*)

CONRAD: Oh good, you've still got it, you better give it to me, it's an illegal weapon, you know, stolen from a dead tart in Armentiers.

GODWIN: (*Waving the gun at* CONRAD *and* PEANUT) You two, get the hell out of here –

CONRAD: (*Shadow boxing*) Oh, it's like that, is it? Put 'em up, put 'em up, see what you're like without the shooter in your hand. Typical bloody conshie. Give 'em a gun and they think they rule the world, put 'em up, put 'em up –

GODWIN: Get out!

PEANUT: I wish you'd say what you mean, Eric.

(*She laughs.* GODWIN *pushes* CONRAD *back.* CONRAD *stumbles.*)

GODWIN: I'll blow your brains out if you don't leave now.

PEANUT: (*An attempt at dignity*) Well. I think we know when we're not wanted, don't we, Conrad?

CONRAD: I should hope so –

PEANUT: I always said you had an ugly nature, Eric.

CONRAD: Never ever heard you mention his nature in your life, Peanut –

(JULIETTE *hurries over to* CONRAD, *speaks quietly and urgently.*)

JULIETTE: Yes, go now and on your way stop off at the police station and tell them we're in need of assistance –

(GODWIN *pulls her away*.)

GODWIN: Sit down, bitch –

CONRAD: (*Overlapping*) Oh no, don't try that on me. I'm having nothing to do with it. *You* fetch the police, I'm having nothing to do with them, isn't that right, Larry?

LARRY: I don't know, I don't know –

GODWIN: I want you out of here! Now!

(*He grabs hold of* CONRAD *and pushes him towards the door*.)

CONRAD: Jesus Christ, what's got into you, Eric?

(GODWIN *advances on* PEANUT, *stops dead, trembling*.)

PEANUT: If you lay a finger on me, I'll scream –

LARRY: Yes, scream, scream, Peanut –

(ERIC *puts the gun away*.)

ERIC: Peanut dear, please, please forgive us. Such unruly behaviour. What you must think of us. He'll be back, of course –

CONRAD: God, you're pissed, Eric, I've never seen you as pissed as this –

ERIC: Believe me, it would be better for all concerned if you leave –

CONRAD: Give me the shooter, Eric –

ERIC: Tomorrow. I need it for protection tonight.

LARRY: Give him the gun, Eric, there's a dear.

ERIC: No. I need it. Believe me. He'll – he'll – you know who I mean – he'll return – and I need to stay alive – somehow –

CONRAD: Come on, Peanut, the pubs will still be open. Let's try The Man in the Moon –

(PEANUT *starts to go*.)

PEANUT: By way of a proper apology, Eric, I shall expect a bouquet of flowers in the morning.

(*They go.* ERIC *follows them. The sound of the door being unlocked and opened*.)

CONRAD: Jesus, it's as yellow as hell out here –

(*Sound of the door being locked. During this, frantic, at speed:*)

LARRY: Oh God, what are we going to do?

JULIETTE: (*Fighting for control*) Let me talk to him, just let me do the talking, I know about these things –

LARRY: D'you think he'd really shoot us?

JULIETTE: Yes –

(ERIC *returns. Silence.*)

ERIC: Thank God they were drunk. It's not right to involve friends, however close, in matters beyond their understanding. No one really understands except Peter, and we are more than friends, more like brothers really. And you, Larry, are owed an explanation. Because I do love you. I want you to believe that.

JULIETTE: (*Affecting calm*) Eric, let's talk about it, isn't that a good idea? For example, can I ask a question, why did you keep Peter so secret?

ERIC: No, no, it was not only me. It was mutually agreed between us. The worlds had to be kept separate. I was ashamed of him, and he of me.

JULIETTE: Why?

ERIC: I myself was not brave enough to create. But I aspired to the heights. He was without fear and without standards. He aspired to the depths.

(*Long silence.*)

GODWIN: There once were two piano-players,
    Who went for to see two soothsayers,
    Beware, beware,
    They were told as a pair,
    Not to drink in the arms of bricklayers.

(*Silence.*)

Things are nearing a conclusion and it's a struggle for me to keep chaos at bay. Give me a drink, I need a drink. We can't have the secret revealed.

(JULIETTE *gives him a drink.* LARRY *takes one, too.*)

JULIETTE: Why not, Peter?

GODWIN: Why not? Why not? Use your limited intelligence, you poxy tart. Once the secret's out, there would be no life hereafter, that's why. They'd hang us with piano wires. They'd come down on us, the judges, KCs, generals, ministers of the Crown, and most of all, the great musical gods. Beware their revenge, whom the gods destroy they first

make mad. That's why they made me rely on him. 'Every
artist needs a critical hand to help him ascend to heaven.' I
was conceived deficient. I can't be exposed. Like a creature
who lives in dark woods, I'd die if exposed to the light. But
it's Wells who's going to die, not me.
(JULIETTE *pours him another drink*.)

JULIETTE: (*Urgent again*) Don't say that, Peter, don't do
anything that'll endanger you. Talk to someone, I know
someone –

GODWIN: (*Exploding*) Doctors, you mean doctors! I don't want
any of your bloody piss-psychology. I'm not seeing a doctor.
You think they're not part of it? You think they're not part
of the conspiracy to belittle and bedevil and bedazzle and
be-de-la-la-ma-ma-da-ma-la- (*He becomes incoherent, spitting
out the short staccato sounds*.)

JULIETTE: Not doctors, Peter. What use are doctors? No, that
man Grace, Rupert Grace, he wants to help, he'd help. Let
him help. He came down to the cottage yesterday, while you
were upstairs, you remember? I lied to him, I said you
weren't there, he believed me, but he said he was anxious to
help –

GODWIN: Just shut your mouth. You talk too much. I know what
you're playing at. You've always talked too much. All you're
good for is penetration.
(*Silence*.)

> There once was a pianist called Pete,
> Who picked up a whore whom he beat.
> He said, 'I'll admit,
> I'm a bit of a shit,
> But it's more fun than beating retreat.'

(*He laughs quietly*.)

ERIC: Peter's the only person who thinks his limericks funny or
clever. (*Silence*.) Larry, perhaps we should leave now,
together, perhaps we could get out of the country before he
finds us –

JULIETTE: Yes, yes, yes, go, go now, both of you, I'll wait here
for him –

ERIC: We have to be clever, quick, ingenious, like the letters, the

writing of the letters, he was cunning, he paid that queenly
guardsman half a crown to deliver his letters, there in the
pub, in front of witnesses, but he got away with it, like a
thief who's a shadow, disappearing disappa-la-na-gra-dza-
dza-

JULIETTE: Why did you write such awful things about him? Why
did you betray him? Why couldn't you let him be?

ERIC: He found me out, alone, in the dark, in the garden of
eternity, trying to hide from the serpent. Yes, he betrayed
me all right. (*Suddenly as if exhausted.*) Oh dear Christ, why
do we need to know right from wrong? (*Turns on* LARRY.)
You. What's your name?

LARRY: (*Terrified*) Laurence Rider.

GODWIN: And you're some sort of queer, are you?

LARRY: (*Barely audible*) Yes.

GODWIN: What? What? Speak up, I can't hear you –

LARRY: Yes.

GODWIN: Yes what? What are you yessing about?

LARRY: You asked me if I was queer. I said yes.

GODWIN: How long have you and Wells been together?

LARRY: Nine months.

GODWIN: Not much fun though, was it? Not a potent sort of
chap, Eric Wells?

LARRY: I love you, Eric, and that's all that counts.

ERIC: (*Turning to* JULIETTE) And I love – and I love – They've
been the happiest nine months of my life, Juliette. Until I
felt bound to expose Godwin. Then it all began to go down
hill. I knew he meant to kill me.

JULIETTE: Why did you expose him, then?

ERIC: Because I knew him to be a fraud. He was not of the front
rank after all. And there is no point in being an artist unless
one is of the front rank. I do not believe they also serve who
only stand and write reviews. His music, his whole life was
deteriorating into slime. No offence, my dear. How long
have you known him?

JULIETTE: About a year –

ERIC: How did you meet?

JULIETTE: I'd heard his music –

ERIC: You sensed a soul-mate, didn't you? Off kilter, askew.
Why did you stay with him?

JULIETTE: I was too frightened to leave.

GODWIN: Balls! You love it, go on, Juliette, admit it, you're not
frightened of me, you can twist me round your little finger.
You wanted me to degrade you. You loved my remorse.
Frightened? You? Balls! You've only to show me your
tongue and I'm cement in your mouth.
(*Sound of footsteps on the stone stairs outside. All freeze.*
GODWIN *produces the gun and threatens them. The doorbell
rings. No one moves. The bell rings again and the door is rattled.*)

RUPERT'S VOICE: Wells? Godwin? It's Rupert Grace, let me in –
(*Silence and stillness in the room.*)
I know you're in there. Open the door.
(LARRY *makes a tentative move.* GODWIN *threatens him with
the gun.*)

RUPERT'S VOICE: (*Near the window*) I'm going to fetch the
police.
(*His footsteps disappear.* LARRY *begins to sob uncontrollably.*)

ERIC: My dear, what's the matter? Don't cry. Go away. Hide.
(*Fighting the inner battle.*) You know as well as I do, Larry,
that if something were to happen to me here in this flat, and
if you were in Birmingham with four thousand others at the
Policeman's Ball, they'd find you, arrest you, charge you and
imprison you. I don't want that to happen. Unlock the door.
You have your own keys, don't you? Don't you?

LARRY: Oh God, I didn't think of my own keys –

ERIC: I love you, Larry. And I do not want you harmed.
(LARRY *doesn't move. The lights go out.* LARRY *screams.*)

GODWIN: I've got the gun, if I hear a noise I'll shoot –
(LARRY *whimpers.*)

LARRY: It's the meter, the meter's run out –

GODWIN: Feed it.
(*Sudden noise of running footsteps, the front door being unlocked,
slammed, the sound of footsteps stumbling up the stone steps, and
disappearing.*)

GODWIN: I'm by the door, I've got the gun, for Christ's sake, find
some money for the meter –

(*A chair is knocked over in the room.* JULIETTE *stifles a scream.*)

GODWIN: Gotcher.

JULIETTE: Let go, Peter, you're hurting me –

GODWIN: You like it –

JULIETTE: I don't, I don't –

(*Sound of a terrible slap and of* JULIETTE *falling. Silence but for her whimpering. After a moment:*)

ERIC: Oh, dear. Has the meter run out? Leave it to me –

(*Movement in the room. Sound of coins in the meter. The light comes on.* ERIC's *head visible above the screen, looking down on* JULIETTE, *who lies on the floor nursing a cut above the eye.* LARRY *has gone.*)

ERIC: Oh, my dear. Have you been hurt? You're bleeding –

(*Looks round; panic.*) Where's Larry?

(*He disappears momentarily, then reappears, charges out of the room to the front door.*)

ERIC'S VOICE: (*Distressed*) Larry! Oh, Larry.

(*Sound of him shutting and locking the door. He returns. He stands over her. She holds out a hand for help but he doesn't take it.*)

GODWIN: 'There once were two men with one head,
  Who liked the same whore in one bed.
  They'd also one cock,
  Which came as a shock
  To the whore who was better off dead.'

(*Silence. He holds the gun steadily.*)

JULIETTE: Don't hurt me any more, Peter, I'm not strong, it's ebbing away from me –

GODWIN: What, what's ebbing away?

JULIETTE: I can't remember.

(*Brief silence.*)

GODWIN: Not long now.

(JULIETTE *gets to her feet. She stares at him and is frightened.*)

JULIETTE: Put away the gun, please, Peter. (*No response.*) Let me leave. I won't tell anyone about – I won't tell anyone the secret. Honest injun.

GODWIN: The little queen got away and I did so want to take him with us.

JULIETTE: Please let me leave, too –

GODWIN: No.

JULIETTE: But why, Peter?

GODWIN: No one must know.

JULIETTE: But Larry's out there now, fetching the police, a doctor –

GODWIN: Who'll believe him? Hysterical, drunken little queen. What will he say? There once were two men with one head? Who'll believe him, Juliette?

JULIETTE: Who'll believe me?

ERIC: Oh, you my dear, you will be believed. You have experience of these things. You have technical terms, a glorious memory and such intricate knowledge of the fractured animus. You will be taken seriously. Not poor Larry, cast out and cut off. No, Juliette. It was our tragedy to cross Peter Godwin's path. (*Sudden stillness*.) He's near. I know it. He's near, I'll have to hide –

JULIETTE: I swear, Eric, I will never speak of these things, never. I swear –
    (*She starts to moan quietly*.)

GODWIN: (*A great cry*) I relied on him! He questioned the notes I recorded. I took sound out of the ether, translated dissonance into ink. You'll die like Judas, I said. And we know how Judas died. Not murdered, no, not sleeping taken, but, but, ut, ut, ut – He was near to it. Oh, so near. A little more courage and the train would have smashed his brains into particles of light. There used to be sounds in my head, celestial harmonies, but no, no, he said, do better, climb higher, aspire, achieve, ascend. It was not my nature, it was his, born in death, sterile of creation, impotent and innocent and intrica-insiga-ontifa-eruda-ga-fa-da-de-(*Silence*.) I'll find harmonies again, I know I will in the heart of the sun where Christ lies buried.
    (*He grabs* JULIETTE *and kisses her fiercely, passionately, starts to rip at her clothes*.)

JULIETTE: (*Struggling*) Please, Peter, let me go, don't –
    (*He is suddenly still*.)

GODWIN: He's here –

(*She makes a dash for it. He grabs her, throws her down. She lands on her knees, cowers. She tries to scream but no sound comes out. Her body is slowly becoming rigid, immobile. He stands over her, raises the gun, points it at her head. Out of her open mouth come gurgling sounds, as though she's choking. He turns the gun on himself, puts the barrel in his mouth and pulls the trigger. Click. The gun is not loaded. He stands trembling, then turns and runs behind the screen. After a moment the sound of hissing gas.*

Distant and unreal, the sound of the 'Shanty for a Dead Love' by Godwin begins to insist itself. JULIETTE, *frozen, kneeling, her mouth open. She coughs but the sound is again like choking. The sound of footsteps on the stone stairs outside. The sound of the door being flung open.*

RUPERT *and a uniformed* POLICEMAN *enter, spluttering and coughing. The* POLICEMAN *rushes to the window, opens it, goes behind the screen. The hissing stops.* RUPERT, *coughing, struggling for breath, stumbles towards* JULIETTE, *tries to lift her but she is rigid, catatonic, impossible to move easily. Unseen, the* POLICEMAN *pushes aside the screen.* ERIC *lies with his head in the gas oven, his face hidden. The* POLICEMAN *struggles and removes the corpse.*

POLICEMAN: Get her out of here, sir, get her out of here –

(*The* POLICEMAN *goes to the telephone, sees the wires ripped, and then runs out. The sound of his whistle being blown is heard.* RUPERT *tries to lift* JULIETTE *but fails. He slips to his knees beside her. The music of Delius gives way to the sound of:*)

TENOR: Let us sail the sea the two of us,
    The two of us,
    But you no more with me,
    No more.

(*The* POLICEMAN *returns. He taps* RUPERT *on the shoulder and points to the body.* RUPERT *rises, crosses to the corpse, looks down.*)

RUPERT: Yes. That's Eric Wells.

(*In the cottage: A hammering on the door. Torchlight shines through the window.*

In the basement flat: The POLICEMAN *covers* ERIC'S *face with his*

tunic. RUPERT *returns to Juliette's side.*
In the cottage: The door is opened. A COUNTRY POLICEMAN
enters, shining his torch.)

COUNTRY POLICEMAN: Mr Godwin? Peter Godwin?
(*He shines his torch across the empty room. He goes towards the
door that leads upstairs and exits. Godwin's song continues and
then:*)

BBC VOICE: At the inquest in Chelsea today into the death of the
music critic, Mr Eric Wells, the coroner's jury returned an
open verdict. In evidence, a Scotland Yard detective said
that the search is continuing for the composer, Mr Peter
Godwin, and for Mr Laurence Rider, both of whom police
believe may be able to help them with their inquiries.
(*The* COUNTRY POLICEMAN *returns. He stumbles over
something in the dark. The sound of two cymbals clapping. He
shines his torch on the monkey toy. The music of Godwin
continues.*
The lights fade to blackout.)

TRAMWAY ROAD

For my sister,
Eve Borland

CHARACTERS

ARTHUR LANGLEY (about 60)
EMIL VISSER (20)
JACOB (about 25)
DORA LANGLEY (about 50)

December 1951. The living room, converted into a small private lending-library, and the stoep of Arthur and Dora Langley's flat in Sea Point, a suburb of Cape Town.

The living room is shabby, small and angular. The walls are covered by shelves which overflow with books. There are also two free-standing shelves. There is a desk, a chair, two filing-cabinets, and a reading-table with chairs.

The front door of the flat is glass-panelled and leads directly from a landing. Another door leads to the rest of the flat. Folding shutters open out on to the stoep.

Tramway Road was first performed at the Lyric Theatre,
Hammersmith on 23 October 1984 with the following cast:

ARTHUR LANGLEY	Freddie Jones
EMIL VISSER	Richard E. Grant
JACOB	William Vanderpuye
DORA LANGLEY	Annette Crosbie

Directed by	David Jones
Set designed by	Timothy O'Brien
Costumes by	Bunny Christie
Lighting by	Dave Horn
Sound by	Richard Borkum

ACT ONE

December 1951. Hot. Evening. A few minutes after 9 p.m.
ARTHUR *and* EMIL *are seated, facing each other.*
JACOB, *a Cape Coloured, removes books from the shelves, dusts and replaces the books.*
ARTHUR: Ah, e: i. (*The 'ah' as in 'but', the 'e' as in 'pin', the 'i' as in 'white'.* EMIL's *speech is affected and too careful.*)
EMIL: Aah, ee: aai.
ARTHUR: No dear. Short ah. Short e: ah, e: i.
EMIL: Ah, e: i.
ARTHUR: I like white.
EMIL: I like white.
ARTHUR: I like white outside.
EMIL: I like white outside.
ARTHUR: I like white is fine. Outside is awful. Ah, oo: ou. Short ah, short oo: out.
EMIL: Ah, oo: out.
ARTHUR: Outside.
EMIL: Outside.
ARTHUR: I like white outside about five-fifteen.
EMIL: I like white outside about five-fifteen.
ARTHUR: Be careful of the ees, Emil dear. No English vowel is made with a smile. Not even ee. Loose mouth, a, e, i, o, u. Forward, forward, loose, loose.
EMIL: A, e. i. o. u.
ARTHUR: As if you're going to kiss someone. Indecently.
EMIL: A, e. i. o. u.
ARTHUR: Much, much, better. Professor Higgins would be proud of you.
EMIL: Who?
ARTHUR: Have you never heard of Professor Higgins?
EMIL: No.
ARTHUR: The leading character in *Pygmalion* by – (*He waits for an answer.*) – by George Bernard – ?
EMIL: Shaw.

ARTHUR: Shaw, that's right, Emil, George Bernard Shaw. Well
then, that's one for your General Culture list.
(*He goes to the shelves, finds a copy of the play and gives it to*
EMIL, *who puts it in a brown paper carrier bag.*)
It's become my wife's private joke. She calls me Professor
Higgins and you she calls – (*Almost without hesitation.*) – in
the play he is a teacher of phonetics but not, alas, of general
culture which is, as we know, our protection against – ? (*He
waits for a suggestion.*) – against barbarism, that's right Emil,
barbarism. Culture is not simply knowledge but feeling. In
speech one must not only enunciate, one must also express.
'Heat me these irons hot; and look thou stand within the
arras: when I strike my foot upon the bosom of the ground,
rush forth and bind the boy which you shall find with me fast
to the chair'. For most of the war I helped out at a school.
What is called in England a Minor Public School. Near
Princes Risborough. That's a town in Buckinghamshire, not
a member of the Royal Family. In the Summer Term – that's
your winter, of course – I produced the Shakespeare play. It
was quite a famous event. One of my Pucks took up acting
professionally and when last heard of was walking on at the
Old Vic. (*Pause.*) Yes, feeling not phonetics. I like white
outside about five-fifteen.

EMIL: I like white –
(*He breaks off, stifling tears.*)

ARTHUR: My dear, what is it?

EMIL: I – I'm not going to – I – I'm not – I, I –

ARTHUR: Emil dear, I know you are blessed with an artistic
temperament but there is no reason to become incoherent.
And let us, even when distressed, not forget our diction. I
haven't. Ah, e: i. I'm not. Not Aai'm not. I'm not. I. I. I.
(*Pause.*)

EMIL: Mr Langley, I haven't got the money to pay you tonight.

ARTHUR: Got is an ugly word, Emil. It is perfectly acceptable to
say, I haven't the money to pay you tonight. Haven't you?
Oh, dear.

EMIL: I'm sorry. I should have told you before we started –

ARTHUR: You haven't the five shillings?

EMIL: No.

ARTHUR: Oh. Well. I daresay I shall still be able to afford breakfast tomorrow morning. (*Pause.*) You really mustn't cry for the want of five shillings.

EMIL: I can't help it. I've taken the lesson under false pretences.

ARTHUR: What a refined conscience you have. And a very soft nature. I like that. (*Pause.*) Emil, will you do me a favour?

EMIL: If I can, Mr Langley.

ARTHUR: Don't mention your lack of funds in front of Mrs Langley. It will only worry her. Unnecessarily. She was not, I make no secret of it, she was not greatly in favour of me giving you lessons. Her reasons were not directed at you personally, you understand but – (*A momentary pause.*) – she would have preferred the library to be less literary and rather more popular in its selection of books. I mean no disloyalty to her but she was keen we should purchase, for example, a second-hand set of Tarzan novels, and Westerns by Zane – ? (*He waits.*) – Grey, that's right, Emil, Zane Grey. And others. (*Pause.*) Curious name, Zane. I think she feels the number of our subscribers ought to be increasing more rapidly. But I would rather, much rather, teach a young person like you than lower my standards. Because I believe, Emil, that one must draw the line somewhere, even here in Sea Point. These shelves bear the glorious weight of Western civilization. (*He turns to the shelves, selecting books at random and handing them to* EMIL.) John Ruskin, André Gide, Daniel Defoe, Hugh Walpole, George – ?

EMIL: Bernard Shaw.

ARTHUR: No, Meredith, Emil, that's right, George Meredith. (*Pause.*) Do me a further favour. Take these two half-crowns (*Giving the coins to* EMIL.) and hand them to me when you leave. In front of Mrs Langley. Ostentatiously. As if it's your five shillings. As if you're paying me for your lesson. Will you?

(EMIL *nods, sniffs and puts the book in his carrier bag.*)
Money is the ugliest of man's inventions. It is one of the two . great anxieties of existence, the other being death. Money is bedfellow to power and the two breed pain. One should

never allow money to come between friends, please bear that in mind at all times. (*Pause*.) A friend is a person one is always pleased to see. (*Pause*.) And I'm always pleased to see you, Emil. I look forward to seeing you. I believe in you. I believe you will win the travel grant. I believe you will go to London. I believe you will gain admission to the Royal Academy of Dramatic Art. I believe you may even win a scholarship. I believe success sits about you as haloes atop the heads of angels. I believe in your talent and in your striking appearance. I believe in –

(DORA *enters*.)

DORA: It's after nine o'clock. How's the little flower-seller this evening?

ARTHUR: Do your vowels for Mrs Langley.

EMIL: A, e, i, o, u.

ARTHUR: Kensington, dear, pure Kensington.

DORA: I hand it to you Arthur. Compared to you Svengali is Enid Blyton.

ARTHUR: I do believe our fiction shelves are a little mixed tonight. (*To* EMIL.) The Wordsworth for Mrs Langley, Emil.

(EMIL *stands, arms stiffly by his side to recite*.)

EMIL: Composed upon Westminster Bridge, September 3, 1802, by William Wordsworth:

Earth has not anything to show more fair:
Dull would he be of soul who could pass by
A sight so touching in its majesty:
This City now doth, like a garment, wear –

DORA: (*Interrupting*) Jacob, stop dusting and make some tea.

ARTHUR: Wouldn't coffee be more suitable?

DORA: I want tea.

(JACOB *goes*.)

ARTHUR: You'll stay for tea, won't you, Emil?

EMIL: Thank you.

DORA: (*To* EMIL) I thought you liked to go early; I thought you were afraid of passing Tramway Road.

ARTHUR: I'll walk with him to the Terminus, dear. He won't be frightened with me beside him, will you, Emil?

DORA: Why, what will you do? Hold his hand?

ARTHUR: Don't be offended by Mrs Langley's interruption of the
Wordsworth, Emil. Any mention of London is apt to be
upsetting. Let us give her instead a real surprise. Animal,
Emil.
(EMIL *takes something from the carrier bag and goes behind one of
the free-standing bookshelves*.)
This will delight you, Dora. The boy is so talented. And so
innocent.

DORA: Has he paid yet?

ARTHUR: Not yet.

DORA: Charity begins at home, Arthur.

ARTHUR: Yes, but not just at this moment, dear –
(EMIL *springs out from behind the bookshelf, wearing the half-
mask of a monkey and performs a brief, passable impersonation of
the animal*.)
(*Watching* EMIL *perform*.) He made the mask himself.

DORA: I can see.

ARTHUR: So well observed. He spent the whole of last Sunday at
the zoo.

DORA: I thought he visited his father in the hospital on Sundays.

ARTHUR: Isn't he clever? (*When* EMIL *finishes*.) Bravo, Emil,
bravo. Even better than earlier. Mr Gielgud will have to look
to his laurels.
(EMIL *removes the mask*.)

EMIL: What does Mrs Langley think?

DORA: I wonder why you need the mask.

ARTHUR: It's another method, dear, of losing the awkwardness of
self. There is more than one way of anaesthetising reality. I
think we should call this the end of the lesson for the evening.

EMIL: Here's the five shillings, Mr Langley.
(*He hands* ARTHUR *the coins*.)

ARTHUR: What? Oh! The five shillings! Thank you! How prompt
you are! Did you see that, Dora? The moment I say the lesson
is over, he pays. Thank you, Emil. I shall make out a receipt.
(*He goes to the desk and writes out a receipt*.)

EMIL: An opera singer came into the opticians today, Mrs Langley.
I thought of you.

ARTHUR: Mrs Langley was never an opera singer, dear, but a

teacher of singing. And Arthur Sullivan rather than
Giuseppe Verdi.

DORA: (*To* EMIL) Who was he?

EMIL: An Italian. In the chorus. He's with the company at the
Alhambra. He'd looked at an eclipse of the sun when he was
a boy and damaged the retina of his right eye –

ARTHUR: Right eye, Emil. Ah, e: i: right eye.

EMIL: His right eye. He wanted a monocle. We don't do
monocles.

(*Pause.*)

ARTHUR: That is a perfect image of this land we live in. One blind
eye.

EMIL: You could see the damage through the ophthalmoscope.
Mr Katz let me look. I sawrit clearly.

ARTHUR: There is no r in saw it, Emil. Not sawrit.

EMIL: Saw it.

ARTHUR: We must watch the intrusive r. Saw it. Law and order.
Sore eyes. The intrusive r is the Iago of speech. A betrayer of
carelessness.

(*He brings* EMIL *the receipt.*)

DORA: Why don't we go to the opera, Arthur?

ARTHUR: Because the library stays open until eight, dear, and the
opera commences at seven-thirty.

DORA: Beniamino Gigli –

ARTHUR: Not now, dear.

DORA: Not now what?

ARTHUR: I thought you were about to give voice.

DORA: Arthur doesn't like opera.

ARTHUR: It's not so much that I don't like it, it's that I don't
know what to believe in when I see it. There is Signor Gigli –
and I mean no disrespect to him, Emil, he is a great artist,
oh, a very great artist – but he is not shaped exactly like Mr
Charles Atlas. A little dynamic tension wouldn't come amiss
as far as Signor Gigli is concerned. There he is complaining
that women are fickle and little wonder when he neglects his
figure the way he does. *Troppo pasta, credo, troppo pasta.*
Never, never neglect your appearance, Emil. Especially
when in England. In England the thin are preferred to the

comely. Always see that your hair is neat, your skin glowing,
your clothes – well, when it comes to clothes the English
really prefer shabbiness to chic. But always have clean
fingernails and take care the back of your neck is washed –
(EMIL *makes a self-conscious gesture to his neck.*)

DORA: Oh, Arthur, stop prattling. You sound like a nervous
virgin about to be deflowered.

ARTHUR: Oughtn't you to go to bed?
(*Embarrassed silence.*)

DORA: Six thousand miles.
(*Music from somewhere: the sound of a small jazz band.*)

EMIL: The Coon Carnival. They're practising for the Coon
Carnival in Tramway Road.

DORA: The Golliwogs' Picnic, I call it.

ARTHUR: That is extremely offensive.

DORA: Why? Jacob isn't here.

ARTHUR: That sort of remark is the first symptom of the
infection.

DORA: Oh, don't be so pompous, Arthur, it was only meant as a
joke.

ARTHUR: I didn't find it funny.

EMIL: What infection, Mr Langley?

ARTHUR: The affliction of your opera singer, Emil. The blind
eye. It is an insidious disease. It happens suddenly like so
much else in this country. Like the dawn and the sunset, like
the rising and the dying of the south-east wind. With the
blind eye there is no pain, no fever. It is a creeping paralysis
of the spirit which, once attacked, basks in its own inertia.
There is no cure, except the conscious will to resist. And that
is hard to come by. And the first symptom is indifference to
the feelings of other human beings.

DORA: Well, of course, if one isn't allowed to make jokes –
(*The music continues.*)

EMIL: The Coons practise all year round for the Carnival, which
takes place on the second day of the New Year –

DORA: Yes, yes, we know all about the Coons –

ARTHUR: Tell me, Emil. I'm not sure I know all about the Coons.

EMIL: They compete in troupes. The best turned-out wins. They black their faces which is funny since they're already Coloured, and paint white mouths. They save every penny they can. They make their own costumes. It's a wonderful parade. Did you see it last year?

ARTHUR: No, but our Jacob belongs to a troupe. And they practise every weekend. I thought I might –

DORA: Why don't we close early one night? We could go to the opera or a play. Or even a film. The bioscope. The bi'scope. Six thousand miles from the centre of things. When you live in London, Emil, you will worship in Mecca, the centre of the world.

ARTHUR: Our travel section seems somewhat higgledy-piggledy, too.

DORA: Six thousand miles.

ARTHUR: We miss home terribly, Emil.

EMIL: I know.

ARTHUR: London is immense and immensely beautiful. You will find it very confusing after Cape Town, Emil. Here, one always knows where one is. The mountain is behind and the sea in front. It's impossible to be lost in Cape Town. But, London. That's a very different map. To be lost in London is one of the glories of the city. London is magnificent for its intricacy. To stumble on hidden alleys, winding streets, a secret mews and not to have the slightest idea of where one is. That is to be truly lost.

DORA: There's always the tube.

ARTHUR: Yes, you'll have to get to know the tube, Emil. The underground arteries of the metropolis. The Circle Line is the most useful. Sloane Square, South Kensington, Gloucester Road, High Street Ken: that was our stamping ground, wasn't it, dear? Sloane Square serves Pimlico, and as a friend of mine used to say, that's only right and proper. We used to live in Pimlico.

DORA: Do you know what I miss most? The Sunday newspapers. *The News of the World, The People, Reynolds News, The Observer, The Sunday Times, The Sunday Graphic.*

ARTHUR: Don't, Dora dear, don't, the very names are a litany of homesickness.

DORA: We used to buy them all. You must promise to send us a bundle occasionally, Emil, I don't care how out of date. A bundle of Sunday newspapers. Heaven. A scoutmaster's disgrace, forty days alone at sea on a raft, an interview with Noel Coward, a photograph of a guardsman in a dead faint at Trooping the Colour.

ARTHUR: And let's not forget Miss C. A. Lejeune and Mr James Agate.

DORA: He's dead now.

ARTHUR: Nevertheless, general culture. Such general culture.

DORA: (*Calling*) Jacob! Jacob! Where is that boy with the tea?
(*She goes.*)

ARTHUR: Mrs Langley is really a very tender-hearted person, Emil. But sometimes, after a long day –

EMIL: My mother was the same.

ARTHUR: Ah.

EMIL: I understand, Mr Langley.

ARTHUR: I try to be patient.
(*Silence, but for the music.*)

EMIL: I have started counting the days. I worked out that, if I win the travel grant, there are two hundred and seventy-eight days before I'd have to leave. I checked at the Union Castle office. I will probably sail on the Edinburgh Castle. Then I bought an exercise book and wrote two hundred and seventy-eight, two hundred and seventy-seven, two hundred and seventy-six, and so on. Tomorrow I'll cross off two hundred and seventy-eight. I hope I'm not tempting fate.

ARTHUR: Yes, well, you have to win the travel grant first.

EMIL: The next day I'll cross off two hundred and seventy-seven.
(*Pause.*) Mr Langley, there is something I have to tell you.
(*Silence, but for the music.*)

ARTHUR: I think I can guess. I hope I can guess. You see, Emil, I can't bear to think of you leaving –

EMIL: You've encouraged me to think of nothing else, Mr Langley. The Union Castle Line. The fourteen days at sea. London fogs. London theatres. London.
(*The music stops.*)

ARTHUR: Of course I want you to go. I want your life to be full of roses and champagne. I'll be able to say, 'I taught him.' I may even end up as a footnote in your biography. Emil Visser was taught by Arthur Langley, an elocution teacher formerly of London, who ended his days in Sea Point, a suburb of Cape Town, six thousand miles from the centre of things. Rather a long footnote. It may have to go over two pages and irritate the reader. (*Pause.*) I hope you'll always acknowledge my help, Emil.

EMIL: Of course, Mr Langley. I'd be nowhere without you.

ARTHUR: Sir Emil Visser, the distinguished South African-born actor, returned to Cape Town today and laid a wreath on the grave of Arthur Langley. Why, no one knows. (*Pause.*) Sir Emil Visser. No, dear, it won't do. We'll have to change your name.

EMIL: Laurence is a good name for an actor.

ARTHUR: I was thinking of Visser. Lee is a fine stage name. Or so dear Ivor Novello always says. Emile Lee. Not bad. Not half bad. Think on't.

(DORA *returns.*)

DORA: That boy Jacob is as thick as Lion's Head. Do you know what he did? He laid out a tray, three cups, three saucers, tea-pot, hot water jug, sugar bowl, milk jug. Only problem was he forgot to put the kettle on. Laid the tray, three cups, three saucers –

ARTHUR: Yes, dear, I think we can all remember the inventory –

DORA: How can anyone be so stupid?

EMIL: An aunt of mine always says the darker the skin the stupider they are.

ARTHUR: Emil, that's a disgraceful thing to say.

EMIL: I don't believe in it myself, Mr Langley. I was merely repeating what this aunt of mine says. She votes for the Nats.

ARTHUR: If you are to be an artist, Emil, you cannot be a Nationalist. Artists do not believe in anything but art. And talent. A person's talent is his identity, his pass book, if you like, his university degree. Art is classless and knows no Colour Bar. I don't approve of judging human beings except by their humanity. Your aunt – forgive me, Emil, I mean no disrespect to her, I'm sure in every other respect she's a worthy woman – but she is quite wrong to imply that dullness of mind can be measured by darkness of skin. To appreciate genuine stupidity one has only to look at the lily-white pallor of our Prime Minister, Dr D. F. Malan. So, please, Emil, let us not subscribe to the Colour Bar. The talent bar, by all means, but nothing else.

DORA: His aunt sounds like your brother. Mr Langley's brother is a judge, Emil. Mr Justice Langley.

ARTHUR: My brother is an ingrown toenail. He knows everything about the law and absolutely nothing about mercy, the quality of which, in his court, is strained to breaking-point. If he were to come here, in the space of twenty-four hours, he would be blind not in one eye but in both. No, Emil, education and general culture are our only protection. That is why Mrs Langley and I keep ourselves to ourselves. Among the native population, if Dr Malan will forgive the term, we have made very few friends. Deliberately.

DORA: Celia Jameson's a good sort.

ARTHUR: I'm not so sure. Judging from some of her remarks, on the few occasions, that is, when I have seen her sober, I have believed her to be in desperate need of a white stick. As for her husband, all that talk of rugby – the game, Emil, not the school – so frightfully hearty and insensitive. And he coughs like a fog horn at Mouille Point.

DORA: (*To* EMIL) How's your father?

EMIL: Not much better, thank you. His temperature is up and down.

DORA: What do the doctors say?

EMIL: They have given him penicillin injections.

ARTHUR: Really? How splendid. Another English discovery.

EMIL: Once every four hours, day and night, they inject him. The nurses wake him up. He says the pain of the injection is worse than the pain in his chest. The penicillin is kept ice cold, and when it's injected and meets his warm blood, the pain, apparently, is excruciating. It's the meeting with the blood.

ARTHUR: But it kills the germs. Pain is often a prerequisite of health.

DORA: (*A little tearful*) I can't bear talk of illness. I can't bear people being ill. Please take your father a book to read. No charge, of course. What sort of books does he like? I can't bear illness.

(JACOB *re-enters with a tray of tea, puts it down and returns to dusting the books and the shelves.* DORA *pours tea.*)

EMIL: He's not a great reader, thank you, Mrs Langley, but perhaps if he could have something on sport. With pictures. He'd like that.

ARTHUR: I'm not sure we have anything of that description.

(*Somewhere, the sound of a woman screaming.*)

ARTHUR: Tramway Road.

DORA: Drunks.

(*The screams continue.*)

DORA: Every night there are screams and fights and arguments and squalor.

ARTHUR: Violence is born of squalor, dear.

DORA: They should clean up Tramway Road.

(*Male shouts. The woman screams again.*)

ARTHUR: One ought to interfere.

DORA: And get killed in the process, no thank you.

EMIL: I remember, during the war, when the Australians stopped at Cape Town, one of their number was taken back to Tramway Road by a girl. Next morning, they found his head in a dustbin. They never found his body.

ARTHUR: I believe the Australians did behave very badly during the war. In Cape Town. I'm sure they were very brave on the field of battle. But when on leave it was quite another conflict.

EMIL: They undressed a policeman, tied him to the front of a motor car and drove him naked up and down Adderley Street shouting, 'Fair dinkum, you boer bastard.'

ARTHUR: (*Disapproving*) Emil.

(*He indicates* DORA.)

EMIL: I'm sorry, Mrs Langley.

DORA: We should look for other premises. We're too close to Tramway Road.

ARTHUR: Do you really think we should move?

DORA: I do. I can't bear the night noises. Listen. Listen.
(*The wailing of the woman.*)

EMIL: I shouldn't worry too much, Mrs Langley. They'll move
Tramway Road soon enough.

ARTHUR: Move Tramway Road?

EMIL: I don't mean they'll move the road. Just the people.

DORA: I'll freshen up the pot.

ARTHUR: I don't think the pot needs freshening, dear –
(*She goes. The cries continue.*)

EMIL: I wish I were leaving tomorrow. I can't say I hate Cape
Town because it's my home. But for as long as I remember
I've wanted to be elsewhere. You can't have known such an
ache, Mr Langley, because you're a Londoner.

ARTHUR: One can be unhappy in London, Emil, I assure you,
one can be unhappy in London.

EMIL: Yes, but that's ordinary unhappiness. Here, it's the sea
mist. It envelopes us daily. It comes with the sunrise, with
the promise of heat. The mist obscures the horizon. We
walk in it and are frightened. I'm twenty years old. And,
night and day, I'm frightened. I'm frightened now.
Because –
(*He breaks off. Silence, but for the woman crying.*)
I shall miss Cape Town. But I shan't miss the sea mist.
(*The crying stops.*)

ARTHUR: We must do something about your esses, Emil. Try,
'Sit, Jessica, sit.'

EMIL: Sit, Jessica, sit.

ARTHUR: The narrowest gap between tongue and ridge of upper
teeth. Sssss. Sit, Jessica, sit.

EMIL: Sit, Jessica, sit.

ARTHUR: You remind me so much of a boy I once knew. Alan
Jones. Not at all educated. He often talked, like you, very
strangely, using unexpected words like misshapen and
impoverished. He was a conscientious objector, as I was. In
the Great War. The war to end wars. He told the Tribunal
violence was a drug which induced feelings of self-
righteousness. They put him in the Medical Corps. That's
where we met. He turned out to be frightfully brave. He was

gassed at Loos. He died some years later, on 4 October 1928, aged thirty-one. He used to say his impoverished lungs were the misshapen parks of London. Dear Alan. He wanted to be a dancer.

(DORA *returns*.)

DORA: Mrs Malan has Coloured blood.

ARTHUR: I beg your pardon?

DORA: Mrs Malan has Coloured blood.

ARTHUR: Really? The Prime Minister's wife?

DORA: How many Mrs Malans do you know?

ARTHUR: Who told you such a thing?

DORA: Celia Jameson. Apparently, according to Celia, you can always tell by looking at the back of the neck. It's where the colour shows. And by the fingernails. The moons are larger and pink. And by the smell, of course. That's why, and this is gospel truth, that's why Mrs Malan secretly imports gallons of French perfume. To cover her natural pungent smell –

ARTHUR: Dora, what does it matter if Mrs Malan has Coloured blood? It's a revolting topic of conversation. At home you wouldn't go around saying so-and-so's Irish, for example, because of his smell. Well, perhaps one would, I don't know, certainly your friend O'Donovan emitted a very unsavoury odour –

DORA: O'Donovan was pale as gin and tonic, and that's beside the point. The point is, Celia says the back of the neck's the giveaway. That's why Mrs Malan always wears chiffon scarves.

ARTHUR: Does she?

DORA: And if you think about it, her husband looks like Beniamino Gigli.

ARTHUR: What about the tea-pot, dear?

DORA: The what?

ARTHUR: You went a moment ago to freshen the tea-pot.

DORA: Yes, yes, yes, yes, yes –

(*She goes.*)

ARTHUR: In London ladies drink in public houses. You mustn't be shocked.

EMIL: It's time for me to go.

ARTHUR: Fancy saying Dr Malan looks like Beniamino Gigli. Too insulting. One oughtn't to insult artists of Signor Gigli's calibre. One ought never to utter the name of a politician in the same breath as an artist. Politicians are only concerned with trivia.

EMIL: I don't think that's true of the Nats, Mr Langley.

ARTHUR: It's true of the Nats and the United Party. In England it's true of those wretched Tories and those wicked Socialists and those unfortunate Liberals. Trivia. History is not written by politicians. History is written by artists. Who was Prime Minister when Jane Austen wrote *Pride and Prejudice?* Who was Chancellor of the Exchequer when Rupert Brooke remembered Grantchester? Who was Home Secretary when Oscar wrote *Dorian Grey?* No one remembers and no one cares. Dust, my dear, dust. And when we are dead and gone they'll remember you, Emil, not Dr Daniel François Malan.

EMIL: You can't describe what the Nats are doing as trivial, Mr Langley. What they do inflicts hourly pain.

ARTHUR: Perfectly true, but that's because politicians, profoundly conscious of their own triviality, retaliate by inflicting pain. It is the only way they can draw attention to themselves. Pain is the creed of the powerful. But let one Coloured man in Tramway Road write one great novel, or a great poem, or produce a celestial symphonic sound, or let there be born in Tramway Road an actor or a singer or a dancer and the power of politicians crumbles as Sparta and Carthage crumbled. A great work of art banishes pain. A great artist is a nation's physician and its spiritual guide. A great artist heals, reveals, redeems.

EMIL: But what about the others?

ARTHUR: What others?

EMIL: Those who are not artists.

(*Silence.* ARTHUR *sips his tea.*)

ARTHUR: I have never in my life met a man or woman who is not to some degree artistic. Jacob here. He cannot read or write, but have you seen his drawings? Fetch your drawings for Master Emil, Jacob.

(JACOB *smiles, shakes his head and goes on dusting.*)

He's shy, painfully shy. And, if the truth be known, his drawings are monstrously rude. But he also plays the banjo. He dances exquisitely. Dance for Master Emil, Jacob. Your Coon Carnival strut, as I call it. Please, Jacob.

(*Sheepishly at first,* JACOB *dances and hums 'Daar Kom die Alabama'.*)

You see? How lithe and suggestive.

(*The woman's cries begin again.* JACOB *stops dancing and goes on with his dusting.*)

As a boy I myself had so many gifts. I acted. I drew. I sang. I danced. I wrote poetry. But I did nothing well, or well enough. So I taught. That is my tragedy. It's a small tragedy, but at least it's mine, all mine. Nevertheless, I believe I was baptised an artist. I was confirmed in art. All I lacked was a true vocation. But you have been called, Emil. You will be ordained. You are a marked man.

EMIL: That's why I want to be where these things are believed in, where these things matter. (*Pause.*) Mr Langley –

(*Silence.*)

ARTHUR: Why, oh why, is one never where one wants to be?

(*The sound of* DORA *singing 'A Wandering Minstrel' from* The Mikado.)

Oh dear.

(DORA *enters. She has put together a makeshift costume. She sings.* ARTHUR *and* EMIL *are embarrassed.* JACOB *is transfixed.* DORA *falters and sits down. She cries quietly.*)

Do you know what Mrs Langley was singing, Emil?

EMIL: No.

ARTHUR: From *The Mikado* by Gilbert and – ?

EMIL: Sullivan.

ARTHUR: Sullivan, that's right, Emil, Gilbert and Sullivan.

(*He goes to* DORA *and gently strokes her hair.*)

Oh Dora dear, oh, Dora, oh, dear, dear Dora.

DORA: You're not the only one with talent, Miss Doolittle. I could have had quite a career, I want you to know –

ARTHUR: (*To* EMIL) Go and choose your father a book. The nearest thing to sport we have is *Three Men in a Boat*.

(EMIL *does not move.*)
Under J. Jerome K. – ? (*No answer.*) Jerome, that's right,
Emil, Jerome K. Jerome.
(EMIL *goes quickly to the shelves.*)

DORA: (*Calling to* EMIL) I had all the chances, all the chances in
the world. I thought I held in my hand keys to doors that
would open and I would enter spacious and gorgeous rooms,
lit by crystal chandeliers, and filled with persons of rank and
renown. But my room was the ground-floor back in
Westbourne Grove, with Mother, all bosom and glass beads,
a teacher of singing who liked the pupils to call her Madame.
And Father, of whom I remember little, a church organist,
blown to bits at Mons. (*Pause.*) We were a very musical
family. (*Pause.*) When Mother died I inherited her pupils,
though they never called me Madame. (*Pause.*) So many lost
opportunities. Keys in a cup but which locks do they fit?
(*Grabbing* ARTHUR'*s hand.*) This is a wonderful man, Emil.
This man is a saint. A good, good, wonderful man –

ARTHUR: You found the cherry brandy.

DORA: I found a saint, Emil. He married me when I was past
forty. We met in the Queen's Elm, Fulham Road. We were
Bohemians. We had tea in a Lyon's Tea Room in the
Gloucester Road. A ha'penny for a pat of butter. And a
penny for a bread roll.

ARTHUR: Your stories, Dora, are remarkable for their detail but
the plots are terribly thin.

DORA: Only one warning, Emil. He's capricious –

ARTHUR: Dora dear –

DORA: Oh yes, changeable is our Arfa! Aincha Arfa?

ARTHUR: Have you found that book for your father, Emil?
(*The sound of two male voices raised in argument. Silence, but
for the voices.* DORA *falls asleep.* ARTHUR *gazes at her, lost in
his own world.* EMIL *comes to him.*)

EMIL: Mr Langley, I have to tell you something.
(*Silence.* DORA *gives a noisy shudder.*)
I had better be going now.

ARTHUR: She's dozed off.

EMIL: My mother was the same.

ARTHUR: Mrs Langley was very beautiful but emotionally extravagant.

EMIL: My mother could fall asleep in the middle of a sentence.

ARTHUR: Certain of my male friends adored her company because they believed she had suffered in love. She had. No one had ever loved her. Ours was a marriage of convenience. For both of us. We sold up everything and with some help from my brother – in all his life he never gave help more willingly – we thought we'd try sunnier climes. But six thousand miles wasn't apparently distance enough to escape the consequences of what we are. One is, I suppose, eternally dogged by one's nature. You see, Emil, you are the sort of person one can talk to. I find I have few secrets from you. Whom do you talk to? You never really confide in anyone. (*The angry voices fade.*)

Do you talk to your father?

EMIL: No.

ARTHUR: Don't you feel the need to talk about your feelings?

EMIL: Yes –

ARTHUR: But you never do.

EMIL: Not really.

ARTHUR: I wonder if someone who never talks about himself was meant to be an actor.

EMIL: I've never wanted to be anything else.

ARTHUR: In the school where I taught, I encouraged the boys to talk to me. English public schools, even the minor ones like mine, can be unfriendly places. Our Headmaster thought that having a crush on someone meant gripping him in a half-nelson. You can talk to me, Emil.

EMIL: I do. I talk to you all the time.

ARTHUR: You never talk of your feelings.

EMIL: I have only two feelings: to go to London, and the fear that I won't.

ARTHUR: Then we must learn to widen our concerns. Let us try to improve the scope of our conversation. Let's pick at random a subject and see how it prospers. Let's talk of intimate matters. For example, oh, I don't know, girl friends. What about your girl friends?

EMIL: I haven't any.

ARTHUR: No little piece of fluff?

EMIL: No.

(*Running footsteps outside, and shouts.*)

ARTHUR: Have you never had a girl friend?

EMIL: I was friendly with Elaine Joubert. She works in
Stuttafords. Her father is in hospital. That was something we
had in common.

ARTHUR: Are you lovers?

EMIL: No.

ARTHUR: You can tell me. I'm not easily shocked. We must learn
to speak frankly of these things.

EMIL: I took her to the bioscope.

ARTHUR: Cinema.

EMIL: Cinema. I wanted to put my arm around her. I got as far as
the back of the seat. I didn't have the nerve to actually hold
her. I couldn't straighten my arm for hours afterwards. She
hasn't talked to me since.

ARTHUR: You split an infinitive, Emil. To actually hold her. Not
good. We can't 'to actually' anything, can we? And, actually,
actually to hold her, besides being correct, is much stronger.
(*Pause.*) Did you have real feeling for her, this Elaine
person?

EMIL: I don't know.

ARTHUR: You see, I have enormous feeling for you, Emil. I think
you know that. But I wonder, do – ? (*Pause.*) Are you in the
least bit – ? (*Pause.*) Teacher and pupil is one side of the
story, father and son another. (*Pause.*) You matter to me. A
good deal. I knew the moment I saw you. Several young
people answered my advert in the *Cape Times*, but I chose
you. I was drawn to you. Instantly. These weekly lessons,
your hopes and fears have meant, I confess freely, a
reawakening. A rebirth. Tell me what you feel.
(*Silence.*)

EMIL: I have things I would like to talk about.
(*Silence.*)

ARTHUR: Please, please, tell me, I want to hear.

EMIL: I have told you some lies.

ARTHUR: Oh dear. Little white lies or great big black ones?
(*Pause.*)

EMIL: Not little white ones.

ARTHUR: I am all expectation, Emil. You cannot shock me. I am
not a moralist.
(*Silence.*)

ARTHUR: Is it about your private life?

EMIL: Yes.

ARTHUR: Come on to the stoep, we don't want to wake Mrs
Langley.
(*They go out on to the stoep.* ARTHUR *pulls the shutter-doors to
behind him.*)
Is it, Emil, that you've discovered you're in some ways
different?

EMIL: No. Not discovered. Always known.

ARTHUR: Oh my dear, my dear –
(*He puts a hand out to* EMIL *but* EMIL *pulls away.*)
I know how shocking it is to come face to face with one's
innermost nature. Speak of it, Emil. I am your friend now,
tomorrow and forever more.
(*The woman's screams come again, closer now.*)

EMIL: I must go.

ARTHUR: Not yet, not yet, talk to me –

EMIL: It's late, I'll miss the last trolley –

ARTHUR: I'll walk with you –

EMIL: No –
(*He goes back into the library and starts to collect up his things.
The woman's screams become more terrible. A police whistle
blows.* ARTHUR *follows* EMIL. DORA *wakes.*)

DORA: Time for bed.

ARTHUR: Emil's just going, dear.

DORA: Don't forget your monkey mask.
(EMIL *picks up the mask and stands for a moment gazing at it.*)

ARTHUR: And what about the book for your father?
(EMIL *puts the mask on.*)
What are you doing, Emil?

EMIL: My father can't read or write.

DORA: Nonsense, what did he say?

EMIL: My father lives in Tramway Road.

ARTHUR: Diction, Emil, diction –

EMIL: They're going to reclassify me.

(JACOB *laughs*.)

DORA: Jacob, stop that noise and get on with your work. (JACOB *subsides*. EMIL *goes to* DORA *and kneels. He bows his head, revealing the back of his neck*.)

What are you doing? What sort of game is this?

EMIL: Is it darker? (*He thrusts out his hands to her*.) Are the moons large and pink? (*He raises both arms*.) Is it my smell that's pungent or is someone else stinking the place out?

ARTHUR: Emil, control yourself, what is all this about?

(EMIL *does his monkey imitation*. DORA *rises and starts to search, opening drawers, looking behind books, in the filing-cabinet*. ARTHUR *is confused, at a loss*. EMIL *dances round, monkey-fashion*.)

EMIL: I don't know if my father is ill or not. He never had penicillin to my knowledge. Elaine Joubert's father had penicillin. I don't know my father. I've never seen my father. They say he lives in Tramway Road.

(*He screeches like a monkey*. DORA *becomes still, but her anxiety does not lessen*.)

They want a written deposition from him. About me. But he can't read or write. So he has to appear in person to give evidence about me. And my mother. My mother was a poor white. She died. A customer knifed her. He was an Australian soldier.

(*He cackles, monkey-fashion*.)

ARTHUR: Emil, stop this, what are you saying, is this true, is it a game, are you improvising?

EMIL: No game, no game. I'm giving you my family tree, the tree where the monkeys live, the tree that grows in Tramway Road.

DORA: What does it mean, Arthur? Reclassified?

(ARTHUR *looks at her helplessly*. EMIL *stops cavorting and becomes still*.)

EMIL: I pass for white outside about five-fifteen. But at five-sixteen, who knows what I'll pass for? My aunt's taking it badly. She's my mother's sister. She's white. She's a dressmaker. She wanted to make me into something. Now, she wants me to leave her home. Colour is contagious and she's scared of catching it.

(*Silence.*)

I'll never go to London now.

(*Silence. Maniacal laughter from somewhere.*)

They don't care whether you're an artist or not, Mr Langley, if your birthright is charred.

(*Silence, but for the distant laughter.*)

I won't be coming again.

ARTHUR: You must. I insist. I won't have you saying that. You can rely on me, Emil. Just remember what I said about being your friend.

(EMIL *takes off the mask and lets it drop.*)

I will not turn the blind eye.

(EMIL *picks up his carrier bag and goes.*)

(*Calling.*) Emil, please come and see me next week –

(ARTHUR *crosses the room and goes out on to the stoep.* EMIL's *footsteps are heard running away.*)

(*Calling down.*) Emil, next week, at the same time –

(*Silence.* ARTHUR *returns to the library.*)

Jacob, lock up. Time for bed.

DORA: (*To* ARTHUR) Where have you hidden the stuff, Arthur, please, tell me, please.

ARTHUR: Perhaps they won't reclassify him, perhaps he's misunderstood. This is such a distressing place. We must do something to help him. That is monstrous, monstrous. Please, Dora, not now, I'm really quite upset. That poor boy –

(*He exits.*)

DORA: (*Following him*) Never mind him, never mind him, charity begins at home –

(JACOB *locks up.*)

JACOB: Ah, e: i. Ah, oo: ou. I like white about five-fifteen outside. (*He laughs and turns off the lights. The woman screams.*)

ACT TWO

Sunday. A few days later. Just before 7.30 a.m.
A high wind.
The shuttered doors are closed. It is shadowy in the library but the first rays of the sun catch the stoep.
DORA is asleep at the desk.
ARTHUR unlocks the front door and enters. He is somewhat dishevelled and exhausted.
DORA wakes.

DORA: Where have you been – ?

ARTHUR: I'm sorry –

DORA: Are you ill – ?

ARTHUR: No –

DORA: What time is it? It's nearly half-past seven, do you realise what time it is? You've been out all night –

ARTHUR: There's a mist –
  (*He sits.*)

DORA: (*Calling*) Jacob, Master's back. Make some tea. Put the kettle on first, then lay the tray, then make the tea. (*To ARTHUR.*) You look dreadful.

ARTHUR: I found myself at Three Anchor Bay watching the sea. There's a south-easter. The table cloth rolled down over the mountain in the later afternoon. And then suddenly the sun was gone. I wished there was dusk as there is at home. No twilight here, no gradual fading of the day. One moment it was light, the next dark. And it was cold.

DORA: I was worried sick. I didn't know whether or not to telephone the police, the hospitals, or – I didn't know what to do. Then I must have fallen asleep. You've been out since yesterday afternoon –
  (*Pause.*)

ARTHUR: I saw Emil.
  (*Pause.*)
  They have, of course, reclassified him. He is now a non-European. He said it was his last day as a person. He must

169

now learn to be a shadow, he said that, you know sometimes
he –

(*He breaks off. The wind howls.*)

DORA: Did he meet his father?

ARTHUR: Yes. A youngish man, Emil said, younger than
expected. He was accompanied by a woman, rather
beautiful, Emil said, the man's wife, he thought, with two
front teeth extracted, you know the way they do, something
sexual – (*Pause.*) The man, Emil's father, identified Emil as
his son. When questioned he was, apparently, unshakable.
He gave the name of Emil's mother, and of her sister. And
although, according to Emil, classification is based on
appearance and general acceptance, no amount of pleading
or argument would shift the authorities. And the irony, Emil
said, was that he himself could see a vague facial resemblance
to the man who claimed to be his father.

DORA: Why didn't you tell me you were going to see him?

ARTHUR: I hadn't planned to. I came out of the G.P.O. –

DORA: Had the money arrived?

ARTHUR: Oh yes. The Judge is prompt with the remittance. He
wants no appeals from his degenerate brother. He requires as
little communication from me as possible. Oh yes, the money
was there all right. Too little to live on but enough to exist.

DORA: How did you meet Emil?

ARTHUR: I came out into Adderley Street and looked at the
Christmas decorations in the stores. The sun was blazing and
hurt my eyes. Then without really knowing what I was
doing, I found myself crossing the Parade and before I knew
it I was standing outside Katz, the optician, looking through
the plate-glass window. There was no sign of Emil. So I went
in and introduced myself to Mr Katz. He said Emil was out
on deliveries but would soon return. Then he informed me
that Emil had been reclassified and that he, Mr Katz, had
been obliged to let Emil go.

DORA: Let him go where?

ARTHUR: He meant he'd given Emil the sack. (*Pause.*) We
talked, Mr Katz and I. One could say we had an illuminating
conversation. For half an hour or more. He seemed

genuinely sorry he had been forced to dismiss Emil. He liked Emil. But his customers, he said, simply wouldn't understand. Or condone. He said it wasn't against the law, but against the life. Against the life. That phrase curdled my smile, I can tell you. Against the life. (*Pause.*) And yet Mr Katz seemed a very decent chap. Very decent, though rather in need of a shave. A very swarthy gentleman with a clammy handshake but awfully decent for all that.

DORA: Yes, he sounds awfully decent. (*Pause.*) Celia Jameson called this afternoon. Or was it yesterday? Well, it all makes – no, never mind. She had been to a matinée of the Italian opera. She'd heard Beniamino Gigli, in *La Bohème*, at the Alhambra – that's that comic theatre with the painted sky and lights that twinkle in imitation of the stars. And just before the curtain rose, Celia said, as the conductor raised his baton for the overture, there was a frightful commotion two rows in front of her. She thought someone had died in their seat, but no, what do you think, Arthur, a Coloured couple, sitting there in the stalls, were forcibly evicted! By the police. Someone had, apparently, complained. I wouldn't be surprised if it wasn't Celia. But then, she said, the curtain rose on pure enchantment. Of course, she thinks *La Bohème* a very silly opera. In Act One they're burning the furniture to keep warm, and that same evening in Act Two they're sitting out of doors in off-the-shoulder frocks. But, she said, she felt so utterly civilized, listening to Gigli singing Puccini. She simply had to tell me. She brought me a bottle of Van der Hum. A sweet liqueur, but such an apt name for a drink after an opera, Van der Hum.

(*Pause.*)

ARTHUR: I made some excuse and left Mr Katz and there, in the street, was Emil. He was, I think, pleased to see me. I told him at once I knew of the decision and that Mr Katz would no longer employ him as an assistant. Yes, Emil said, Mr Katz could not have tainted hands examining untainted eyes. So, in a show of bravado, I invited him to tea at the Waldorf, where we ate anchovy toast and listened to Basil Metaxas and his Band playing 'We'll gather lilacs in the spring again'.

(*Silence.* ARTHUR *breaks down. He weeps silently, struggling to control his anguish.*)

Oh Dora dear, oh dear, dear Dora, I'm so tired of misfits.

(*Somewhere a tin can is blown by the wind.*)

I nursed Alan for almost ten years. I had all that agony with Oliver. I've had my ration of pain. I want the end of my life to be unsullied and uneventful. I want animal comforts. I want no more danger or despair. Oh, Dora, Dora, I've done a terrible thing. I'm racked with conscience. I don't know how to put it right, I don't know whether I should.

DORA: Tell me, Arthur.

ARTHUR: All the time Emil and I sat in the Waldorf listening to the chatter of others and to the music, I had a rising feeling of guilt, uncontrollable, like nausea. Against the life. I felt, as I've always felt, outside the law, as though everyone in the place was watching us, knowing that Emil was forbidden to be there, and that we were criminals. I dreaded, as I've always dreaded, the heavy footfall of uniformed authority. (*He weeps.*)

DORA: Arthur dear, what did you do that's so terrible?

ARTHUR: I told Emil I didn't want to see him again. I told him he must never come near this flat. I told him – (*Pause.*) I said he was to return our books, collect his mask, and that I simply could have nothing more to do with him.

DORA: That wasn't kind, Arthur, that wasn't kind.

(ARTHUR *weeps silently.* JACOB *enters with the tea but stands, staring at* ARTHUR.)

Jacob, put the tea down and then you may go to your Coon rehearsal. And lock the back door.

(JACOB *puts the tray down and goes.*)

ARTHUR: I am drained by a monumental feeling of loss. But I've done the right thing, haven't I, you agree with me, don't you, it would be impossible to continue as before – ?

(DORA *pours the tea.*)

DORA: God Almighty, he hasn't put tea in the tea-pot. (*Calling.*) Jacob! Jacob! (*To* ARTHUR.) We'll have to install a bell. (*Calling.*) Jacob!

(JACOB *returns, half-undressed.*)

There's no tea in the tea-pot. Jacob, you're a cretin, an
absolute cretin.

(*He takes the tea-pot and goes.*)

Servants, servants. They're more trouble than they're worth.

(*She rises and starts to look in drawers, behind books.* ARTHUR
watches her for a moment.)

ARTHUR: I hid one behind the philosophy section, dear.

DORA: I found that last night.

ARTHUR: Then the other's in the filing-cabinet. Somewhere
between Arthur Ransome and Edith Sitwell.

(DORA *hurries to one of the filing-cabinets, finds a half-bottle of
brandy and pours herself a teacupful.* JACOB *returns with the
tea-pot and goes.* ARTHUR *pours himself tea and adds a little
brandy.*)

I'll have a drop. Just a drop. To warm me.

DORA: Bottoms up.

(*She drinks.*)

ARTHUR: God bless, dear.

(*He sips his tea.*)

DORA: This is nice. Nothing stirs memories more tenderly than
'bottoms up' and 'God bless, dear'. I remember when we
first met. A month after Mother died. The Queen's Elm.
Full of poets and prophets and artists' models.

ARTHUR: And us.

DORA: Time gentlemen, please, but never time, ladies. And later,
the Lord Nelson, Chelsea, you telling me that Greenwood,
the music master, had been called up and that I'd make a
dashing replacement. You could fix it, you said. Dashing,
you said.

ARTHUR: Dashing, did I?

DORA: And those evenings in Courtfield Gardens. With Annie
and Ken and Oliver and Philip and Brian. After the pub. In
the holidays. The bombs falling. Heedless of danger. Talk,
talk, talk. Misfits together. Bottoms up and God bless, dear.
So cosy. I miss Oliver and Brian most of all.

ARTHUR: By the fire.

DORA: Looking for shillings for the gas meter.

ARTHUR: Talk, talk, talk.

(*Pause.*)

DORA: It's a crime, Arthur, don't you think it's a crime?

ARTHUR: Everything one does seems to be a crime.

DORA: I haven't slept for days.

ARTHUR: Yes, you have, dear –

DORA: Not a wink –

ARTHUR: You were asleep when I came in –

DORA: Then, yes, then, then, but I've lain awake for hours on
end, I assure you, thinking of Emil, thinking of hard-faced
men telling him his life is to be shattered. That's the crime to
which I was referring, Arthur. What's your opinion?

ARTHUR: It's the law, dear. I didn't make the law.

DORA: I thought you had a crush on him –

ARTHUR: Please, Dora, dear, please –

DORA: You shouldn't have told him you didn't want to see him
again. That wasn't kind, Arthur.
(*A sudden gust of wind. Somewhere a door begins to bang
intermittently.*)

ARTHUR: It's for the best, dear.
(*Pause.*)

DORA: You disgust me.

ARTHUR: There's nothing to be done.
(*Pause. She pours herself more brandy and adds another drop to
his tea.*)

DORA: You've behaved as you always behave: capriciously.

ARTHUR: Please don't make it haunt us, Dora dear. We have
between us enough phantoms to last a lifetime. And more.

DORA: To whom, in my case, are you referring?

ARTHUR: No one in particular, dear. I was speaking generally.

DORA: Oh, no you weren't. I know you. Who were you getting at
me for? Are you still harping on O'Donovan?

ARTHUR: No –

DORA: O'Donovan, let me remind you, was not Emil Visser.
O'Donovan was a deeply cultured man –

ARTHUR: O'Donovan? Cultured? Please, Dora dear, O'Donovan
moved his lips when reading.

DORA: At least he tried, he tried, Arthur. He joined Alcoholics
Anonymous.

ARTHUR: He joined Alcoholics Anonymous because he thought he could drink without anyone knowing his name. Emil Visser is worth a hundred O'Donovans.

DORA: Then why did you do what you did?

(*Pause.*)

ARTHUR: We made a conscious, careful decision to come here. To give up all we knew and loved. To start again. We are making a life for ourselves here. We have a certain ease we have never known before. Or used to have.

(*Pause.*)

DORA: You disgust me.

ARTHUR: Dora dear, you really mustn't go on at me. What else could I have done?

DORA: You could have shown him some human kindness.

ARTHUR: You're a bitch, Dora dear, a thorough-going, double-dyed bitch.

(*Pause.*)

DORA: No travel grant for Emil Visser now. No London. No general culture.

(*Pause.*)

ARTHUR: Why do the numbers two-seven-seven keep buzzing in my head?

DORA: Search me.

ARTHUR: Two, seven, seven. Like a code. As though in a dream. Two, seven, seven, as if it's a key to something.

(*Pause. She pours more brandy for both of them.*)

DORA: I never liked Emil Visser. I still don't like him. His affectations appal me. His ingratiating manner makes me want to vomit. I have no opinion of his talent. When he came for his lessons I felt excluded and threatened. I loathed your flirting and twittering and showing-off. I always behaved badly on those nights and hated myself for doing so. I warned him you were changeable –

(*The fog horn at Mouille Point sounds.*)

No. I am not a fan of young Emil Visser. But I'm not strong enough to witness slow torture without at least making an effort to staunch the flow of the victim's blood.

ARTHUR: You are stronger than I am, Dora dear. Always have

been, always will be.
(*Pause.*)

DORA: You'll miss his five shillings.

ARTHUR: Yes.

DORA: He was a good little payer.

ARTHUR: Very prompt.

DORA: How could anyone in the Waldorf have known he was a non-European? The decision had only just been made, hadn't it? He didn't suddenly turn brown, did he? How could anyone possibly have known? (*Pause.*) I bet they're not going to reclassify Mrs Malan.
(*Silence, but for the wind and the occasional banging of the door.*)

ARTHUR: Pain before pleasure.
(*The fog horn sounds.* ARTHUR *sings quietly.*)
Eternal Father, strong to save,
Whose arm hath bound the restless wave,
Who bidd'st the mighty ocean deep
Its own appointed limits keep:
O hear us when we cry to Thee
For those in peril on the sea.

DORA: Such a gifted boy, you said. And so innocent.

ARTHUR: I didn't think the back of his neck was particularly dark.
(*Pause.*)

DORA: What did he do when you told him you didn't want to see him again?

ARTHUR: He spat in my tea.
(*Stillness.* DORA *pours the rest of the bottle into her cup and the last drop or two into* ARTHUR'*s.*)

DORA: He'd have been better off in England.

ARTHUR: Hear-hear! Hear-hear!

DORA: He won't travel on the Circle Line now.

ARTHUR: Sloane Square, South Kensington, High Street Ken, Notting Hill Gate, Bayswater.

DORA: You've missed out Gloucester Road.

ARTHUR: No I didn't, dear.

DORA: You did, you did, you bloody well did. Sloane Square,

South Kensington, Gloucester Road, then High Street Ken and Notting Hill Gate.

ARTHUR: Gloucester Road is on the Piccadilly Line, dear.

DORA: It's on the Circle Line as well –

ARTHUR: Have it your own way –

DORA: Never mind my way, it's the bloody way the tube goes that matters. Sloane Square, High Street Ken – no, no, Sloane Square, South Kensington, Gloucester Road, High Street Ken, Notting Hill Gate, Bayswater. Don't tell *me*, don't tell *me*.

ARTHUR: How quickly one forgets.

DORA: I haven't forgotten; you've bloody well forgotten.

ARTHUR: Round and round, round and round, two, seven, seven, the Circle Line, Ah, oo, round. Ah, i, line.

DORA: But not for Emil.

ARTHUR: No. He said non-Europeans aren't given passports. But can that be true, do you really think that can be true? I think he exaggerates, don't you?

DORA: He'd be much better off in England.

ARTHUR: Or France. The French have always been kind to negroes. Especially talented negroes. Paris was full of black jazz musicians in the thirties. *Ils sont bons types, les français.*

DORA: And what's that supposed to mean?

ARTHUR: It means the French are very good sorts.

DORA: That's not what you said in 1940.

ARTHUR: It's what I say now.

DORA: He'd have been much better off in Australia, too, whatever he might say about their soldiers.

ARTHUR: Perhaps we should have gone to Australia.

DORA: Or New Zealand.

ARTHUR: Yes, yes, they say New Zealand is very like home.
(*Pause.*)

DORA: I see what you mean.

ARTHUR: How especially, dear?
(*Pause.*)

DORA: Did he call you Master?

ARTHUR: No.
(*Pause.*)

177

DORA: Is there really nothing to be done?

ARTHUR: The law's the law, dear. They make the law. Even at home they make the law. They make the law everywhere. In France. In Australia. Even in Peru. They make the law.

DORA: They, They, They? Who are They? I'm sick to death of They. Who? Who? They say, They will, They do, They might. To hell with They. Who are They who cripple and maim us? Who are They who stand at the border asking for passwords and documents and family histories? Who are They? Bugger They and all their descendants.

ARTHUR: Alan used to say that They is always us.

DORA: Bugger us, too.
   (*Pause.*)

ARTHUR: I told Emil to hold his head high. Hold you head high, I said, even when the bullets fly. It's the only way to survive. I speak from personal experience. Hold your head high.
   (*Pause.*)

DORA: You can't suddenly be a person one day, and not a person the next. (*Pause.*) Can you?
   (*Pause.*)

ARTHUR: Pain before pleasure, pain before pleasure. A little penicillin wouldn't come amiss, however cold or warm the blood. Nothing matters so long as we're kind to each other.

DORA: That's a fine thing for you to say.

ARTHUR: I'll tell you another fine thing for me to say: history is a tidal wave.

DORA: So what?

ARTHUR: The great thing is to be nowhere near when it breaks.

DORA: That's a question of agility and physical fitness.
   (*The wind howls.*)

ARTHUR: Oh God, I feel such chaos mounting. I found myself standing at the water's edge, knowing I'd be enveloped by the waves, the great tidal waves not of our making. History is a tidal wave, dear.

DORA: So you said.

ARTHUR: I watched the sea pounding the rocks, felt the spray on my face, feared the fear of drowning, stood on the ocean bed and swam in my grave while all the future flashed before me,

the dilution of blood and sperm, the erosion of flesh and
bone. I raised my arm and begged the water to recede but I
continued to drown.

DORA: We're very poetic tonight, I must say.

(*The wind screams. The door bangs. Shouts from somewhere.*)

ARTHUR: I must have slept. When I woke the wind had risen
and a sea mist floated like gauze on the water. I'm not
drunk at all.

DORA: It's South Africa brandy, that's why.

(*Pause.*)

ARTHUR: I wish They would show us some mercy from time to
time.

DORA: Some hope.

ARTHUR: The south-easter will blow the chaos away.

(*Pause.*)

DORA: What did he do after he spat in your tea?

ARTHUR: Rose in a very dignified manner and departed into the
shadows.

DORA: Yes, he was very dignified.

ARTHUR: I don't think spitting in my tea was very dignified,
dear.

DORA: It all depends on who does the spitting.

(*Pause.*)

ARTHUR: I like white outside about five-fifteen.

(*Pause.*)

DORA: What's Peru got to do with it?

ARTHUR: I don't follow your drift.

DORA: Nor do I. (*Pause.*) London, London, London. (*Pause.*)
England.

ARTHUR: I know where London is, dear.

DORA: I wish I were in London now that summer's here.
London. We must go to London.

ARTHUR: You sound like the Three Sisters.

DORA: How can I? I was an only child.

ARTHUR: We're South Africans now, dear.

DORA: I shall never learn Afrikaans. Totsiens is all I shall ever
say, and that means goodbye.

ARTHUR: I know what totsiens means.

DORA: All right, all right, pardon me for breathing. (*Pause.*) I
never learned French either.
(ARTHUR *weeps silently.*)
ARTHUR: He had the makings of a true artist.
DORA: They put a stop to that.
ARTHUR: And all because he is misshapen and impoverished.
DORA: You disgust me.
ARTHUR: You're repeating yourself, Dora dear. That's a bad
sign, oh yes, indeedy, that's a very bad sign.
DORA: You're a fine one to talk. I've lost count of how many tidal
waves we've had tonight.
ARTHUR: In my long life, Dora, of having to watch my step, I've
frequently noticed that when it comes to matters moral,
those who observe always believe they'd behave better than
those who partake. I just thought I'd throw that in.
DORA: Is that a dig at me?
ARTHUR: If the shovel fits.
DORA: Well, it doesn't –
ARTHUR: Oh, doesn't it, doesn't it? Let's not forget, Dora dear, it
was you who suggested marriage and persuaded me to let
Oliver face the music. Alone. The moment we learned that
the Headmaster had asked him to find another school to
teach in, you said marriage would protect me from guilt by
contamination.
DORA: Well, it did, didn't it? You weren't sacked –
ARTHUR: No, I wasn't and the ruse certainly worked, it did, it
did, but all I'm saying is, I took no pleasure in seeing Oliver
blubbing in front of the Upper Sixth, and having to tell him
to cut along. And then I wept, and had to take out my
handkerchief, pretending I was mopping my brow instead of
my tears.
DORA: If you're not tiddly, Arthur, I'd like to know what tiddly
is.
ARTHUR: All I'm saying is, that it's easy to be wise before the
event. People are always weaker than they hope they'll be.
(*The wind begins to die.*)
DORA: Just think, if Gilbert and Sullivan were reclassified they'd
never have written *The Mikado*.

ARTHUR: That's true of William Wordsworth.

DORA: But he didn't write *The Mikado*.

ARTHUR: Nor Rupert Brooke. (*Pause.*) Or Beniamino Gigli, come to that.

DORA: They were extremely fortunate no one discovered their fathers lived in Tramway Road.

ARTHUR: They weren't standing on the wrong beach.

DORA: They must have been in Peru at the time.

ARTHUR: Or New Zealand.

DORA: Very probably.

> (*Pause. The wind has almost died away.*)

ARTHUR: It takes such strength to stand up against a tidal wave.

DORA: You ought to have tried, you rotten old bastard. You ought to have said, Emil, I'm your friend no matter what, I'm your support, your anchor, your refuge, your safe harbour. Instead you deserted the poor little sod in his hour of need. You're despicable, Arthur, utterly despicable.

ARTHUR: I know, I know.

> (DORA *takes* ARTHUR's *face in her hands and kisses him fondly on the forehead.*)

DORA: Goodnight, dear, I'm going to bed.

ARTHUR: But it's already morning.

DORA: Is it?

> (*She opens the shutters and lets in the light, which dazzles her.*)
> What day is it?

ARTHUR: Sunday.

DORA: Is it?

ARTHUR: All day.

> (*She sits. Silence.*)
> The south-easter has blown itself out. (*Pause.*) How suddenly things happen here.

DORA: That sounds too ominous for me.

> (*She dozes off. The sound of the Coon Band approaching.*
> ARTHUR *listens.*)

ARTHUR: The Coons, Dora, dear. The Coons.

> (DORA *sleeps.* ARTHUR *listens.*)
> Jacob's troupe from Tramway Road. Satins and silks, top hats and canes, sequins and bows, strutting and dancing. (*He*

listens.) The music of abandon and emancipation.
(*The music is loud now and it draws* ARTHUR *out on to the stoep.
He watches.*)
(*Calling out.*) Jacob! Come and look, Dora, he's waving. I see
you, Jacob, I see you. You must come and show Madam
your costume.
(ARTHUR *waves excitedly. The procession passes and the music
begins to fade. He returns to the library.*)
What a surprising, heartwarming, utterly delightful
spectacle. A brilliant, rhythmic ribbon of shining white and
glittering gold. Jacob makes a splendid Coon, blackened face
and big white mouth, like a minstrel in the music hall. So
elegant and slim and rubbery. And the little skolly boys,
Dora, strutting beside their elders as though in training for
the real thing in time to come. Jacob's troupe will win this
year for certain. That must be the cry in Tramway Road.
(DORA *wakes.*)

DORA: Arthur? Arthur? Oh, there you are. I thought you were
lost.

ARTHUR: The wind died and the sea mist lifted. How fortunate
for the Coons. I haven't enjoyed myself so much since VE
day. You should have seen the little skolly boys, Dora,
dressed in the costume of the troupe. Too adorable.

DORA: Think if it had happened to us.

ARTHUR: If what had happened to us, dear?
(*Pause.*)

DORA: I wish the place weren't so beautiful. I wish they had pubs.
I wish they had Sunday newspapers. I wish we had friends.
(*Pause.*)

ARTHUR: I miss friends most of all. Such decent fellows. All
Cambridge men with first-class minds.

DORA: Yes, and curious private habits.

ARTHUR: At least we had a vision of the future. We wanted
Jerusalem in England's green and pleasant land.

DORA: But not, apparently, in Gloucester Road.
(*Pause.*)

ARTHUR: The Coons, you know, are an expression of culture,
rhythmic, vibrant, raw. When Emil returns our books I shall

talk to him about it, he may find that rather rewarding, the exploration and assimilation of a new world. Perhaps that's what I felt instinctively at the Waldorf.

DORA: That's what you felt, was it, instinctively, at the Waldorf? You felt that Emil was much better off now that he's been reclassified. You felt that instinctively, did you?

ARTHUR: Don't scoff, Dora, I can see great things for him. I once told him that should Tramway Road produce an artist of the front rank all the barriers would crumble. I believe he may have a mission. And I shall tell him so. I hope I may give him inspiration.

DORA: Give him inspiration? You couldn't even give him tea at the Waldorf.

ARTHUR: We have lives, too, Dora.

DORA: (*Crying mawkishly*) I can't abide cruelty –

ARTHUR: Don't become maudlin, Dora, I beg you, I don't think I could bear that –

DORA: I've always believed a time would come when we'd all behave kindly to each other –

ARTHUR: And so it will, dear, so it will –

DORA: But when? When? Not soon enough for Emil Visser.

ARTHUR: Oh yes, dear, soon enough for him. We'll vote United Party. We'll see changes. I've no doubt of that.

DORA: Yes, but what changes?

ARTHUR: Give it twenty, thirty years. You'll see. You'll see.

DORA: No, I won't, I'll be in my grave before then.

ARTHUR: Not you, dear, not you –

DORA: Yes, I bloody well will.

ARTHUR: It's the way of things.

DORA: A terrible wrong has been inflicted.

ARTHUR: I refuse to take the blame for that, Dora dear.

DORA: I have only ever expected one thing from you, Arthur. Not love, not children, but human kindness.

ARTHUR: And I've only ever expected one thing from you, Dora dear, and that is that you don't become maudlin.
(*Pause.*)

DORA: I wouldn't go to see the Coon Carnival if you paid me.

ARTHUR: We're here, Dora. There's no going back, no changing course, no other anchorage. This is where we've been washed up.

DORA: Are we flotsam or jetsam? I never know the difference.

(*Two banjo chords strike. The door opens and* JACOB *enters in his silks and satins. He plays the banjo and struts and dances.* DORA *watches expressionless.* ARTHUR *beams and claps to the rhythm.*)

ARTHUR: He came to show you his costume. Smile, Dora dear, smile –

(*The glass of the front door is suddenly smashed.* EMIL's *carrier bag of books has been heaved through the panes. For a fleeting second,* EMIL *is visible.* DORA *screams.* ARTHUR *takes cover.* JACOB *cowers, too, at first, but then begins to shiver from head to foot.* DORA *becomes hysterical. Cautiously,* ARTHUR *goes to her.*)

Stop it, Dora, take hold of yourself – (*To* JACOB.) Jacob, will you please go and get Madam some water? Jacob! Jacob! Dora, it was probably just a skolly boy, that's all. Jacob, stop shivering! Between the pair of you, you'll drive me to tears. I'm upset, too, you know, I should like to cry, too –

(*He shakes* DORA. *She continues to cry and laugh. He takes the jug of milk from the tea-tray and throws the contents over her. She begins to subside.*)

DORA: A drink, I must have a drink, please Arthur –

(ARTHUR *turns and sees the carrier bag. He reaches inside and takes out some of his books. An envelope drops to the floor.* ARTHUR *retrieves it, tears it open and reads the note inside.*)

Please, Arthur, show me where you hid the drink.

ARTHUR: This is monstrous. Read what he's written. It's reprehensible.

(*He hands her the note.*)

DORA: Lend me your glasses.

(*He hands her his glasses. She reads and begins to cry again.*)

ARTHUR: As if *I* made the decision. How dare he threaten? He must learn to grow up, must Master Emil Visser. And how would he carry out such a threat? Put his head in a gas oven? Drink poison?

(*The screech of brakes from somewhere, and the sound of a car colliding.* DORA *exits.*)

Jacob, guard the door. We are at home to no one.

(*A police siren.* JACOB *takes his banjo and sits by the front door.*
ARTHUR *tears up the note and drops the pieces in a wastepaper
basket. He sees* EMIL's *monkey mask.*)

Here, Jacob, you can have this.

(JACOB *puts on the mask and tries to see his reflection in a
fragment of broken glass.* DORA *returns.*)

DORA: Of course, Celia Jameson says they always show their true
colours.

ARTHUR: It's best forgotten. It's an ugly incident like that awful
woman effing and blinding on Paddington Station. Do you
remember?

DORA: The one who said she felt a little queer, and we all
laughed?

ARTHUR: No. The other one, the foul-mouthed slut.

DORA: No –

ARTHUR: That's because it's best forgotten.

DORA: Fancy calling you such names. And in writing.

ARTHUR: Put it from your mind.

DORA: Celia says that insolence and lying come naturally to them.

(JACOB *begins to strum on the banjo. Pause. Shouts. The sound
of an ambulance.*)

ARTHUR: I'm suddenly famished. I wonder if the Greek shop's
open. I have a great fancy for fresh fruit.

DORA: There's roast beef for lunch.

ARTHUR: In this heat? If only we could break the habits of home.
Roast beef and two veg on Sundays. I sweat at the thought
of it. (*Pause.*) You know what we ought to do, dear?

DORA: No, dear, what ought we to do?

ARTHUR: We ought to braai on Sundays as our neighbours do.
Hot charcoal, steaks and chops and boerewors, whatever that
may be. Jacob could manage cooking meat on a braaivleis. It
doesn't take much skill.

(*Pause.*)

DORA: Anyway, he returned the books.

(*She begins to put them back on the shelves.*)

ARTHUR: I suppose, if shove comes to push, we could invite Celia
and her husband. Merge a little more than we do. We must
allow ourselves to be accepted.

DORA: Yes, but what about Christmas Day? Will we go down to
Saunder's Rocks and eat roast turkey and plum pudding
while acquiring a tan?
(*Silence.*)

ARTHUR: When in Rome.
(*A church bell tolls.*)

DORA: If only I could get his face out of my mind.

ARTHUR: I think I shall go to church today. It always makes me
feel better.

DORA: It always makes me feel worse.

ARTHUR: I shall put another advert in the *Cape Times*. We could
do with the extra money, couldn't we, dear?

DORA: I never felt the benefit of his five shillings.
(ARTHUR *takes up paper and pen and begins to write.*)

ARTHUR: How about this? 'Former London Teacher offers
classes in elocution and general culture. Five shillings an
hour.' (*Pause.*) But this time I think I'd better add,
'Europeans only need apply'. What do you think, Dora dear?
(*She continues to put away the books.* ARTHUR *strolls out on the
stoep.* JACOB *strums on his banjo and sings quietly.*)

JACOB: Daar kom Alabama,
    Alabama kom oor die see.
    Noi, Noi, die riet koi noi,
    Die riet kooi is gemaak,
    Die riet kooi is vir my gemaak
    Om daarop te slaap.
    Die Alabama,
    Die Alabama,
    Die Alabama kom oor die see.
    Januarie, Februarie, Maart,
    April, Mei, June, Julie,
    August, September, Oktober,
    November, Desember.
(DORA *is suddenly motionless, caught by some memory.* ARTHUR
takes out his handkerchief and seems to mop his brow.
*Somewhere a man or a woman gives vent to terrible, mournful
wailing.* JACOB *continues to sing.*)

THE ORDEAL OF GILBERT PINFOLD

from the novel by
Evelyn Waugh

INTRODUCTION

Evelyn Waugh, who for most of his life was a conscientious diarist, made no record of the events between 12 January 1954 and 19 June 1955. Michael Davy, editor of the author's diaries, speculates that a record probably was made of the period but later destroyed. It is known, however, that Waugh, reacting against the bitterly cold winter of 1954, and against sleeplessness, forgetfulness and rheumatism, set off on a sea-voyage to Ceylon. It is also known that after his return some months later he said to a friend, 'I haven't seen you for a long time, but then I've seen so few people because – did you know? – I went mad.' By February 1956 he felt strong enough to describe in detail what happened during the voyage. The result was a short novel, *The Ordeal of Gilbert Pinfold*.

Waugh never denied that the book was closely autobiographical, beginning as it does with a ruthlessly honest self-portrait that is instantly recognisable. His biographer, Christopher Sykes, remarks that in *Pinfold* Waugh seems not only to have drawn heavily on his raw material, but also to have left it raw. This assertion seems to me, however, to miss the essential point which is that the events aboard the ship were interpreted, and thereby transformed, by a novelist with a novelist's imagination and that the experiences described are exorcised by the writing of the novel. In that sense it does not much matter whether we call the novelist Pinfold or Waugh.

The book had, as they say, a mixed reception. Hostility was shown by those critics disgusted by the social values inherent in the self-portrait. J. B. Priestley led the field, attacking Pinfold and, of course, by implication Waugh, in a long review in the *New Statesman*. Priestley was offended by what he saw as Waugh's denial of his artistic nature by asssuming the pose of a Catholic landed gentleman, asserting that the two were incompatible. Waugh elected to defend himself – in *The Spectator*, of course – by fighting, and fighting brilliantly, on the ground Priestley had chosen. By doing so, I believe he perversely obscured the central theme of his creation.

The social values, it seems to me, expressed by Pinfold (and by Waugh), and the criticism levelled at them, are wholly irrelevant to what Waugh put in hazard, and detract unfairly from the book as a work of art and a work of self-revelation. What Evelyn Waugh did by writing *The Ordeal of Gilbert Pinfold* was to expose his own vulnerability – a quality for which he was not famed – and to acknowledge, especially through the role of the girl, Margaret, his own deficiencies not as artist or Catholic or social animal but, most importantly, as a human being. There is an element of self-hatred revealed in *Pinfold* that is present in none of Waugh's other works. It is as if, like Ibsen's Brand, Pinfold has to learn that He is the God of Love. I believe this to be the theme of the book and the quality that gives it universality.

Waugh took another view of the book's universality. In copies which he gave to friends he used to inscribe: 'Watch out. Your turn next.'

R.H.

CHARACTERS

GILBERT PINFOLD
MRS PINFOLD
REGGIE GRAVES-UPTON/IST GENERAL
DR DRAKE/2ND GENERAL
ANGEL
MARGARET/IST YOUNG GIRL
FOSDYKE/FOSKER/SPANISH OFFICIAL
MURLOCK/MURDOCH
INDIAN STEWARD
ENGLISH STEWARD
CAPTAIN STEERFORTH
GLOVER
MR SCARFIELD
MRS SCARFIELD/MOTHER
NORWEGIAN LADY/GONERIL
YOUNG GENTLEMAN
2ND YOUNG GIRL
VARIOUS VOICES

The play is set in the mid-1950s and takes place
in Lychpole and on board the SS *Caliban*.

The Ordeal of Gilbert Pinfold was first presented at The Royal Exchange Theatre, Manchester, on 15 September 1977. The cast was as follows:

GILBERT PINFOLD	Michael Horden
MRS PINFOLD	Margaret Inglis
REGGIE GRAVES-UPTON/1ST GENERAL	Lockwood West
DR DRAKE/2ND GENERAL	Willoughby Gray
ANGEL	Geoffrey Bateman
MARGARET/1ST YOUNG GIRL	Lindsay Duncan
FOSDYKE/FOSKER/SPANISH OFFICIAL	Ian Hastings
MURLOCK/MURDOCH	Ken Randle
INDIAN STEWARD	Derrick Branche
ENGLISH STEWARD	Ron Emslie
CAPTAIN STEERFORTH	Myles Hoyle
GLOVER	Gareth Forwood
MR SCARFIELD	Frank Crompton
MRS SCARFIELD/MOTHER	Gwen Cherrell
NORWEGIAN LADY/GONERIL	Dilys Hamlett
YOUNG GENTLEMAN	Jeffrey Perry
2ND YOUNG GIRL	Tilly Tremayne

Directed by	Michael Elliott
Designed by	Stephen Doncaster

The play was presented in London, at the Round House, on 14 February 1979, with the following change of cast:

FOSDYKE/FOSKER/SPANISH OFFICIAL	Geoffrey McGivern
CAPTAIN STEERFORTH	John Ringham
MRS SCARFIELD/MOTHER	Pauline Jameson
NORWEGIAN LADY/GONERIL	Carol Gilles

ACT ONE

Lychpole. Pinfold's study.
Light on GILBERT PINFOLD *at his desk. He is reading what he has written.*

PINFOLD: 'The ordeal of Gilbert Pinfold. A Conversation Piece. Chapter One. Portrait of the Artist in Middle Age. It may happen in the next hundred years that the English novelists of the present day will come to be valued as we now value the artists and craftsmen of the late eighteenth century. The originators, the exuberant men, are extinct and in their place subsists and modestly flourishes a generation notable for elegance and variety of contrivance. It may well happen that there are lean years ahead in which our posterity will look back hungrily to this period, when there was so much will and so much ability to please. Among these novelists Mr Gilbert Pinfold stood quite high. At the time of his adventure – '
(He stops abruptly and stares into space, remembering with a faint smile of amusement.
Morse code sounds, and a distant oratorio.
The music fades away. Morse code continues then fades as:)
When did it begin? When? Ah!
(Two BBC engineers – FOSDYKE and MURLOCK – enter, unravelling cable which they lead to a table where they will fix a microphone and other equipment for a broadcast. PINFOLD *lays down his pen and glances at his pocket watch. He pours himself a brandy and downs it.* MRS PINFOLD, *some years younger than her husband, enters. She wears a duffle-coat and gumboots.)*

MRS PINFOLD: Gilbert, the men from the BBC are here.

PINFOLD: The electricians.

FOSDYKE: } Morning.
MURLOCK: }

MRS PINFOLD: I'll leave you to it. I'm going to see if that wretched man Hill has cleared off yet.
(She begins to go, then stops.)

I hope they're not intending to stay to luncheon.
(*She exits.* PINFOLD *rises with arthritic difficulty.* ANGEL, *a bearded BBC interviewer, enters.* PINFOLD *goes to meet him.*)

ANGEL: Mr Pinfold, how d'you do? My name's Angel. From the BBC.
(*They shake hands.*)
This is a very great honour.
(*A pause.* PINFOLD *says nothing to ease* ANGEL'*s awkwardness.*)
I cannot thank you enough for agreeing to be interviewed.
(*Pause.*) My colleagues are nearly ready. Lychpole is an awfully pretty village. I must say the countryside's very lovely. I have an aunt nearby. We slept at her house last night.
(*Pause.*) We'll have to leave before lunch.
(*He is forced to glance at the paintings on the wall.*)
Ah, a collector of paintings, I see. The last house we visited had a gouache by Rouault.

PINFOLD: I didn't know he ever painted in gouache. Anyway, he's a dreadful painter.

ANGEL: (*With enormous relief*) Ah! That's very nice. Very nice indeed. We must try and work that into the broadcast.
(FOSDYKE *steps forward.*)

FOSDYKE: We're ready for you.
(PINFOLD *and* ANGEL *go towards the table where the microphone is set with a great many wires.*)

ANGEL: As I think I explained in my letter we're doing a series of these interviews, looking for an informal, short, pithy, spontaneous discussion with various celebrities. The French have done something similar. Rather successfully. Do be careful of the wires.
(PINFOLD *reacts as though something of special significance has been said.* ANGEL *glances at him with a little concern. The moment passes.*)
May I introduce my colleagues, Mr Fosdyke and Mr Murlock?
(*The two men mumble greetings.* PINFOLD *stiffens at something apparently only he has heard.*)

PINFOLD: (*To* ANGEL) Please understand that you pronounce my name *Pin*fold.

ANGEL: Yes, of course, I know that.

PINFOLD: I distinctly heard one of you say Pinefold.

(ANGEL *laughs until he sees that* PINFOLD *is in earnest.*)

ANGEL: Shall we sit?

(ANGEL *and* PINFOLD *sit at either side of the table,* PINFOLD *with much difficulty and discomfort.*)

(*To the* ENGINEERS.) All right?

(*They give the thumbs-up sign.*)

(*To* PINFOLD.) I wonder if we could just have some level. Would you care to say something?

PINFOLD: Something.

ANGEL: (*With a nervous laugh*) We need a little more than that.

PINFOLD: 'I'm Gilbert, the filbert,

The knut with the K

The pride of Piccadilly

The blasé roué.'

ANGEL: Very nice, splendid. (*To the* ENGINEERS.) All right?

(*They give the thumbs-up sign again.*)

Fine, fine. Are we ready, then? I prefer not to prepare my victims in any way, so we'll just begin, shall we?

(*The* ENGINEERS *set the equipment in motion and signal to begin.*)

MURLOCK: Running.

ANGEL: The Angel interview with Gilbert Pinfold, take one. Gilbert Pinfold, I wonder if we could start by trying to get a picture of your life here at Lychpole. How do you spend your time?

PINFOLD: My days are passed in writing, reading and managing my own small affairs.

ANGEL: You live in a large house by today's standards, with a good deal of land, in a style perhaps more fitting to the eighteenth or nineteenth century. Presumably you have a good many servants.

PINFOLD: Certainly not. I've never employed a secretary. And for the last two years I've been without a manservant.

ANGEL: Is that something you regret?

PINFOLD: I'm perfectly competent to answer my own letters, pay my bills, tie my parcels and fold my clothes.

(ANGEL *nods with pleasure and to encourage.*)

ANGEL: But wouldn't you say you were someone really who hankers for a bygone age and that the modern world is not to your liking?

PINFOLD: I would say I'm too old a dog to learn new tricks.

ANGEL: What is it particularly that you don't like about contemporary society?

PINFOLD: Plastics, Picasso, sunbathing and jazz.

ANGEL: Everything, in fact, that's happened in your own lifetime.

PINFOLD: Yes.

ANGEL: And I suppose you're shocked by a great many of the things you see going on?

PINFOLD: Yes.

ANGEL: What for instance?

PINFOLD: A bad bottle of wine, an impertinent stranger, or a fault in syntax.

(ANGEL *smiles and nods.*)

ANGEL: Are you a lonely man?

PINFOLD: Solitary, not lonely. Since the end of the war my life has been strictly private.

ANGEL: Are you bored?

PINFOLD: Easily.

ANGEL: You have no pastimes?

PINFOLD: Time was, I rode to hounds, went for long walks, dug my garden, felled small trees. Now I spend most of my days in an armchair.

ANGEL: I wonder if we could come now to some of your views and beliefs. You are, of course, a Roman Catholic. When were you converted?

PINFOLD: I was received into the Church – 'conversion' suggests an event more sudden and emotional than the calm acceptance of the propositions of my faith – I was received into the Church in early manhood, at the time when many Englishmen of humane education were falling into communism. Unlike them I've remained steadfast.

ANGEL: Your critics would say that you were bigoted rather than pious.

PINFOLD: I accept without much resentment the world's estimate of myself. It's part of the price I pay for privacy.

ANGEL: What about politics?

PINFOLD: I have never voted in a parliamentary election.

ANGEL: Isn't that a sort of old-fashioned Toryism?

PINFOLD: Idiosyncratic rather than old-fashioned, I think. But I can see that many people would regard my views as being almost as sinister as socialism.

ANGEL: Presumably you favour capital punishment.

PINFOLD: Only for certain crimes. Notably murder.

ANGEL: But supposing that you were ordered to carry out the hanging yourself. What would you say then?

PINFOLD: I'd say there was something very odd about Home Office administration if novelists were called upon to perform an operation which I believe requires training and considerable technical skill.

ANGEL: But if for the sake of argument you *were* ordered to do it. Would you?

PINFOLD: Yes.

(ANGEL *smiles*.)

ANGEL: You have not much sympathy for the man in the street, have you, Mr Pinfold?

PINFOLD: You must understand that the man in the street does not exist. There are individual men and women, each one of whom has an individual and immortal soul, and such beings need to use streets from time to time.

(ANGEL *smirks*.)

ANGEL: You're in your fifties, you've written a dozen books. Looking back, how would you assess your novels?

PINFOLD: I don't think novelists should assess their novels. They mustn't do literary critics out of a job. Besides, I regard my books as objects which I've made, things quite external to myself to be used and judged by others.

ANGEL: Well then, what about the future – as regards your work?

PINFOLD: A novelist is condemned to produce a succession of novelties, new names for characters, new incidents for his plots, new scenery, but I've always maintained most men harbour the germs of one or two books only; all else is professional trickery of which the most daemonic of the novelists – Dickens and Balzac even – were flagrantly guilty.

ANGEL: Gilbert Pinfold, thank you very much. (*Pause.*)
Splendid. Absolutely splendid.
(*Pause.*)

PINFOLD: Mr Angel, would you and your electricians care for a
glass of sherry?

ANGEL: That'd be very welcome, thank you.
(PINFOLD *rises and goes to pour sherry. While he does so,*
ANGEL *and the* ENGINEERS *confer in whispers.* PINFOLD *is a
little disconcerted. He brings them their sherry and breaks up their
conference.*)
Thank you, thank you. How kind. Cheers.

PINFOLD: Who is your next subject to be?

ANGEL: We're going to Stratford to interview Sir Cedric Thorne.

PINFOLD: You evidently have not seen this morning's paper.

ANGEL: No, we left before it came.

PINFOLD: Cedric Thorne has escaped you. He hanged himself
yesterday evening in his dressing room.

ANGEL: Good heavens, are you sure?

PINFOLD: It's in *The Times*.

ANGEL: May I see?
(PINFOLD *hands* ANGEL *the newspaper.*)
Yes, yes. That's him. I half expected this. He was a personal
friend. I must get on to his wife. May I phone?
(PINFOLD *indicates the telephone.* ANGEL *dials.*)

PINFOLD: I apologise for breaking the news with such levity.
(*Awkward pause for* PINFOLD.)

ANGEL: Yes, yes it is a terrible thing – not wholly unexpected
though. Well – this rather changes my plans. I shall have to
return directly to London and prepare an obituary for tonight.
(MRS PINFOLD *enters but remains in the background.*)
We must leave immediately. Thank you again for your time
and hospitality. I shall let you know when our conversation is
to be broadcast. I hope you'll enjoy listening to it. Goodbye.

PINFOLD: Goodbye.
(ANGEL *and the* ENGINEERS *exeunt.*)

MRS PINFOLD: You didn't like those people much, did you?

PINFOLD: Hm? No. They seem to believe that anyone sufficiently eminent to be interviewed must have something to hide, must be an imposter whom it's their business to trap and expose. That man – Angel was his name? – became slightly sinister, the insidiously plebian voice, menacing. There was the hint of the underdog's snarl I recognise also in my press-cuttings.

MRS PINFOLD: Well, I have some good news for you: Hill has finally moved.

PINFOLD: No.

MRS PINFOLD: The fields are ours again. Do you realise he's been trying to hold on to them for over four years? We no longer have a sitting tenant.

PINFOLD: I am pleased.

MRS PINFOLD: I saw Colonel Bagnold and told him. He said had I acted at once in 1945, Hill would have been out with his nondescript herd of cattle and his compensation that Michaelmas. The Bag said I was tender-hearted and Hill was adroit. I said that in an odd way it seemed as if the war was finally over.

PINFOLD: I suppose Hill will boast of his cleverness and his comfortable profit.

(REGINALD GRAVES-UPTON – *the Bruiser* – *enters. He is a refined, fastidious old gentleman. He whistles and calls his dog.*)

REGGIE: Here, Megs, Megs, here!

MRS PINFOLD: There's the Bruiser. Shall I ask him in?

PINFOLD: Do.

MRS PINFOLD: Reggie! Reggie! Care for a sherry?

REGGIE: I say, that's awfully civil of you. Heard about Hill. Well done. I expect Megs is sniffing around by the stables. Gilbert in?

(MRS PINFOLD *helps him off with his coat.* PINFOLD *pours a sherry.*)

Gilbert, good morning. Saw the BBC van. How did the interview go?

PINFOLD: They tried to make an ass of me. I don't believe they succeeded.

REGGIE: I bet they didn't. Cheers. Mind you, I will say this for them, they put out some first rate programmes. There's a

thoroughly good series of talks at the moment on
contemporary writers. Chap called Clutton-Cornforth.
D'you know him?

PINFOLD: Yes, I do. I've known him for almost thirty years.

REGGIE: There you are. Very, very interesting.

MRS PINFOLD: Excuse me Reggie – I must see to luncheon.
(MRS PINFOLD *exits*.)

REGGIE: And music! From Vienna! Imagine! All those sound
waves going through the air. Extraordinary. And a most
interesting play two nights ago about the last mutiny at sea
aboard a British vessel. Awfully well done. Heaven knows
how they manage the sound effects – absolutely life-like. I
wish you'd heard it. Of course, wireless is still a miracle to
me, you know. I don't really understand how it works. I say,
isn't it good about Hill clearing off your land at last?

PINFOLD: Isn't it.

REGGIE: How are the aches and pains?

PINFOLD: Intermittent.

REGGIE: Are you sleeping any better?

PINFOLD: As a matter of fact, I am. I've found a splendid way of
taking my sleeping draught, you know, the chloral and
bromide mixture I buy on my old prescription in London. It
was composed largely of water. I suggested to the chemist
that it would save trouble to have the essential ingredients in
full strength and to dilute them myself.
(*He produces the bottle from his desk drawer and shows it to*
REGGIE.)
Well, the taste was bitter but after various experiments I
found a most palatable way of taking it.

REGGIE: How?

PINFOLD: In crème de menthe.

REGGIE: Gilbert, Gilbert. Does Mr Drake know about it?

PINFOLD: Certainly not. Nor will I tell him.

REGGIE: And you won't let me try The Box on you?

PINFOLD: No.

REGGIE: They're everywhere now, you know. Really, Gilbert,
there's nothing to it. It looks like a makeshift wireless set.
And it works, really works. You don't have to take my word

for it. There are hundreds of devotees all over the country.
The Box definitely exercises diagnostic and therapeutic
powers. All you do is take some part of a sick man or animal – a
hair, a drop of blood preferably – bring it to The Box and then
I 'tune in' to the lifewaves of the patient, discern the origin of
the malady and prescribe treatment. It's all to do with radio
waves.

(MRS PINFOLD *re-enters*.)

MRS PINFOLD: Reggie, won't you stay to luncheon?

REGGIE: No, thank you. Must be off. Think about it, Gilbert.
(*He exits, calling his dog.* MRS PINFOLD *sees* REGGIE *out. They
talk in undertones.* PINFOLD *strains to hear what they say.*
REGGIE *exits.* MRS PINFOLD *returns.*)

PINFOLD: (*Enraged*) I know what you two have been talking about!

MRS PINFOLD: Do you? I was hearing about the Fawdle's row with
the Parish Council –

PINFOLD: You've been giving him my hair for his box!

MRS PINFOLD: Nonsense, Gilbert.

PINFOLD: I could tell by the way he looked at me he was measuring
my Life Waves.

MRS PINFOLD: (*Sadly*) You really are in a rather bad way, aren't
you, darling?

PINFOLD: (*Subsiding*) Damn, damn, damn. Why does everyone
except me find it so easy to be nice?
(*Pause.*)

MRS PINFOLD: Why don't you try it?

PINFOLD: What?

MRS PINFOLD: The Box. For your rheumatism. I think there
might be something in it. Did I tell you about Lady Fawdle-
Upton's nettle-rash. Well, they tried the Box on it without her
knowledge and she had immediate relief. It's simply a matter
of increasing the Life Waves.

PINFOLD: An extremely dangerous device in the wrong hands.

MRS PINFOLD: No, no. That's the beauty of it. It can't do any
harm. You see, it only transmits *Life* forces. Fanny Graves
tried it on her spaniel for worms but they simply grew
enormous with all that Life Force going into them. Like
serpents, Fanny said.

PINFOLD: I should have thought The Box counted as sorcery. You ought to confess it.

MRS PINFOLD: D'you really think so?

PINFOLD: No, not really. It's just a lot of harmless nonsense . . .

(MRS PINFOLD *exits.*

The lights fade except on PINFOLD, *who mixes his sleeping draught with crème de menthe. Radio pips sound a little distorted.*)

I was half-way through another novel and had stopped work in early summer. The completed chapters had been typed, rewritten, retyped and lay in a drawer in my desk. I was entirely satisfied with them. I knew in a general way what had to be done to finish the book and I believed I could at any moment set myself to do it. It was as if the characters I had quickened had fallen into a light doze and I left them benevolently to themselves. Hard things were in store for them. Let them sleep while they could. And I too wanted sleep. There are periods of literary composition when I find the sentences I have written during the day running in my head, the words shifting and changing colour kaleidoscopically, so that again and again I climb out of bed, pad down to the library, make a minute correction, return to my room and lie in the dark dazzled by the pattern of vocables until obliged once more to descend to the manuscript. After even the idlest day I demand six or seven hours of insensibility. In order to achieve them I have to take even larger doses of my sleeping draught.

(*Lights out. In the darkness* PINFOLD *cries out. Lights snap on.* MRS PINFOLD *enters.*)

MRS PINFOLD: What's the matter?

PINFOLD: Look, there are crimson blotches on the backs of my hands.

MRS PINFOLD: You're a very odd colour altogether. Either you're drinking too much or doping too much or both.

PINFOLD: I must get away. I must go somewhere sunny and finish my book.

MRS PINFOLD: Yes, I think you ought. I'll make a plan and come too.

PINFOLD: No, you can't, you can't leave the farm.

MRS PINFOLD: I'm worried about you, you know. You ought to
     have someone to look after you.
PINFOLD: I'll be all right. I work better alone.
     (*He tries to rise but cannot manage it.*)
MRS PINFOLD: What is it?
PINFOLD: My feet and ankles and knees. I've never known the
     aches so bad.
MRS PINFOLD: I'm going to call in Dr Drake.
     (*She exits.*)
PINFOLD: No, it's not necessary. I won't have it . . .
     (*Lights change.* DR DRAKE, *lean, horsey, and weatherbeaten,
     enters. He examines* PINFOLD's *hands and face.*)
DRAKE: Can't have him coming out in blotches, can we? Right.
     Let's have a look at you. Looks like an allergy.
PINFOLD: Allergic to what?
DRAKE: Ah, that's hard to say. Almost anything can cause an
     allergy nowadays. It might be something you're wearing or
     some plant growing near. The only cure really is a change.
PINFOLD: I've been thinking of going abroad after Christmas.
DRAKE: Yes, that's the best thing you could do. Anyway, don't
     worry. No one ever died of an allergy. It's allied to hayfever.
     And asthma. But I've got something for your aches and
     pains.
     (DRAKE *rummages in his bag.*)
PINFOLD: There is something else troubling me. The behaviour
     of my memory. It's begun to play me tricks.
DRAKE: Not to worry. I can't remember things from one day to
     the next.
PINFOLD: No, I'm not growing forgetful. I remember everything
     in clear detail but I remember it wrong. Did I tell you about
     the wash-hand stand?
DRAKE: The wash-hand stand?
PINFOLD: A massive freak of fancy that a friend in London,
     James Lance, offered me as a present, just the sort of trophy
     I most value. I hurried up to London, studied the object with
     exultation, arranged for its delivery and impatiently awaited
     its arrival. A fortnight later it came. To my horror, an
     essential part was missing. There should have been a

prominent, highly ornamental copper tap in the centre, forming the climax of the design. In its place there was merely a small socket. The carriers asserted this was the condition of the piece when they fetched it. There was a brisk exchange of letters, the carriers denying all responsibility. Finally, I wrote to James Lance asking for corroboration. James Lance replied: there never had been any tap such as I described.

DRAKE: Yes, yes, a warm climate, that'll do the trick. Try these for the aches and pains.

(*He hands over the first bottle.*)

They're something new and pretty powerful. Are you sleeping at all? Take two of these at night.

(*He hands over the second bottle.*)

They'll make all the difference. But do go easy on those. Right, then, Gilbert. I'll see you on Thursday.

PINFOLD: Thursday – if I'm spared.

(*Lights dim.* DRAKE *exits.* PINFOLD *rises, mixes his chloral and bromide with the crème de menthe, and adds the new pills, and the new sleeping draught, and swallows them all. He pours a brandy and downs it, then pours another. He goes to the telephone. He dials. While he waits he again mixes his crème de menthe mixture.*)

(*Into the telephone.*) Telegrams please. I wish to send a telegram. Lychpole 312. Subscriber's name Pinfold, G. Global Travel Agency, Albemarle Street, London, W.1. Kindly arrange immediate passage West Indies, East Indies, Africa, India, anywhere hot, luxury preferred, private bath, outside single cabin essential. Gilbert Pinfold.

(*He swallows his sleeping draught.*

Blackout.

Radio pips sound long and more distorted.

Lights up as MRS PINFOLD *enters with a large envelope, which she hands to* PINFOLD *who is now seated. He opens it quickly to find inside travel brochures and a letter, which he reads.*)

PINFOLD: (*Becoming frantic*) 'We await your further instructions.' They haven't done what I asked! I said arrange immediate passage and all they do is to send me folders from which to choose. I don't want to choose! I gave my instructions. Why can't they do as they are told! I shall send a telegram to every member of the board of directors, I don't care how many there are. To all of them, at their private addresses dispatch this message: 'Kindly investigate wanton inefficiency your office. Pinfold.'

(*Lights snap out.*
Radio pips very long and irregular and distorted.
Lights up on PINFOLD *asleep.* MRS PINFOLD *shakes him gently.*
He is comatose and in pain.)

MRS PINFOLD: Gilbert, the telegrams seem to have done some good. There's little choice at the moment. But they've booked you on a ship sailing in three days for Ceylon: the *Caliban*.

PINFOLD: Caliban?

MRS PINFOLD: It's a one-class ship.

PINFOLD: Ban, ban, Caliban.

(*He is barely able to take in the information. He winces with pain.*)

MRS PINFOLD: You're doped, darling, up to the eyes.

PINFOLD: Yes. It's those rheumatism pills. Drake said they were very strong.

(*He reaches out for his medicine but the bottle slips from his fingers.*)

I shall give up the sleeping draughts as soon as I get to sea. I always sleep better at sea. I shall cut down on drink, too. As soon as I can get rid of these damned aches, I shall start work. I can always work at sea. I shall have the book finished before I get home.

MRS PINFOLD: Of course you will. Once you're on board all will be well.

PINFOLD: I must take foolscap paper . . . in large quantities . . . and pens . . . and nibs. And any clothes you think necessary. You can always get a Chinaman anywhere out of Europe to make you a suit of clothes in an afternoon . . .

(*He mixes his medicine, drinks it and takes his other pills.*)

Yes, yes I know I'm taking too much. I'll finish what I've got and never order any more. (*He looks at the back of his hands.*) I'm sure it's not really good for me . . .

MRS PINFOLD: I don't believe you ought to be going alone. Wait
for another ship and I'll come too.

PINFOLD: No, no, I shall be all right.

(PINFOLD *hobbles out and the lights fade.*

Ship's hooter. Morse Code very fast.

Lychpole gives way to the SS Caliban.

Lights up as CAPTAIN STEERFORTH *enters and the passengers
begin to come aboard:* MR *and* MRS SCARFIELD, GLOVER, *the*
NORWEGIAN LADY, TWO YOUNG GIRLS, TWO YOUNG MEN
– one of them FOSKER *– and* MR MURDOCH, *a solitary
gentleman. An* ENGLISH STEWARD *hands* MRS SCARFIELD *the
passenger list.*)

ENGLISH STEWARD: Passenger list, Madam? Allow me to show
you to your cabin.

SCARFIELD: (*As they follow*) Anyone we know?

MRS SCARFIELD: (*Reading as she goes*) Dr Abercrombie . . .
Adison, Angel, Benson, Blackadder, Glover . . . the usual
crowd . . . oh, and there's a Mr G. Pinfold. He's new . . .
(*They exeunt as* PINFOLD *enters painfully, with an* INDIAN
STEWARD *carrying his bags.*)

PINFOLD: (*Looking about; mournfully to himself*) One-class
ship . . .

(*The* INDIAN STEWARD *leads* PINFOLD *to his cabin, which has
a single bunk, a chair and a table. The* INDIAN STEWARD *goes.*
PINFOLD *unlocks and opens his suitcase with great difficulty,
then tries to unpack but is in too much pain.* PINFOLD *rings a
bell. The* INDIAN STEWARD *re-appears.*)

I'm not very well. I wonder if you could unpack for me.

INDIAN STEWARD: Dinner seven-thirty o'clock, Sir.

PINFOLD: I said, could you unpack for me?

INDIAN STEWARD: No sir. Bar not open in port, Sir.

(*He smiles, bows and goes.* PINFOLD *sits and stares. The*
ENGLISH STEWARD *enters.*)

ENGLISH STEWARD: Sir. The passenger list, some forms to fill in
and, the Captain's compliments, Sir, he'd like the honour of
your company at his table in the dining room.

PINFOLD: Now?

ENGLISH STEWARD: No, Sir. During the voyage. Dinner is at

7.30. I don't expect the Captain will be dining in the saloon tonight.

PINFOLD: I don't think I shall either. Thank the Captain. Very civil of him. Another night. Someone said something about the bar not being open. Can't you get me some brandy?

ENGLISH STEWARD: Oh yes, Sir, I think so, Sir. Any particular brand?

PINFOLD: Brandy. Large one. And I want to send a telegram.

ENGLISH STEWARD: There's a boy taking messages at the head of the gangway, Sir.

PINFOLD: I'm not feeling very well. I wonder if you could write it for me.

ENGLISH STEWARD: Sorry about that, Sir. Pleased to be of any help.

(*The* ENGLISH STEWARD *takes up pen and paper.*)

PINFOLD: To Pinfold, Lychpole.

ENGLISH STEWARD: Is Lychpole sufficient address, Sir?

PINFOLD: Oh yes. There's only one Lychpole in the country. 'Safely embarked. Everyone in ship most helpful. All love.'

ENGLISH STEWARD: I've got that, Sir.

PINFOLD: I wonder if you could unpack for me.

ENGLISH STEWARD: Certainly sir.

(*He unpacks.* PINFOLD *finds his medicines and puts them out carefully. With difficulty he finds some silver and gives it to the* ENGLISH STEWARD.)

Thank you very much, Sir. If there's anything you need . . .

PINFOLD: Thank you. And don't forget the brandy.

(*The* ENGLISH STEWARD *exits.*)

TANNOY: Could I have your attention please, would friends and relatives of the passengers kindly leave the ship. Thank you.

(*The* ENGLISH STEWARD *returns with the brandy and exits.*
PINFOLD *takes a swig from his bottle of sleeping draught, swallows a pill and gulps the brandy. He lies on the bed. He sleeps fitfully.*
Lights out.
Ship's hooter. Sea noise. Lights up.
PINFOLD *rocks on his bunk to and fro with the motion of the ship. He wakes, and glances at his watch. The* INDIAN

STEWARD *enters and puts a cup of tea down on the table.*
PINFOLD *comes properly to with a start.*)

INDIAN STEWARD: No good today. Plenty passengers sick.
(*He exits.*)

PINFOLD: (*Sipping the undrinkable tea*) I'm not surprised.
(PINFOLD *rises, still in some pain, and combs his hair. He steps out of his cabin. He uses his blackthorn walking-stick.
Sea noise rises. Wind.* PINFOLD *walks with the rolling of the ship.* 1ST YOUNG GIRL, *wearing a thick sweater, tacks past.*
PINFOLD *watches her.* GLOVER, *a young Englishman, staggers past and into the saloon area where the* ENGLISH STEWARD *enters to take his order.* PINFOLD *follows, nods to* GLOVER *and sits down. The* ENGLISH STEWARD *approaches* PINFOLD.)

ENGLISH STEWARD: Good morning, Sir. Not many about this morning. You must be a good sailor, sir.

PINFOLD: Brandy and ginger-ale, please.
(*The* ENGLISH STEWARD *goes and in passing* GLOVER *whispers to him obviously about* PINFOLD. GLOVER *takes his drink – orange juice – and approaches* PINFOLD.)

GLOVER: Mr Pinfold? My name's Glover. My cabin's next to yours. May I join you?

PINFOLD: Please do.
(GLOVER *sits down. A pause.*)

GLOVER: I'm a manager of a tea plantation in Ceylon. Can't wait to get back. I've been home for a couple of months. But I miss the life out there. We live on horseback.
(*The* ENGLISH STEWARD *brings* PINFOLD *his drink.*)
Cheerio.

PINFOLD: (*Pointedly*) Cheerio.

GLOVER: Do you play golf?

PINFOLD: No.

GLOVER: We get these long leaves, you know. I spend them at the golf club. It's rather a demanding game. Golf. Physically. As a matter of fact, to keep myself in condition I have a weighted club, the head's on a spring, and I swing it a hundred times morning and evening.
(PINFOLD *is not really able to take in what is being said.*)
We have to share a bathroom. When do you like your bath?

PINFOLD: What? Oh. Well, really, I hardly ever take a bath at sea. One keeps so clean and I don't like hot salt water. I tried to book a private bathroom. I can't think why.

GLOVER: There aren't any private baths on the ship.

PINFOLD: So I learned. It seems a very decent sort of ship.

GLOVER: Yes, everyone knows everyone else. The same people travel in her every year. People sometimes complain they feel out of things if they aren't regulars.

(PINFOLD *rises*.)

PINFOLD: It can't be too quiet for me. Now, if you'll excuse me.

(*He rises, bows and leaves* GLOVER. *Sea noise and wind rises. As he goes* PINFOLD *suddenly stops and looks about uneasily as if he is looking for someone he can't see. Again,* IST YOUNG GIRL *crosses his path but, as before, doesn't look up or notice him. She exits.* PINFOLD *enters his cabin.*)

It can't be too quiet for me.

(*As if over a tannoy he hears the strains of a jazz band. He stands perfectly still, puzzled.*)

(*Realising.*) It's the golfer! The young man next door. He's got a gramophone.

(*Outside the cabin the sound of a* DOG *padding along.*)

What's more, he's got a *dog*! (*He listens.*) I bet he's not allowed it. I've never been in a ship where they've allowed dogs in the cabins. I daresay he bribed the steward. Anyway, one can't reasonably object. I don't mind. He seems a very pleasant fellow.

(*He notices his pills and takes one, then lies down and picks up a book, which quickly slips from his hands. He falls asleep. The sounds stop.*

Lights change to an evening light.

As PINFOLD *stirs, a new sound insists itself, coming from under his bunk.*)

CLERGYMAN'S VOICE: And, my brethren, let me say this unto you: if you abuse yourselves you will end in hell-fire and everlasting damnation.

(PINFOLD *is alert and startled.*)

You cannot hide your sins from Almighty God. Sin against yourself and you sin against the Lord. It matters not to God how long you are at sea. What matters to the Almighty is that you keep yourselves pure. As in Deuteronomy 18, verse 12: 'For all that do these things are an abomination unto the Lord.' Amen.

(*An organ plays the introduction to a hymn. Male voices sing 'Pull for the shore, sailor. Pull for the shore.' At intervals* PINFOLD *inclines his head to listen to the singing coming from 'below'. The hymn ends.*)

PINFOLD: Anglican community.

CLERGYMAN'S VOICE: I want to see Billy alone after you dismiss. Well, God Bless you all, Amen.

(*A great shuffling of feet and pushing about of chairs. A hush.*)

Well, Billy, what have you got to say to me?

(*The sound of* BILLY *sobbing.* PINFOLD *becomes more anxious and uneasy.*)

Billy, you must tell me yourself. I am not accusing you of anything. I am not putting words into your mouth.

(*The sound of* BILLY *sobbing.*)

Billy, you know what we talked about last time. Have you done it again? Have you been impure, Billy?

BILLY'S VOICE: Yes, Sir, I can't help it, Sir.

CLERGYMAN'S VOICE: God never tempts us beyond our strength, Billy. I've told you that, haven't I? Do you suppose I do not feel these temptations, too, Billy? Very strongly at times. But I resist, don't I? You know I resist, don't I? Billy?

(PINFOLD *is horror-struck. He takes his walking-stick and beats strongly on the floor. A pause.*)

Did you hear anything then, Billy? A knocking. That is God knocking at the door of your soul. He can't come and help you unless you are pure, like me.

(PINFOLD *becomes more alarmed. He tries to hurry his dressing.*)

BILLY'S VOICE: I can't help it, Sir. I want to be good. I try. I can't.

CLERGYMAN'S VOICE: You've got pictures of girls stuck up by your bunk, haven't you?

BILLY'S VOICE: Yes, Sir.

CLERGYMAN'S VOICE: Filthy pictures.

BILLY'S VOICE: Yes, Sir.

CLERGYMAN'S VOICE: How can you say you want to be good when you keep temptation deliberately before your eyes? I shall come and destroy those pictures.

BILLY'S VOICE: No, please, Sir, I want them – I want them – I want them.

(PINFOLD *hobbles out of the cabin.*
The voices stop.
PINFOLD *crosses to the saloon area. The* ENGLISH STEWARD *enters to be in attendance.*)

PINFOLD: A white lady, please.

(*The* ENGLISH STEWARD *goes to get the drink. The* YOUNG PEOPLE *enter, talking gaily among themselves. The* ENGLISH STEWARD *brings* PINFOLD *his drink.*)

Does this ship carry a regular chaplain?

ENGLISH STEWARD: Oh no, Sir, the Captain reads the prayers on Sunday.

PINFOLD: There's a clergyman then among the passengers?

ENGLISH STEWARD: I haven't seen one, Sir. Here's the list.

(*He gives* PINFOLD *a passenger list.* PINFOLD *studies it.* GLOVER *enters.*)

PINFOLD: No prefix indicating Holy Orders. A strange ship. Laymen are allowed to evangelise a presumably heathen crew.

(GLOVER *watches* PINFOLD *talking to himself.*)

Religious mania perhaps on the part of one of the officers.

(*He notices* GLOVER.) Nice to see you again.

(GLOVER *is slightly startled.*)

GLOVER: I've been down in my cabin.

PINFOLD: I had to come up. I was embarrassed by that prayer meeting. Weren't you?

GLOVER: Prayer meeting? No.

PINFOLD: Right under our feet. Couldn't you hear it?

GLOVER: I heard nothing.

PINFOLD: (*To* GLOVER) Have a drink?

GLOVER: I won't thanks. I don't. Have to be careful in a place like Ceylon.

PINFOLD: How's your dog?

GLOVER: My dog?

PINFOLD: Your crypto-dog. The stowaway. Please don't think
I'm complaining. I don't mind your dog. Nor your
gramophone for that matter.

GLOVER: But I haven't a dog. I haven't a gramophone.

PINFOLD: (*Huffily*) Oh well, perhaps I'm mistaken.

(*The* INDIAN STEWARD *enters and bangs the dinner gong.*)

GLOVER: See you at dinner.

(*He exits.* PINFOLD *finishes his drink and rises. Three tables are
brought on. One is laid for six, the second for four, the third for
two. The* YOUNG PEOPLE *sit at the table for four,* MURDOCH *at
the table for two. The* INDIAN STEWARD *stands in attendance.*
PINFOLD *crosses to the table for six. The* INDIAN STEWARD
puts a plate of soup before him then stands to the side of
PINFOLD, *but not too close, looking at him. Pause.*)

INDIAN STEWARD: Fuck.

(PINFOLD *stiffens.*)

Piss.

(PINFOLD *is still.*)

Shit.

(PINFOLD *turns and glares at him. The* INDIAN STEWARD
sidles up to PINFOLD.)

Yes, Sir, something to drink, Sir?

(PINFOLD *hesitates. The* INDIAN STEWARD's *manner is
completely innocent, with no hint of mockery.*)

PINFOLD: Wine.

INDIAN STEWARD: Wine, Sir?

PINFOLD: You have some champagne on board, I suppose?

INDIAN STEWARD: Oh yes, Sir. Three names. I show list.

PINFOLD: Don't bother about the name. Just bring a half bottle.

(*The* INDIAN STEWARD *goes.* GLOVER *enters and sits opposite*
PINFOLD.)

GLOVER: I say, have you noticed on the stairs, a bronze plaque
commemorating the use of this ship by the Royal Navy
during the war? She served in the landings in North Africa
and Normandy.

(PINFOLD *is struck by the information.*)

Almost impossible to imagine now –

PINFOLD: I owe you an apology. It wasn't your gramophone.

GLOVER: I've told you. I haven't a gramophone.

PINFOLD: Of course you haven't. No, no, it must be part of the naval equipment left over from the war.

GLOVER: (*Uneasy*) Oh. That's it, is it?

PINFOLD: It seems the most likely explanation.

GLOVER: Perhaps it does.

PINFOLD: During the war, I travelled on a troop ship which was fitted with amplifiers on every deck. I shall have to enquire if there's some way of having it cut off.

(*The* INDIAN STEWARD *brings* PINFOLD *his champagne and retires.*)

(*Confidentially.*) Very odd language the servants use.

GLOVER: They're from Travancore.

PINFOLD: No. I mean the way they swear. In front of us, I mean. I daresay they don't mean to be insolent but it shows bad discipline.

GLOVER: (*More uneasy*) I've never noticed it.

(CAPTAIN STEERFORTH *enters with* MR *and* MRS SCARFIELD *and the* NORWEGIAN LADY. *They all take their seats at* PINFOLD's *table.*)

CAPTAIN: Good evening. I'm Captain Steerforth. May I introduce Mr and Mrs Scarfield? And this is our Norwegian friend Mrs . . . (*He mumbles the name.*) You must be Mr Pinfold. This is Mr Glover.

(*Greetings are exchanged.*)

PINFOLD: Forgive me for not standing, and for not changing for dinner. I'm temporarily a cripple. My doctor has given me some awfully strong pills to take. They make me feel rather odd. You must forgive me if I'm a dull companion.

MRS SCARFIELD: We're all very dull, I'm afraid. You're the writer, aren't you? I'm afraid I never seem to get any time for reading.

PINFOLD: I wish I didn't.

(*He tries to pour his champagne but knocks over the glass.* MRS SCARFIELD *looks sideways at him.* PINFOLD *feels the need to explain.*)

They're big grey pills. I don't known what's in them. I don't believe my doctor does either. Something new.

MRS SCARFIELD: That's always exciting, isn't it?

(*The* NORWEGIAN LADY *leans across* PINFOLD.)

NORWEGIAN LADY: There are two books of yours in the ship's library, I find.

PINFOLD: Ah.

NORWEGIAN LADY: I have taken one. It is named *The Last Card*.

PINFOLD: *The Lost Chord*.

NORWEGIAN LADY: It is a humorous book, yes?

PINFOLD: Some people have suggested as much.

NORWEGIAN LADY: I find it so. Is it not your suggestion also? I think you have a peculiar sense of humour, Mr Pinfold.

PINFOLD: Ah.

NORWEGIAN LADY: That is what you are known for, yes, your peculiar sense of humour?

PINFOLD: Perhaps.

MRS SCARFIELD: May I have it after you? Everyone says I have a peculiar sense of humour too.

NORWEGIAN LADY: But not so peculiar as Mr Pinfold?

MRS SCARFIELD: That remains to be seen.

SCARFIELD: I think you're embarrassing the author.

MRS SCARFIELD: I expect he's used to it.

NORWEGIAN LADY: He takes it all with his peculiar sense of humour.

(*An uneasy pause.*)

GLOVER: How's the timber trade, Scarfield? Teak, isn't it?

SCARFIELD: Yes. Oh, same as ever. It doesn't matter how hard one works, or how much knowledge one has, or how sharp one is, there's no winning against politicians. They keep changing their policies.

PINFOLD: In a democracy men do not seek authority so that they may impose a policy. They seek a policy so that they may achieve authority.

(*Silence.*)

SCARFIELD: Fascinating.

CAPTAIN: Is that not being rather harsh?

PINFOLD: (*Becoming oblivious of his audience*) I happen to know most of the Government Front Bench. Some are members of my club. Bellamy's. I was up at Oxford with both Oliver

Pearson and Wilfred Prince-Bentham. Or Winifred as we
used to call him. The Prime Minister was my brother's fag.
Until he was expelled. The Prime Minister. Not my brother.
In the case of Winifred he's crossed the floor twice and he did
so not because he believed in his opponents' policies, but
because he believed in the possibility of their assuming
authority. As an undergraduate he switched his allegiances
even more frequently, attaching himself to three Presidents
of the Union, one after the other, some thought for rather
unhealthy motives. On the day he introduced a higher rate of
supertax, I heard him, at the bar of the club, ask a reputable
banker how one opened a numbered account in Switzerland.
(*The others at the table exchange glances.* PINFOLD *begins to
notice.*)
And just the other day the Prime Minister said that he didn't
give a –
(*He stops in mid-sentence. He bows his head, embarrassed and
ashamed of himself.*)

MRS SCARFIELD: (*Covering the awkwardness*) It must be very
exciting to move behind the scenes. We only know what we
see in the papers.

PINFOLD: Oh, I hardly ever read the political columns.

MRS SCARFIELD: (*Without a trace of spite or irony*) You don't have
to, do you, getting it all first hand?
(*Pause.* PINFOLD *attempts to rise.* GLOVER *goes to his assistance
and helps him away from the table.*)

PINFOLD: I don't know anything about politics.

GLOVER: No?

PINFOLD: Tell him I don't know anything.

GLOVER: Tell who?

PINFOLD: The Captain.

GLOVER: The Captain? But –

PINFOLD: Oh well, it doesn't matter.
(GLOVER *returns to the table and he, the* CAPTAIN, *the*
SCARFIELDS *and the* NORWEGIAN LADY, *put their heads
together and whisper.* PINFOLD *stands and listens, then hobbles
away.*
The tables give way to PINFOLD's *cabin.*

PINFOLD *enters the cabin area and hurriedly swallows a pill. He holds up the sleeping draught bottle to see how much is left.*)
Only three tablespoons left. I won't take any tonight. At least not until after midnight.
(*He lowers himself into the chair and picks up a book. He turns a page.*
The jazz band strikes up, the sound coming from beneath PINFOLD's *bunk.*)

FOSKER'S VOICE: Let's try the Pocoputa Indian one.

1ST YOUNG GIRL'S VOICE: Oh not *that*. It's so *beastly*!

FOSKER'S VOICE: I know. It's the three-eight rhythm. The Gestapo discovered it independently, you know. They used to play it in the cells. It drove the prisoners mad.

1ST YOUNG GIRL'S VOICE: Yes. Thirty-six hours did for anyone. Twelve was enough for most. They could stand any torture but that.

ASSORTED VOICES: (*overlapping*)
It drove them absolutely mad.
Raving mad.
Stark staring mad.
It was the worst torture of all.
The Russians use it now.
The Hungarians do it best.
Good old three-eight.
Good old Pocoputa Indians.
They were mad.

1ST YOUNG GIRL'S VOICE: I suppose no one can hear us?

FOSKER'S VOICE: Don't be so wet, Mimi. Everyone's up on the main deck. Ready? All right then. The three-eight rhythm.
(*Music blasts out, a throbbing, overpowering beat.*)

PINFOLD: I can't think – I can't –
(*He tries to read but throws aside the book. He covers his ears. The music continues. He rises and drains the bottle of sleeping draught. He stumbles to the bed. He falls into unconsciousness. The music ceases.*
Lights out.
Dawn light.
PINFOLD *wakes. Silence.*

216

A dragging sound as though an enormous chain-harrow is being hauled over the deck above him. In a foreign language – gibberish – the sounds of men complaining mutinously.)

OFFICER'S VOICE: Get on with it, you black bastards. Get on with it.

(The men shout back.)

I'll call out the Master-at-Arms. By God, I'll shoot the first man of you that moves.

(The complaints increase.)

Get on with it.

(There is a crash – a huge percussion of metal – followed by a wail of agony.)

(Like a nanny.) There, just see what you've gone and done now!

(PINFOLD puts on his cabin light and rises.
Subdued murmurs from above and the whimpering of the injured man.)

Steady there. Easy does it. He's trapped all right. We'll have to cut him free. You, run along to the sick-bay and get the surgeon. You, go up and report to the bridge.

(A confusion of sounds: running footsteps, metallic hammering, and voices from various parts of the ship.)

VOICES: Sir, there's a man trapped on the upper deck.

Nurse, the surgeon's needed on deck.

There's a man trapped.

A man trapped.

Trapped.

Trapped.

(PINFOLD dazed and half asleep, begins to search the cabin. He looks under the bunk. He stands with great difficulty on the bunk, then sits down. The hammering metallic noises continue.)

PINFOLD: There's a fault in the wiring. It *must* be something surviving from the war. It's all coming into my cabin. I remember once . . . during the Blitz . . . an hotel . . . I was given a bedroom which had just been vacated by a – by a visiting allied politician – statesman. I lifted the telephone to order, but – but – I was on a private line direct to the Cabinet Office. That's it. That's what's happened. During the war this cabin . . . must have been . . . some operation headquarters . . .

OFFICER'S VOICE: Right! Cut him out!

(*A terrible metallic saw screeches. The victim screams in agony. The operation is very quick. The victim cries out with relief.*)

Bloody thing's ruined. Throw it overboard.

(*A dragging sound and a huge splash.*)

PINFOLD: An unhappy ship.

OFFICER'S VOICE: Take him to the sick-bay.

PINFOLD: The engineers . . . should have disconnected . . . the wiring.

OFFICER'S VOICE: Nurse, he's in a pretty poor state, I'm afraid. I'll leave him with you.

(*The victim cries.*)

NURSE'S VOICE (MARGARET): You must be brave. I will say the rosary for you. You must be brave.

(*Morse code is tapped out. It stops. The sound of running footsteps.*)

MAN'S VOICE: Nurse, we've received a message from the shore. They suggest the following treatment – here –

CAPTAIN'S VOICE: I'm not going to be bothered with a sick man on board. We'll have to signal a passing homebound ship and have him transferred.

(*The victim whimpers.*)

NURSE'S VOICE (MARGARET): Now, this won't hurt. Just a pin-prick. Something to make you sleep.

(*The victim moans.*)

Now try and sleep . . . Ave, Maria, gratia plena: tecum; benedicta tu in mulieribus, et benedictus fructus ventris tui . . .

(PINFOLD *becomes drowsy and falls asleep.*

The noises stop.

On the deck CAPTAIN STEERFORTH *enters on his rounds and exits.*

Lights change to morning light.

The INDIAN STEWARD *enters* PINFOLD's *cabin with a cup of tea.*)

INDIAN STEWARD: Good morning, Sir.

PINFOLD: Good morning. Very disagreeable businesss that last night.

INDIAN STEWARD: Yes, sir.

PINFOLD: How is the poor fellow?

INDIAN STEWARD: Eight o'clock, Sir.

PINFOLD: Have they managed to get in touch with a ship to take him off?

INDIAN STEWARD: Yes, Sir. Breakfast eight-thirty, Sir.

(*The* INDIAN STEWARD *goes.* PINFOLD *drinks his tea. He picks up a book and reads. The intercom clicks.*)

CAPTAIN'S VOICE: This is your captain speaking.

PINFOLD: Oh yes?

CAPTAIN'S VOICE: I want you to know that a great quantity of valuable metal was sacrificed last night for the welfare of a single seaman. The metal was pure *copper*. I want you all to appreciate that only on a British ship would such a thing be done. In the ship of any other nationality it would have been the seaman not the metal that was cut up. And another thing, instead of taking the man with us to Port Said and the filth of a Wog hospital, I had him carefully transhipped and he's now on his way to England. I know the hospital he's going to; it's a sweet pretty place. It's the place all seamen long to go to.

(*Shuffling and muttering – the sounds of a meeting dispersing.*)

GONERIL'S VOICE: Well, that should teach them not to grumble.

(*The voice is harsh, grating.* PINFOLD *winces at the sound of it.*)

CAPTAIN'S VOICE: Yes, we've settled that little mutiny, I think. We shouldn't have any trouble now.

GONERIL'S VOICE: I liked your touch about the sweet, pretty hospital.

CAPTAIN'S VOICE: Yes, they little know the Hell-spot I've sent him to. Spoiling my copper indeed. He'll soon wish he were in Port Said.

GONERIL 'S VOICE: (*Laughing*) Soon wish he were dead.

(PINFOLD *is appalled. Click: new voices:*)

1ST GENERAL'S VOICE: What a splendid Skipper! I think the passengers should be told, don't you, General?

2ND GENERAL'S VOICE: Yes, General, we ought to call a meeting.

It's the sort of thing that so often passes without proper recognition. We ought to pass a vote of thanks.

1ST GENERAL'S VOICE: A ton of copper, you say.

2ND GENERAL'S VOICE: Pure copper, cut up and chucked overboard. All for the sake of a nigger. It makes one proud of the British service.

1ST GENERAL'S VOICE: Yes, we'll call a meeting.

2ND GENERAL'S VOICE: Yes, a meeting.

(*Silence.*)

PINFOLD: I must attend that meeting. It's my duty to report what I know of the true characters of the Captain and his female associate. (*Pause.*) But how will I prove my charges?

(*Soft music: an oratorio sung by a great but distant choir.*)

(*Rising.*) That *must* be a gramophone record. Or the wireless. They can't be performing this on board.

(*He takes up his box of pills, looks at it, and takes a pill. He sits down. The music continues but becomes more distant as* PINFOLD *slowly falls asleep.*

Lights out.

Lights up on the four YOUNG PEOPLE *playing quoits, laughing and jostling each other.* GLOVER *is swinging his golf club.* MR *and* MRS SCARFIELD *enter the saloon area and drink. The* NORWEGIAN LADY *sits in a deck-chair, a rug over her legs, and reads her Pinfold.* MURDOCH, *the solitary man, is also in a deck-chair, reading. The* ENGLISH STEWARD *serves in the saloon area. The* INDIAN STEWARD *serves beef tea to the others.* CAPTAIN STEERFORTH *does his rounds.* PINFOLD *enters, walking with a stick and limping. He stands and watches* GLOVER. GLOVER *smiles self-consciously.*)

GLOVER: It's all follow-through, you know.

PINFOLD: Noisy night, wasn't it?

GLOVER: Oh, I didn't hear anything.

PINFOLD: You must sleep very sound.

GLOVER: As a matter of fact I didn't. I usually do, but I'm not getting the exercise I'm used to. I was awake half the night.

(*Laughter draws their attention to the* YOUNG PEOPLE.)

PINFOLD: Odd that such healthy, good-natured creatures should rejoice in the music of the Pocoputa Indians.

GLOVER: (*Uneasy*) Yes . . .
  (*He continues to swing the club.*)
PINFOLD: By the way, have you been asked to attend the
  meeting?
GLOVER: The meeting?
PINFOLD: The two elderly military gentlemen. Have you seen
  them aboard?
GLOVER: Two elderly military gentlemen . . .?
PINFOLD: Yes. Major-Generals, I imagine. Retired now.
GLOVER: Major-Generals?
PINFOLD: Yes, you know the sort . . . (*Improvising.*) . . . passed
  over for active command in '39, but served loyally in offices.
GLOVER: What are their names?
PINFOLD: I don't know.
GLOVER: Oh.
PINFOLD: I wondered if you'd seen them.
GLOVER: No.
PINFOLD: Or anyone resembling them.
GLOVER: No.
  (PINFOLD *continues on his way to the saloon area.* GLOVER
  watches him suspiciously then continues to swing his club. MR
  SCARFIELD *greets* PINFOLD.)
SCARFIELD: Ah, Mr Pinfold, may I buy you a drink?
PINFOLD: Thank you.
SCARFIELD: What'll it be?
PINFOLD: Brandy.
SCARFIELD: Anything with it?
PINFOLD: Yes. Crème de menthe.
  (SCARFIELD *and his wife exchange a look.* SCARFIELD
  summons the ENGLISH STEWARD *and orders the drinks.*)
  I say, I'm afraid I was an awful bore last night.
MRS SCARFIELD: Were you? Not while you were with us.
PINFOLD: All that nonsense I talked about politics. It's those pills
  I have to take. They make me feel rather odd.
MRS SCARFIELD: I'm sorry about that, but I assure you, you
  didn't bore *us* in the least. I was fascinated.
PINFOLD: Anyway, I shan't hold forth like that again.
MRS SCARFIELD: Please do.

(*The* ENGLISH STEWARD *brings a glass of brandy and one of* crème de menthe. PINFOLD *very deliberately pours one into the other and drinks it.* CAPTAIN STEERFORTH *and* GLOVER *enter the saloon area.*)

SCARFIELD: Captain Steerforth, Glover, what'll it be?

CAPTAIN: My usual, steward.

GLOVER: Orange juice, please.

PINFOLD: (*To* GLOVER) And you didn't hear the accident last night?

GLOVER: No.

MRS SCARFIELD: Accident? Was there an accident last night, Captain?

CAPTAIN: No one told me of one.

PINFOLD: (*Muttering*) The villain. Remorseless, treacherous, lecherous, kindless villain.

(*All stare at* PINFOLD. SCARFIELD *surreptitiously indicates* PINFOLD'*s drink.*)

MRS SCARFIELD: (*To cover*) What accident, Mr Pinfold?

PINFOLD: Perhaps I was mistaken. I often am.

(*He downs his drink, rises, bows stiffly and leaves. The moment he goes their heads come together and they whisper.* PINFOLD *pauses and hears:*)

MRS SCARFIELD: Tight as a tick.

CAPTAIN: Are you sure?

SCARFIELD: Simply plastered.

(PINFOLD *moves further away.* CAPTAIN STEERFORTH *leaves the group and exits.* PINFOLD *hobbles painfully to his cabin and takes a pill.*)

GONERIL'S VOICE: You've got to teach him a lesson.

CAPTAIN'S VOICE: I will.

PINFOLD: Captain Steerforth!

GONERIL'S VOICE: A good lesson. One he won't forget.

CAPTAIN'S VOICE: Bring him in.

(*Scuffling and whimpering.*)

GONERIL'S VOICE: Tie him to the chair.

PINFOLD: (*Involuntarily*) 'Bind fast his corky arms.' Who said that? Goneril? Regan? Cornwall?

GONERIL'S VOICE: Tie the knots tighter.

PINFOLD: Goneril.

CAPTAIN'S VOICE: All right, you can leave him to me.

GONERIL'S VOICE: And to me.

> (*Retreating footsteps. A door slams.*)
> This man, Captain, entered my cabin at 0900 hours
> precisely. I was lying on my bunk, the bedclothes pulled up
> to my neck. The man stood just inside my cabin. He licked
> his lips. He took a step towards me. The ship was steady, yet
> he pretended, *pretended*, to sway with the movement, falling
> forward, pulling up the sheets off my body. I sleep naked.
> He had his knee on the bunk and he was staring at me. Then,
> he unbuttoned his trousers, and – and – fell heavily on me. I
> fought with him, but, but . . .

PINFOLD: Guilty.

> (*A brief pause.*)

CAPTAIN'S VOICE: Guilty. Pass me the whip.

> (*A hiss of satisfaction from* GONERIL. *A pause. The crack of a
> whip. A cry of pain. The whipping continues and a dull thudding
> sound. The victim moans and sobs.*)

GONERIL'S VOICE: More. More. Again. Again. Again. You
haven't had anything yet, you beast. Give him some more,
more, more, more.

> (PINFOLD *cannot endure the sound.*)
> That's enough.
> (*The torture ceases. Pause.*)

CAPTAIN'S VOICE: If you ask me, it's too much.

GONERIL'S VOICE: He's shamming.

CAPTAIN'S VOICE: He's dead.

GONERIL'S VOICE: Well, what are you going to do about it?

CAPTAIN'S VOICE: Untie him.

GONERIL'S VOICE: I'm not going to touch him. I never touched
him. It was all *you*.

CAPTAIN'S VOICE: As master of this ship I shall make out a death
certificate and have him put overboard after dark.

GONERIL'S VOICE: How about the surgeon?

CAPTAIN'S VOICE: He must sign too. The first thing is to get the
body into the sick-bay. We don't want any more trouble with
the men. Get Margaret.

(*Pause. Footsteps.* PINFOLD *does not move.*)

MARGARET'S VOICE: Poor boy, poor boy. Look at these ghastly
marks. You can't say these are 'natural causes'.

CAPTAIN'S VOICE: The best thing you can do, young lady, is to
see nothing, hear nothing, and say nothing.

MARGARET'S VOICE: But the poor boy. He must have suffered so.

CAPTAIN'S VOICE: Natural causes.

(*Silence.* PINFOLD *slowly straightens and relaxes. Then he is
horrified. He lurches rapidly across the cabin, but stops dead,
realising he is no longer in pain. He rotates his wrists. He rises on
his toes. He bends his knees. Amazed and delighted, he proceeds
to do a series of exercises, swinging his arms, bending at the waist
and knees.*)

PINFOLD: Whatever has to be done need not be done now. I can't
burst alone into the Captain's cabin and denounce him.
What's the proper procedure, if it exists, for putting a
Captain in irons on his own ship? I shall have to take advice.
I must find those military men. They'll know what to do. (*He
puts his walking-stick in the corner.*) I shan't need that again.
(*He goes out on to the deck area, walking easily. His spirits rise.
He breathes the fresh air. There is no one about now except the
INDIAN STEWARD, sweeping the deck. PINFOLD, making sure
he is not observed, does a little skipping movement; he looks
heavenwards as if in gratitude, closing his eyes.* MARGARET
(1ST YOUNG GIRL) *pads round, head down, noiseless, and
comes up to* PINFOLD, *his back to her.*)

MARGARET: Poor boy. He must have suffered so.

(PINFOLD *spins round but she disappears.
Lights begin to fade.*
PINFOLD *remains alarmed and mystified.
Blackout.*)

ACT TWO

Lights up on PINFOLD *in his cabin. He is performing his exercises —
knee bends, arms swinging. He stops and looks at the back of his
hands. He glances at himself in the mirror.*

PINFOLD: I feel better than I have done for weeks.

    (*Click.*)

ANNOUNCER'S VOICE: This is the BBC Third Programme. Here
    is Mr Clutton-Cornforth to speak on 'Aspects of Orthodoxy
    In Contemporary Letters'.

CLUTTON-CORNFORTH'S VOICE: If one is asked – and one often
    is asked – to give a name which typifies all that is decadent in
    contemporary literature, one can answer without hesitation –
    Gilbert Pinfold.

PINFOLD: Really!

CLUTTON-CORNFORTH'S VOICE: The basic qualities of a Pinfold
    novel seldom vary and may be enumerated thus:
    conventionality of plot, falseness of characterisation, morbid
    sentimentality, gross and hackneyed farce alternating with
    grosser and more hackneyed melodrama; cloying religiosity,
    which will be found tedious or blasphemous according as the
    reader shares or repudiates his doctrinal preconceptions –

PINFOLD: How unlike the Third Programme –

CLUTTON-CORNFORTH'S VOICE: – an adventitious and offensive
    sensuality that is clearly introduced for commercial motives.

PINFOLD: My word, I'll give that booby such a kick on the
    sit-upon next time I see him waddling up the steps of the
    London Library –

CLUTTON-CORNFORTH'S VOICE: All this is presented in a style
    which, when it varies from the trite, lapses into positive
    illiteracy. Worst of all . . .

    (PINFOLD *switches on the tannoy:*)

FEMALE SINGER'S VOICE: 'I'm Gilbert, the filbert,
      The knut with the K,
      The pride of Piccadilly,
      The blasé roué.

For Gilbert, the filbert,
The Colonel of the Knuts.'
(Silence, PINFOLD *listens intently. Gradually he becomes
alarmed by a growing feeling that all is not well, like a
premonition that something is about to happen.*)

FOSKER'S VOICE: He's gone to bed.

YOUNG GENTLEMAN'S VOICE: We'll soon get him out.

FOSKER'S VOICE: Music.

YOUNG GENTLEMAN'S VOICE: Music.

FEMALE SINGER'S VOICE: 'I'm Gilbert, the filbert,
The knut with the K,
The pride of Piccadilly,
The blasé roué

Oh Hades, the ladies
Who leave their wooden huts
For Gilbert, the filbert,
The Colonel of the Knuts.'

(*During the song* PINFOLD *sits heavily on the bunk, covering his
face with his hands despairingly.*

FOSKER *and the* YOUNG GENTLEMAN *enter, carrying a bottle,
and singing. They are shadowy figures.*)

FOSKER: Come on, Gilbert. Time to leave your wooden hut.

(PINFOLD *does not look up.*)

PINFOLD: Damned impudence. Oafs, bores.

YOUNG GENTLEMAN: Do you think he's enjoying this?

FOSKER: He's got a most peculiar sense of humour. He's a
peculiar man. Queer, aren't you, Gilbert? Come out of your
wooden hut, you old queer.

(PINFOLD *rises and goes to draw the wooden shutters across the
window.*)

He thinks that'll keep us out. It won't, Gilbert. We aren't
going to climb through the window, you know. We shall
come in at the door and then, by God, you're going to cop it.
(*Pause.*) Now he's locked the door.

PINFOLD: I haven't –

FOSKER: Not very brave, is he? Locking himself in. Gilbert
doesn't want to be whipped.

YOUNG GENTLEMAN: But he's going to be whipped.

FOSKER: Oh yes, he's going to be whipped all right.

(PINFOLD *takes up his walking-stick and stealthily prepares to leave the cabin. He raises the stick and steps out.* FOSKER *and the* YOUNG GENTLEMAN *run off.* PINFOLD *looks for them in all directions.*

From above come shrieks of laughter.)

FOSKER'S VOICE: (*From above*). No, no. Gilbert, you can't catch us that way. Go back to your little hut, Gilbert. We'll come for you when we want you. Better lock the door.

(PINFOLD *returns to the cabin. He sits, stick in hand, listening.* FOSKER *and the* YOUNG GENTLEMAN *re-enter.*)

YOUNG GENTLEMAN: We'd better wait till he goes to sleep.

FOSKER: Then we'll pounce.

YOUNG GENTLEMAN: He doesn't seem very sleepy.

FOSKER: Let's get the girls to sing him to sleep. Come on, Margaret, give Gilbert a song.

(MARGARET *and the* 2ND YOUNG GIRL *enter.*)

MARGARET: Aren't you being rather beastly?

FOSKER: No, of course not. It's all a joke. Gilbert's a sport. Gilbert's enjoying this as much as we are. He often did this sort of thing when he was our age – singing ridiculous songs outside men's rooms at Oxford. He made a row outside the Dean's rooms. That's why he got sent down. He accused the Dean of the most disgusting practices. It was all a great joke.

MARGARET: Well, if you're sure he doesn't mind.

(*The* 2ND YOUNG GIRL *joins her in singing angelically:*)

MARGARET: ⎱ 'When first I saw Mabel,
GIRL: ⎰ In her fair Russian sable,
    I knew she was able
    To satisfy me.

    Her manners were careless,
    Her hmm-hmm was hairless
    I knew she'd wear less
    To satisfy me.'

FOSKER: Did you enjoy Mabel, Gilbert?

YOUNG GENTLEMAN: Like music, don't you, Gilbert?

(*The* 1ST GENERAL *enters.*)

1ST GENERAL: Go to bed, you two. You're making an infernal nuisance of yourselves.

FOSKER: We're only mocking Pinfold. He's a beastly man.

1ST GENERAL: That's no reason to wake up the whole ship.

FOSKER: He's a Jew.

1ST GENERAL: Is he? Are you sure? I never heard that.

FOSKER: Of course he is. He came to Lychpole in 1937 with the German refugees. He was called Peinfeld then.

YOUNG GENTLEMAN: We're out for Peinfeld's blood. We want to beat hell out of him.

FOSKER: I hate him. I hate him. I hate him. I hate him. I've got my own score to settle with him for what he did to Hill.

1ST GENERAL: The farmer who shot himself?

FOSKER: Hill was a decent, old-fashioned yeoman. The salt of the country. Then this filthy Jew came and bought up the property. The Hills had farmed it for generations. They were thrown out. That's why Hill hanged himself.

1ST GENERAL: Well, you won't do any good by shouting outside his window.

YOUNG GENTLEMAN: We're going to do more than that. We're going to give him the hiding of his life.

1ST GENERAL: Yes, you could do that, of course. But I'm certainly not going to hang around and be a witness. He's just the sort of fellow to take legal action. All the same, I wish I was young enough to help. Good luck to you. Give it to him good and strong. Only remember, if there's trouble, *I* know nothing about it.

(*The* 1ST GENERAL *exits.* MARGARET *and the* 2ND YOUNG GIRL *sing 'Mabel' again.* FOSKER *and the* YOUNG GENTLEMAN *swig from a bottle.* PINFOLD *stands helplessly holding his stick.* MOTHER *enters.*)

MOTHER: It's no good, my son, I can't sleep. You know I can never sleep when you're in this state. My son, I beg you to go to bed. Mr Fosker, how can you lead him into this escapade? Margaret, darling, what are you doing here at this time of night? *Please* go to your cabin, child.

MARGARET: It's only a joke, Mother.

MOTHER: I very much doubt whether Mr Pinfold thinks it's a joke.

YOUNG GENTLEMAN: I hate him.

MOTHER: Hate? Hate? Why do all young people *hate* so much? You were not brought up to *hate*. Why do you hate Mr Pinfold?

YOUNG GENTLEMAN: I have to share a cabin with Fosker. That swine has a cabin to himself.

MOTHER: I expect he paid for it.

YOUNG GENTLEMAN: Yes, with the money he cheated Hill out of.

MOTHER: He behaved badly to Hill certainly. But he isn't used to country ways. I've not met him, though we've lived so near all these years. I think perhaps he rather looks down on all of us. We aren't so clever as he, nor as rich. But that's no reason to *hate* him. Come along, girls.

(MOTHER *exits, followed by* MARGARET *and the* 2ND YOUNG GIRL. *Pause.* PINFOLD's *alarm grows because of the silence.*)

FOSKER: Murderer!

YOUNG GENTLEMAN: You let your mother die in destitution, Gilbert.

FOSKER: Ashamed of her, weren't you? Why, Gilbert? Because she was an illiterate immigrant?

YOUNG GENTLEMAN: Gave her a pauper's funeral!

FOSKER: How much did you pay to sit at the Captain's table, Peinfeld?

YOUNG GENTLEMAN: Religious humbug!

FOSKER: Snob.

YOUNG GENTLEMAN: Sodomite.

FOSKER: You will be chastened and chastised.

(*They begin to circle, prancing, becoming more and more savage.* PINFOLD *swings round this way and that, trying to keep up with them.*)

YOUNG GENTLEMAN: We'll have your blood, Gilbert.

FOSKER: Blood.

YOUNG GENTLEMAN: We'll batter your brains out.

FOSKER: Castrate you, you old queer.

YOUNG GENTLEMAN: Chop it off.

FOSKER: Jew.

YOUNG GENTLEMAN: Queer.

FOSKER: Chop it off.

YOUNG GENTLEMAN: We'll have your blood.

FOSKER: Blood.

YOUNG GENTLEMAN: Blood!

FOSKER: Blood!

YOUNG GENTLEMAN: Now's the time. Ready, Fosker?

FOSKER: Ready.

> (PINFOLD *turns out the light in the cabin and stands by the door, walking-stick raised. Darkness.*)

YOUNG GENTLEMAN: In we go then. You first, Fosker.

> (*Pause.*)

FOSKER'S VOICE: (*Near the cabin*) I can't get in. The bastard's locked the door.

YOUNG GENTLEMAN'S VOICE: Go on, what you waiting for?

FOSKER'S VOICE: I tell you he's locked us out.

YOUNG GENTLEMAN'S VOICE: That's torn it. (*Pause.*) I feel awfully sick suddenly.

> (*Sound of vomiting.*
> MOTHER *re-enters with a candle.*)

MOTHER: I haven't been to bed, dear. I couldn't leave you like that. I've been waiting and praying for you. You're ready to come now, aren't you?

YOUNG GENTLEMAN'S VOICE: Yes, Mother. I'm ready.

MOTHER: I love you so. All love is suffering.

> (MOTHER *exits.*
> *Silence.*
> PINFOLD *puts away his stick. Dawn light. Slowly he opens the door of the cabin and peers out. Back in the cabin he considers his next move.*)

PINFOLD: I must think clearly. Some of the charges are totally preposterous. Others are inconsistent. If, for example, I were a newly arrived immigrant, I could not have been a rowdy undergraduate at Oxford. But how did they know about Hill? Did they not say they came from my part of the country? If that's the sort of thing that's being said in the district, I must correct it. Something must be done. I must

lay the matter before the Captain, the natural guardian of law
on this ship. The Captain? But he's guilty of murder! Wasn't
I going to have him arrested at the earliest opportunity? I
must think clearly. (*Pause.*) Of course! I must seek the
villains out and identify them. Then . . . I shall act.
(*He leaves the cabin. On deck he breathes fresh air.* MARGARET
and the 2ND YOUNG GIRL *enter.*)

MARGARET: Look, he's left his cabin. Now's our chance to give
him our presents. It's much better than giving them to his
steward as we meant to. Now we can arrange them ourselves.

2ND YOUNG GIRL: D'you think he'll like them?

MARGARET: He ought to. We've taken enough trouble. They're
the best we could possibly get.

2ND YOUNG GIRL: But Megs, he's so grand.

MARGARET: It's because he's so grand he'll like them. Grand
people are always pleased with little things.

2ND YOUNG GIRL: Suppose he comes in and finds us.

MARGARET: You keep *cave*. If he comes, sing.

2ND YOUNG GIRL: 'When I first saw Mabel'?

MARGARET: Of course. *Our* song.
(*Pause.* PINFOLD *is pleased.* MARGARET *goes into his cabin,
hides the present and rejoins the* 2ND YOUNG GIRL.)
I've hidden it. He hasn't moved, has he?

2ND YOUNG GIRL: No. What d'you suppose he's thinking
about?

MARGARET: Those beastly boys, I expect.

2ND YOUNG GIRL: Do you think he's very upset?

MARGARET: He's so brave.

2ND YOUNG GIRL: Often brave people are the most sensitive.

MARGARET: Well, it will be all right when he gets back to his
cabin and finds our present. *Cave, cave, cave.*
(PINFOLD *sets off for his cabin. Once inside, he searches
everywhere for the present, but cannot find anything. As he steps
out again he sees the* INDIAN STEWARD *coming along, beating a
gong for breakfast.*)

PINFOLD: I say, did a young lady leave anything for me in my
cabin?

INDIAN STEWARD: Yes, Sir, breakfast now, Sir.

PINFOLD: No. Listen, I think something was left for me here a short time ago.

INDIAN STEWARD: Yes, Sir, gong for breakfast just now.

(*He exits.* MARGARET *and the* 2ND YOUNG GIRL *re-enter.*)

MARGARET: Oh, he hasn't found it.

2ND YOUNG GIRL: He must *look*.

(*They run round the cabin at speed.*)

MARGARET: (*As they tear round*) *Look* for it, Gilbert, *look*.

(PINFOLD *returns to the cabin and looks again but can find nothing.*)

He can't find it. He can't find anything. The sweet brave idiot, he can't find anything.

(*Dejected,* PINFOLD *leaves his cabin.*

Three dining tables. PINFOLD *sits at the Captain's table. The* INDIAN STEWARD *approaches him with a menu.*)

PINFOLD: Coffee . . . fish, scrambled eggs . . . and fruit.

(*He sits patiently. The rose-shaded electric lamp on the table comes into action as a transmitter.*)

FOSKER'S VOICE: Good morning, Gilbert.

PINFOLD: Good morning.

FOSKER'S VOICE: Can you hear me?

PINFOLD: Yes.

FOSKER'S VOICE: Did you think you could hide? Come on, fetch him out.

(*The* INDIAN STEWARD *serves* PINFOLD, *oblivious to the noises.*)

YOUNG GENTLEMAN'S VOICE: Come out, Peinfeld. We know where you are. We've got you. Run, Peinfeld, run. We can see you. We're coming for you.

(PINFOLD *eats stolidly.*)

FOSKER'S VOICE: Jew.

YOUNG GENTLEMAN'S VOICE: Queer.

FOSKER'S VOICE: Sodomite.

YOUNG GENTLEMAN'S VOICE: Come and meet us, Gilbert.

FOSKER'S VOICE: You're afraid, Peinfeld.

YOUNG GENTLEMAN'S VOICE: We want to talk to you Peinfeld.

FOSKER'S VOICE: You're hiding, aren't you? You can't, you know.

YOUNG GENTLEMAN'S VOICE: Meet us on D. Deck, Gilbert. Turn right. Got that? You'll see some lockers. The next bulk-head. We're waiting for you.

FOSKER'S VOICE: Better come now and get it over. You've got to meet us some time you know.

YOUNG GENTLEMAN'S VOICE: We've got you, Gilbert. There's no escape.

FOSKER'S VOICE: Better get it over.

(PINFOLD *pushes his plate away.*)

Off your feed, Gilbert? You're in a funk, aren't you? Can't eat when you're in a funk, can you?

(*Exasperated,* PINFOLD *pulls the lamp towards him.*)

PINFOLD: (*Into the lamp*) Pinfold to Hooligans. Rendezvous Main Deck 0930 hours. Out.

(GLOVER *enters and comes to the table.*)

GLOVER: Hello, something gone wrong with the light?

PINFOLD: I tried to move it. I hope you slept better last night.

GLOVER: Like a log. No more disturbances, I hope?

PINFOLD: No. If you'll excuse me . . .

(PINFOLD *leaves the dining area. As he does so he passes the solitary little man,* MURDOCH, *and watches him.*
The tables give way to the four YOUNG PEOPLE, *who suddenly burst on playing a game, which requires three of them to keep a ball away from the fourth. Much laughter and high spirits.*
PINFOLD *watches them closely. They take no notice of him.*)
(*Calling tentatively.*) Fosker? Margaret?

(*The* YOUNG PEOPLE *continue their game and exeunt playing.*
PINFOLD *checks his watch. He walks up and down.* MR *and* MRS SCARFIELD *pass and stare strangely at him as he talks to himself.*)

9.30, Main deck – where are they? (*He paces up and down.*) Now what will I say to them? Let me remind you that you are subjects to British Law – no – better a plain statement of fact. You are subject to British law on the SS *Caliban* just as much as on land . . . now, something about defamation of character and threatened physical assault being grave crimes – I'll throw the whole book at them. (*He looks at his watch.*) Where are they?

(*At his feet:*)

FOSKER'S VOICE: We'll talk to Pinfold when it suits us and not a moment before.

PINFOLD: The wiring in this ship is in need of an overhaul.

YOUNG GENTLEMAN'S VOICE: Who'll do the talking?

FOSKER'S VOICE: I will, of course.

PINFOLD: For all I know there may be a danger of fire!

YOUNG GENTLEMAN'S VOICE: What are we waiting for?

FOSKER'S VOICE: To let him get into a thorough funk. Remember at school one was always kept waiting for a beating? Just to make it taste sweeter? Well, Peinfold can wait for *his* beating.

YOUNG GENTLEMAN'S VOICE: He's scared stiff.

FOSKER'S VOICE: He's practically blubbing now.

(PINFOLD *begins to go.*)

He's going away.

YOUNG GENTLEMAN'S VOICE: He's running away.

FOSKER'S VOICE: Funk.

(PINFOLD *sees the* ENGLISH STEWARD *crossing the deck.*)

PINFOLD: I wish to send a telegram. To Pinfold. Lychpole. England: 'Entirely cured. All love. Gilbert.'

(*Blackout.*

Lights up.

The 2ND GENERAL *enters, pursued by the* 1ST GENERAL.)

1ST GENERAL: I say, old friend, have you heard? The Spaniards are going to seize Gibraltar. They're stopping and searching all ships passing through the Straits in what they define as their territorial waters. They're demanding we put into Algeciras for examination of cargo and passengers. Franco's orders.

2ND GENERAL: Tin-pot dictator.

1ST GENERAL: Twopenny-halfpenny Hitler.

2ND GENERAL: Dago.

1ST GENERAL: Priest-ridden puppet.

2ND GENERAL: What incenses me is that our bloody government is prepared to truckle to him.

1ST GENERAL: It's nothing short of a blockade. If I were in command I'd call their bluff, go full steam ahead and tell them to shoot and be damned.

1ST GENERAL: That would be an act of war, of course.

1ST GENERAL: Serve 'em right. We haven't sunk so low we can't lick the Spaniards, I hope.

2ND GENERAL: It's all this bloody United Nations.

(*Lights out.*
Lights up on the upper level as CAPTAIN STEERFORTH *appears with a* SPANISH OFFICIAL.)

SPANISH OFFICIAL: This is not a pleasant task for me, Captain Steerforth, but I am only carrying out orders. I am instructed by our Head of State to say that if a sum of one hundred million pounds sterling is forthcoming from London the *Caliban*'s free passage would immediately be ensured. You have until midnight, after which if no satisfactory arrangements are made, the *Caliban* will be taken under escort to Algeciras.

CAPTAIN: Piracy. Blackmail.

SPANISH OFFICIAL: We cannot allow such language about our Head of State.

CAPTAIN: Then you can bloody well get off my bridge.

(*Lights out.*
Lights up on deck as GLOVER *begins to swing his golf club.*
PINFOLD *enters.*)

PINFOLD: Did you see the Spaniards come on board?

(GLOVER, *as usual, is alarmed by* PINFOLD.)

GLOVER: Spaniards? Come on board? How could they? When?

PINFOLD: They're causing a lot of trouble.

GLOVER: I'm awfully sorry. I simply don't know what you're talking about.

PINFOLD: You will. Soon enough, I fear.

(GLOVER *moves off to find a place to swing his club.* PINFOLD *goes to the saloon area where the* ENGLISH STEWARD *and the* INDIAN STEWARD *are in attendance.* PINFOLD *sits down. The* ENGLISH STEWARD *begins to mix drinks, talking to the* INDIAN STEWARD, *whose English is suddenly fluent.*)

ENGLISH STEWARD: The Spanish bastards are asking for whisky.

INDIAN STEWARD: I won't serve them.

ENGLISH STEWARD: Captain's order.

INDIAN STEWARD: What's come over the old man? It isn't like him to take this lying down.

ENGLISH STEWARD: He's got a plan . . . Trust him. Don't forget the whisky and I hope it poisons them. (*He sees* PINFOLD.) Evening, Sir. Brandy and crème de menthe, Sir?

(*He gives* PINFOLD *his drink.* PINFOLD *downs it in one.*)

CAPTAIN'S VOICE: Gentlemen –

PINFOLD: Yes?

CAPTAIN'S VOICE: I must take you into my confidence: there is particular reason why we cannot allow this ship to be searched. You all know we have an extra man on board. He's not one of the crew. He doesn't appear on any list. He's got no ticket or papers. I don't even know his name myself. I daresay you've noticed him sitting all alone in the dining saloon. All I've been told is that he's very important to H.M.G. He's on a special mission. It's him of course, the Spaniards are after. All this talk about territorial waters and right of search is pure bluff. We've got to see that the man gets through. Now I've got an idea that I think will work. I shall have to take the passengers into my confidence – not all of them of course, and not fully into my confidence. But I'm going to collect half a dozen of the more responsible men and put them in the picture. I'll ask them up here, casually, after dinner. With their help the plan *may* work.

(*Lights out.*

Lights on in the saloon area where passengers are collected for pre-dinner drinks, PINFOLD *is among them.* MURDOCH, *the solitary man, stands aloof. When* CAPTAIN STEERFORTH *enters,* PINFOLD *detaches himself and stands rather hopefully in the* CAPTAIN'*s path.* CAPTAIN STEERFORTH *nods and passes him to join the others.* PINFOLD *is crestfallen and then overhears as the* ENGLISH STEWARD *serves* GLOVER.)

ENGLISH STEWARD: (*Whispering to* GLOVER) Captain's compliments, Sir, and he would be grateful if you could find it convenient to join him for a few minutes after dinner.

(*The* ENGLISH STEWARD *comes to* PINFOLD, *who inclines his ear for a whispered message.*)

Brandy and crème de menthe, Sir?

MRS SCARFIELD: When do we go through the Straits?

CAPTAIN: Early tomorrow morning.

NORWEGIAN LADY: It ought to be warmer then, yes?

CAPTAIN: Not at this time of year. You must wait for the Red Sea before you go into whites.

SCARFIELD: Will you join us for a rubber after dinner?

CAPTAIN: Not this evening, I'm afraid. I've one or two things to see to.

(*The gong sounds. All, except* PINFOLD, *begin to exit.*)

MRS SCARFIELD: Aren't you coming in to dinner, Mr Pinfold?

(*He is lost in thought. She shrugs and exits.*
Lights out.
Lights up on the upper level. CAPTAIN STEERFORTH *enters with shadowy male figures.*)

CAPTAIN: That, gentlemen, is a resumé of the situation.

(*Male murmurs.*)

I have to report that I've been unable to obtain authorization for the company to pay the hundred million pounds sterling. The alternative offer – to put into Algeciras until the matter is settled between Madrid and London would be a betrayal of every standard of British seamanship. The *Caliban* will not strike her flag.

(*Applause.*)

So, here's the plan: at midnight the Spanish ship will come alongside. They intend to take me under arrest and a party of hostages, to tranship us, and to put an officer of their own on my bridge to sail her into the Spanish port. But . . . In the dark, on the gangway, our resistance will disclose itself: we'll overpower the Spaniards, throw them back into their ship and if one or two get into the drink in the process so much the better. Then *Caliban* will make full steam ahead. You are all agreed?

MEN: Agreed. Agreed. Agreed.

CAPTAIN: I knew I could trust you. I'm proud to have you under my command. Are there any questions?

1ST GENERAL: How about Pinfold? Shouldn't he be here?

CAPTAIN: There is a role assigned to Captain Pinfold. I don't think I need go into that for the moment.

2ND GENERAL: He has received his orders?

CAPTAIN: Not yet. We have some hours before us. I suggest, gentlemen, that you go about the ship in the normal way, turn in early, and rendezvous here at 23.45. The time is now 22.52. Midnight is zero hour. Perhaps, General, you will remain behind for a few minutes. For the present, goodnight gentlemen.

MEN: Goodnight, goodnight.

(*All exit except* CAPTAIN STEERFORTH *and the* 1ST GENERAL.)

CAPTAIN: Well, how did that sound?

1ST GENERAL: Pretty thin, Skipper, I must say, but I take it that what we've just heard is the cover plan.

CAPTAIN: Precisely. I could hardly hope to deceive an old campaigner like you. I'm sorry not to have been able to take your companions into my confidence, but in the interest of security . . .

1ST GENERAL: Of course.

CAPTAIN: The role of the committee who have just left us is to create sufficient diversion to enable us to carry out the real purpose of the operation.

1ST GENERAL: Which is?

CAPTAIN: To prevent a certain person falling into the hands of the enemy.

1ST GENERAL: Pinfold?

CAPTAIN: No, no, quite the contrary. Captain Pinfold has, I fear, to be written off. The plan briefly is this: Captain Pinfold is to impersonate the agent. He will be provided with papers identifying him. The Spaniards will take him ashore and the ship will sail on unmolested.

(*Pause.*)

1ST GENERAL: It might work.

CAPTAIN: It *must* work.

(*Lights up slowly on* PINFOLD *in his cabin. He is listening, gazing upwards. He is in shock.*)

1ST GENERAL: Why Pinfold?

CAPTAIN: He is the obvious man, really. No one else would take the Spaniards in for a moment. Pinfold looks like a secret agent. He's a sick man and therefore expendable. And, of course, he's a Roman Catholic. That ought to make things a little easier for him in Spain.

1ST GENERAL: Yes, yes. I see all that. But all the same I think it's pretty sporting of him to agree.

CAPTAIN: Oh, *he* doesn't know anything about it.

1ST GENERAL: The devil he doesn't?

CAPTAIN: No, that would be quite fatal to security. Besides he might *not* agree. He has a wife, you know, and a large family. No, Captain Pinfold must be kept quite in the dark. That's the reason for the counter-plan, the diversion. There's got to be a schemozzle on the gangway so that Captain Pinfold can be pushed into the corvette. Perhaps, Sir, you'd be responsible for hauling him out of his cabin and planting the papers on him.

1ST GENERAL: Of course. That boy of mine will laugh. He took against Pinfold from the start. Now he hears he's deserted to the enemy . . .

(*Lights fade on the upper area.*
Lights up on PINFOLD. *He is horrified and enraged.*)

PINFOLD: I am alone. I am alone, without hope of reinforcements. My sole advantage is that I know, and they do not know that I know, their plan of action.

(*He rises, begins to collect up various papers, and his stick.*)

Whatever outrage the night brings forth shall find me ready. Passport, travellers' cheques . . . blackthorn.

(*He prepares to leave the cabin.*)

It's a clumsy plan. The Spanish will open fire if the *Caliban* attempts to sail away. For myself I have little concern. If this man is really of vital importance to the country, he must be protected. I will gladly protect him. But I will not be tricked into it. Captain Steerforth and his cronies must understand that if I go, I go voluntarily as a man of honour. And my wife must be fully informed of the circumstances. I will go to the sacrifice a garlanded hero.

(*Sounds of Spanish and English calls from ship to ship and running feet of crew, chains, orders: sounds of continuous and growing activity.* PINFOLD *rises.*)

I shall deliver my terms to Captain Steerforth.

(*He grips his blackthorn and leaves his cabin as the sounds are at their loudest and most intense. As he steps out the noise stops abruptly and completely. Dead silence. A slight wind rises and there is a gentle rush of the sea.* PINFOLD *is victim to real fear. He goes this way and that in the hope of seeing someone. All is deserted and silent.*)

Oh, let me not be mad, not mad, sweet heaven.

(*He is in agony. From several points comes the sound of peal upon rising peal of mocking laughter –* GONERIL's: *a harsh, obscene cacophony. As though the laughter brings relief,* PINFOLD *begins slowly to smile.*)

A hoax. The hooligans have hoaxed me. A hoax.

(*He returns to his cabin and falls on his bunk.*

MARGARET, FOSKER *and* MOTHER *enter.*)

MARGARET: It was an absolutely beastly joke and I'm glad it fell flat.

FOSKER: It came off very nicely. Old Peinfeld was gibbering with funk.

MARGARET: He wasn't – and he isn't called Peinfeld. He was a hero. When I saw him standing alone on deck I thought of Nelson.

FOSKER: He was drunk.

MOTHER: He says it's not drink, Mr Fosker. He says it's some medicine he has to take.

FOSKER: Medicine from a brandy bottle.

MARGARET: I know you're wrong. You see it just happens I *know* what he's thinking and you don't.

GONERIL'S VOICE: (*Nearby*) I can tell you what he was doing on deck. He was screwing up his courage to jump overboard. He longs to kill himself, don't you, Gilbert? You wish you were dead, don't you, Gilbert? And a very good idea, too. Why don't you do it. Gilbert? Why not? Perfectly easy. It would save us all – you, too, Gilbert – a great deal of trouble.

MARGARET: Beast.

(*She sobs.*)

FOSKER: Oh God, now you've turned on the water-works again.

(MARGARET, FOSKER *and* MOTHER *exeunt.*)

PINFOLD: (*Weary but relieved*) I might be unpopular. I might be ridiculous. But I'm not mad. Sleep. I must sleep. I haven't slept for forty hours . . . I must sleep.
(*The lights fade to blackness.*

MARGARET *enters. She stands gazing at* PINFOLD. *A pause.*)

MARGARET: Gilbert, Gilbert. Why don't you speak to me? You passed quite close to me on deck and you never looked at me. *I* haven't offended you, have I? You know it isn't me who's saying all these beastly things. Answer me, Gilbert. I can hear you.

PINFOLD: Where are you? I don't even know you by sight. Why don't we meet, now? Come and have a cocktail with me.

MARGARET: Oh Gilbert, darling, you know that's not possible. The *Rules*.

PINFOLD: What rules? Whose? Do you mean your father won't let you?

MARGARET: No, Gilbert, not *his* rules, the Rules. Don't you understand? It's against the *Rules* for us to meet.

PINFOLD: What do you look like?

MARGARET: I mustn't tell you that. You must find out for yourself. That's one of the Rules.

PINFOLD: You talk as though we were playing some kind of game.

MARGARET: That's all we were doing – playing a kind of game. But there's one thing I would like to say.

PINFOLD: Well?

MARGARET: You won't be offended?

PINFOLD: I don't expect so.

MARGARET: Are you sure, darling?

PINFOLD: What is it?

MARGARET: Shall I tell you? Dare I? You won't be offended? (*Pause; then in a thrilling whisper:*) You need a shave!

PINFOLD: But I shaved this morning. You're not asking me to shave again?

MARGARET: Oh, Gilbert, I think you're sweet. Is your chin a little bit rough, darling? How long after you shave does it get rough again? *I think* I should like it rough.
(PINFOLD *runs a hand over his chin. He is flattered by*

MARGARET's *attention*.)

PINFOLD: Well, perhaps it is a little rough . . .

(*He rises. A little self-consciously he begins to shave*.)

MARGARET: Oh Gilbert, darling, I do love you. I adore you. I
worship you. How wonderful you'll look when you've
shaved: younger, smarter, loveable.

(PINFOLD *glows*.)

I love you, Gilbert, with all my heart and soul. No one has
ever loved as I love you. Oh my brave, good, wonderful
darling. I glory in you. Just to gaze on you is to be reminded
of spring, of warmth, of goodness. I love you, Gilbert
darling. I love, love, love you.

(*She runs off.* PINFOLD *wipes his face. He cannot stop smiling.
He lies down on the bunk and sighs with pleasure.*
MOTHER *and* MARGARET *enter*.)

MOTHER: Mr Pinfold, Mr Pinfold. Surely you haven't gone to
sleep? Surely you haven't forgotten your promise to
Margaret?

MARGARET: (*Strained, almost hysterical*) Mother, he didn't make
any promise. Not really. Not really what you'd call a *promise*.

MOTHER: When I was young, dear, any man would be proud of a
pretty girl taking notice of him. He wouldn't try and get out
of it by pretending to be asleep.

MARGARET: I asked for it. I expect I bore him. He's a man of the
world. He has hundreds of other girls, all sorts of horrible,
fashionable, vicious old hags in London and Paris and Rome
and New York. Why should he look at *me*? But I *do* love him
so.

(*She whimpers – it is the same sound that the victims have made
in earlier scenes.*)

MOTHER: Don't cry, my dear. Mother will talk to him.

MARGARET: Please, *please* not, Mother. I forbid you to interfere.

MOTHER: 'Forbid' isn't a very nice word, is it, dear? You leave it
to me. I'll talk to him. Mr Pinfold. Gilbert! Wake up.
Margaret's got something to say to you. He's awake, dear,
now, I know. Just tell her you're awake and listening.
Gilbert.

PINFOLD: I'm awake and listening.

MOTHER: (*Like a telephone operator*) All right, then, hold on. Margaret's going to speak to you. Come along, Margaret, speak up.

MARGARET: I can't, Mother, I can't.

MOTHER: You see, Gilbert, you've upset her. Tell her you love her. You do love her, don't you?

PINFOLD: (*Desperately*) But I've never met her. I'm sure she's a delightful girl, but I've never set eyes on her.

MOTHER: Oh, Gilbert, Gilbert, that's not a very gallant thing to say, is it? Not really like you, not like the real you. You just pretend to be hard and worldly, don't you? And you can't blame people if they take you at your own estimate. Everyone in the ship has been saying the most odious things about you. But I know better. Margaret wants to come and say goodnight to you, Gilbert, but she's not sure that you really love her. Just tell Mimi you love her, Gilbert.

PINFOLD: I can't, I don't. I'm sure your daughter is a most charming girl. It so happens I've never met her. It also happens that I have a wife. I love *her*.

MOTHER: Oh, Gilbert, what a very middle-class thing to say.

MARGARET: (*Wailing*) He doesn't love me, he doesn't love me.

MOTHER: Gilbert, Gilbert, you're breaking my little girl's heart.

PINFOLD: I'm going to sleep now. Goodnight.

MOTHER: Margaret's coming to see you.

PINFOLD: Oh, shut up, you old bitch!

(*The* YOUNG GENTLEMAN *and the* 1ST GENERAL *enter and join the women.*)

YOUNG GENTLEMAN: My God, Peinfold, you'll pay for that. If you think you can talk to my mother like –

(*The* 1ST GENERAL *chuckles heartily.*)

1ST GENERAL: Upon my soul, my dear, he called you an old bitch. Good for Peinfeld. That's something I've been longing to say to you for thirty years. You *are* an old bitch, you know, a thorough old bitch. Now perhaps you'll allow *me* to handle the situation. Clear out the lot of you. I want to talk to my daughter.

(MOTHER *and the* YOUNG GENTLEMAN *go.*)

Come here, Meg, Peg o'my heart, my little Mimi. (*His accent*

243

becomes Celtic, his tones sentimental.) You'll not be my little Mimi ever again, any more after tonight, and I'll not forget it. You're a woman now and you've set your heart on a man as a woman should. He's old for you, but there's good in that. An old man can show you better than a young one. He'll be gentler, kinder and cleaner; and then, when the right time comes you in your turn can teach a younger man – and that is how the art of love is learned and the breed survives. I'd like dearly to be the one myself to teach you, but you've made your own choice and who's to grudge it you?

MARGARET: But Father, he doesn't love me. He said not.

1ST GENERAL: Fiddlesticks. You're as pretty a girl as he'll meet in a twelvemonth. Go in and get him, lass. How do you think your mother got me? Not by waiting to be asked, I can tell you. She was a soldier's daughter, she always rode straight at her fences. She rode straight at me, I can tell you. Don't forget you're a soldier's daughter, too. If you want this fellow Pinfold, go in and take him. But for God's sake come on parade looking like a soldier. Get yourself cleaned up. Wash your face, brush your hair, take your clothes off. She's coming, Gilbert, she won't be long.

(*Music: angelic voices chant an epithalamium. The* 2ND YOUNG GIRL, *dressed like a bridesmaid, enters.* MARGARET *begins to disrobe and is covered in a diaphanous material. The* 2ND YOUNG GIRL *attends her.* MOTHER *joins the* 1ST GENERAL *and they watch proudly.* PINFOLD *rises. He attends to his appearance. He takes off his jacket, loosens his collar and puts on a dressing gown. He faces* MARGARET.)

PINFOLD: Come. Come speedily. I am strongly armed.

(MOTHER *and the* 1ST GENERAL *inspect* MARGARET.)

MOTHER: Oh my darling, my own. You're so young. Are you sure? Are you quite sure you love him?

MARGARET: Yes, Mother, I love him.

MOTHER: Be kind to her, Gilbert. My daughter's happiness is in your hands. Treat her *husbandly*. I'm entrusting something very precious to you.

1ST GENERAL: That's my beauty. Go and take what's coming to

you. Listen, my Peg, you know what you're in for, don't you?

MARGARET: Yes, Father, I think so.

IST GENERAL: It's always a surprise, but there's no going back now. Come and see me when it's all over. I'll be waiting up to hear the report. In you go, bless you.

(MOTHER *and* IST GENERAL *exeunt. Pause.*)

MARGARET: Gilbert, Gilbert. Do you want me?

PINFOLD: Yes, of course, come along.

MARGARET: Say something sweet to me.

PINFOLD: I'll be sweet enough when you get here.

MARGARET: Come and fetch me.

PINFOLD: Where are you?

MARGARET: Here. Just outside your cabin.

PINFOLD: Well, come along in. I've left the door open.

MARGARET: I can't. I can't. You've got to come and fetch me.

PINFOLD: Oh, don't be such a little ass. I've been waiting here for goodness knows how long. Come in, if you're coming. If you're not. I want to go back to bed.

(MARGARET *bursts into tears*, MOTHER *enters*.)

MOTHER: Gilbert, that wasn't kind. It wasn't like you. You love her. She loves you. Can't you understand? A young girl; the first time; woo her, Gilbert, coax her. She's a little wild, woodland thing.

(*The* IST GENERAL *enters*.)

IST GENERAL: What the hell's going on? You ought to be in position by now. Isn't the girl over the Start Line?

MARGARET: Oh, Father, I can't. I *can't*. I thought I could, but I *can't*.

IST GENERAL: (*Going*) Something's gone wrong, Pinfold. Find out. Send out patrols.

(*He exits.*)

MOTHER: (*Going*) Come and find her, Gilbert. Lure her in, tenderly, *husbandly*. She's just there, waiting for you.

(*All, except* MARGARET, *exeunt*. PINFOLD *walks out of the cabin. The sound of* MARGARET *crying, quite close, on the far side of the deck where he cannot see her.*)

PINFOLD: Where are you? I can hear you. I can hear Glover snoring. But where *are* you?

(MARGARET's *sobbing continues.* PINFOLD *goes back into the cabin.*)

I'm sorry, Margaret. I'm too old to start playing hide and seek with schoolgirls. If you want to come to bed with me, you'll have to come and join me there.

(*He lies on the bunk. He turns off his light. Darkness.*
MARGARET *enters his cabin, stands looking at him, then runs out, closing his door.* PINFOLD *sits up and turns on his light. There is no one there. He turns off the light.*)

MARGARET'S VOICE: I did go to him, I did. I did. I did. And when I got there he was lying in the dark, snoring.

MOTHER'S VOICE: Oh, my Margaret, my daughter. You should never have gone. It was all your father's fault.

1ST GENERAL'S VOICE: Sorry about that, Peg. False appreciation.

GONERIL'S VOICE: Snoring. Shamming. Gilbert knew he wasn't up to it. He's impotent, aren't you, Gilbert? Aren't you? (*Pause.*)

PINFOLD: (*Sleepily*) It was Glover snoring.
(*Silence.*
Morse code begins to sound.
Lights up on PINFOLD, *who stirs from sleep as the* ENGLISH STEWARD, *the* YOUNG GENTLEMAN, FOSKER *and the* 2ND YOUNG GIRL *enter with telegrams.*)

ENGLISH STEWARD: Listen to this – 'Entirely cured. All love, Gilbert.'

YOUNG GENTLEMAN: Cured! Ha. Ha.

2ND YOUNG GIRL: Entirely cured!

FOSKER: Our Gilbert, entirely cured, oh that's delicious, read us some more.

ENGLISH STEWARD: 'Everyone in ship most helpful.'

FOSKER: Ah, that's a good one.

2ND YOUNG GIRL: Everyone.

YOUNG GENTLEMAN: I wonder if poor Gilbert thinks that now.

ENGLISH STEWARD: Oh, this is marvellous. 'Kindly arrange immediately luxury private bath. Kindly investigate wanton inefficiency your office.'

YOUNG GENTLEMAN: He sent out dozens of those.

2ND YOUNG GIRL: Thank God for our Gilbert. What should we do without him?

FOSKER: Was his luxury private bath inefficient?

2ND YOUNG GIRL: 'Wanton' is good coming from Gilbert. Does he wanton in his bath?

YOUNG GENTLEMAN: Love from Gilbert. All love, Gilbert.

FOSKER: Love. Love from Gilbert – that's funny.

(*They go.* PINFOLD *leaves his cabin in a rage and confronts* CAPTAIN STEERFORTH, *who is crossing the deck.*)

PINFOLD: Captain Steerforth, may I speak to you for a moment?

CAPTAIN: Surely. What can I do for you?

PINFOLD: First, I want to know whether radiograms sent from your ship are confidential documents.

CAPTAIN: I'm sorry, I'm afraid I don't understand you.

PINFOLD: Captain Steerforth, since I came on board I have sent out a large number of messages of an entirely private character. This morning, early, there was a group of passengers reading them aloud.

CAPTAIN: How many of these radiograms were there?

PINFOLD: I don't know exactly. About a dozen.

CAPTAIN: And when did you send them?

PINFOLD: At various times during the early days of the voyage.

CAPTAIN: (*Perplexed*) This is only our fifth day out, you know.

PINFOLD: (*Disconcerted*) Are you sure?

CAPTAIN: Yes, of course I'm sure.

PINFOLD: It seems longer.

CAPTAIN: How were these radiograms sent, Mr Pinfold?

PINFOLD: One of the stewards wrote the forms for me. I haven't been too well – one I sent myself –

(CAPTAIN STEERFORTH *summons the* ENGLISH STEWARD.)

CAPTAIN: Steward, this is Mr Pinfold, a passenger.

ENGLISH STEWARD: Yes, Sir, I've seen him before.

CAPTAIN: He wants to enquire about some radiograms he says you wrote out for him. Could you ask the wireless operator for his file?

ENGLISH STEWARD: Very good, Sir.

(*He exits.*)

CAPTAIN: We'll soon get to the bottom of this.

PINFOLD: I hope so. (*Pause.*) I hope so.

(*The* ENGLISH STEWARD *returns with a file.*)

ENGLISH STEWARD: Wireless Op. says we've had very little private traffic, Sir. Easy to check.

CAPTAIN: (*Taking the file*) Yes. Here we are. The day before yesterday. Just the one. 'Entirely cured. All love.'

PINFOLD: (*Bewildered*) But the others?

ENGLISH STEWARD: There were no others, Sir.

PINFOLD: A dozen or more.

ENGLISH STEWARD: Only this one, Sir.

PINFOLD: What about the one I sent the evening I came aboard?

ENGLISH STEWARD: That would have gone by Post Office Telegraph, Sir.

PINFOLD: And you wouldn't have a copy here?

ENGLISH STEWARD: No, Sir.

PINFOLD: Then how was it possible for a group of passengers to read it aloud at eight o'clock this morning?

CAPTAIN: Quite impossible, Mr Pinfold. I was on duty myself at that time and there were few passengers about. And the wireless office does not open until nine. (*Pause.*) Does that satisfy all your questions, Mr Pinfold?

PINFOLD: Not quite. May I speak to you privately?

(CAPTAIN STEERFORTH *dismisses the* ENGLISH STEWARD.)

Captain Steerforth, I am the victim of a practical joke.

CAPTAIN: Something of the sort, it seems.

PINFOLD: Not for the first time. Ever since I came on board this ship – you say it's only been five days?

CAPTAIN: Four, actually.

PINFOLD: Ever since I came on board, I have been the victim of hoaxes and threats. Mind you, I'm not making any accusation. I don't know the names of these people, I don't even know what they look like. I am not asking for an official investigation – yet. What I do know is that the leaders comprise a family of four.

CAPTAIN: I don't believe we have any families on board. Except the Angels. I hardly think they're the sort of family to play practical jokes on anyone. A very quiet family.

(PINFOLD *is alerted by something the* CAPTAIN *has said; some memory has stirred. He is becoming excited but doing his best to conceal his feelings with a degree of cunning.*)

PINFOLD: And I don't suppose there are people travelling who aren't on the passenger list?

CAPTAIN: No one, I assure you.

PINFOLD: What about Fosker?

CAPTAIN: No, we haven't anyone aboard called Fosker.

PINFOLD: And that dark little man who always sits alone?

CAPTAIN: Him? I know him well. He often travels with us. Mr Murdoch. He's on the list.

(PINFOLD *abruptly walks away as though something has been confirmed.* CAPTAIN STEERFORTH *shrugs and continues on his rounds.*)

PINFOLD: No families on board except –

(*He stops himself from saying any more. He looks about. His excitement is difficult to contain.*)

Oh God! Of course! I am near to a full explanation! I have followed so many false clues, reached so many absurd conclusions. But now I know the truth! I understand it all! I am in a position to name the villain! Angel!

(*Blackout.*

Lights up on ANGEL, *who stands on an upper level in a commanding position.*)

ANGEL: Keep him under continual observation. Immediate reports are to be made to headquarters of his every move. I want the reports concise, factual and accurate.

(*Lights snap on the others; except for* MARGARET *their voices are the voices of automata.*)

MOTHER: Gilbert has sat down at his table. He's reading the menu. Take over, Baker.

FOSKER: O.K. Abel. He's ordering wine. He's ordered a plate of cold ham. Take over, Charlie.

2ND YOUNG GIRL: O.K. Baker. He's eating. (*Pause.*) Take over, Dog.

1ST GENERAL: O.K. Charlie. Gilbert coming up to main deck. Take over, Easy.

2ND YOUNG GIRL: O.K. Dog. Gilbert now approaching door on port side, going out on deck. Take over, Fox.

YOUNG GENTLEMAN: O.K. Easy. Gilbert walking the deck anti-clockwise. He's approaching the main door, starboard side. Take over, George.

2ND GENERAL: O.K. Fox. He's sitting down with a book.

ANGEL: O.K. George. Stay on duty in lounge. Report any move. I'll have you relieved at three.

MOTHER: A to H.Q. A to H.Q.

ANGEL: Come in, Abel.

MOTHER: His head's lolling. Gilbert seems punch-drunk.

2ND GENERAL: G to H.Q. G to H.Q.

ANGEL: Come in, George.

2ND GENERAL: Confirm A's report. Gilbert's in a sort of daze.

MOTHER: Gilbert's falling asleep . . .
> (*Lights dim.*
> *Pause.*
> *Lights snap on.*)

2ND GENERAL: Gilbert's awake again. Fifty-one minutes.

ANGEL: That's better than the time before.

MARGARET: But it isn't enough.

ANGEL: Give him the Swiss therapy.

MARGARET: Swiss therapy?

ANGEL: For neurotic industrial workers. The most soporific noises are those of a factory.
> (*Loud clanging of machinery.*
> *Lights snap on on* PINFOLD *in his cabin.*)

PINFOLD: You bloody fools. I'm not a factory worker. You're driving me mad.

ANGEL: No, no, Gilbert, you *are* mad already. We're driving you sane.
> (*Factory noise continues.*)
> Gilbert not asleep yet? Report please.

1ST GENERAL: 0312 hours. 'You bloody fools. I'm not a factory worker.'

ANGEL: Well, nor he is.

1ST GENERAL: 'You're driving me mad.'

ANGEL: I believe we are. Turn off that record. Give him something rural.
> (*Factory noise stops. Singing nightingales take over.*

PINFOLD *rises and leaves his cabin, coming to the ship's rail.*)
GONERIL'S VOICE: Go on, Gilbert. Jump. In you go.
(*He backs away.*)
Water-funk.
PINFOLD: (*Desperate*) I know all about that actor, you know.
Cedric Thorne. The friend of Angel's who hanged himself in
his dressing-room.
ANGEL: Why do you call me Angel?
PINFOLD: Because it's your name. I know exactly what you're
doing for the BBC. I know exactly what you did to Cedric
Thorne. I know exactly what you're trying to do to me.
ANGEL: Liar.
GONERIL'S VOICE: Liar.
MARGARET: I told you, Gilbert's no fool.
PINFOLD: (*Driving home his advantage*) You have the technical
skill to use the defects of the ship's communication system.
You 'half-expected' Cedric Thorne to kill himself. You bore
a grudge for the poor figure you cut at Lychpole, found me
by chance alone and ill and defenceless, ripe for revenge. I
shall expose you.
(PINFOLD *marches into his cabin, sits down and begins to write a
letter at speed.* ANGEL *signals for the others to go. Alone, his
manner is wheedling*:)
ANGEL: Look here, Gilbert, you've got us all wrong. What we're
doing is nothing to do with the BBC. It's a private enterprise
entirely. And as for Cedric – that wasn't our fault. He came
to us too late. We did everything we could for him. He was a
hopeless case.
(PINFOLD *writes furiously.*)
Why don't you answer? Can't you hear me, Gilbert? Why
don't you answer?
(PINFOLD *continues to write.*)
Gilbert, what are you doing?
PINFOLD: I'm writing to my wife!
(*Lights out on* PINFOLD *and* ANGEL.
MRS PINFOLD *enters, reading.*)
MRS PINFOLD: 'Darling, this has not proved a happy ship and I
have decided to get off at Port Said and go on by aeroplane.

Do you remember the tick with a beard called Angel who came to Lychpole from the BBC? He is on board with a team bound for Aden. These BBC people have made themselves a great nuisance to me on board. They have something that is really a glorified form of Reggie Upton's Box. Angel's Box is able to speak and hear. In fact I spend most of my days and nights carrying on conversations with people I never see. They are trying to psychoanalyse me. I know this sounds absurd. The Germans at the end of the war were developing this Box for the examination of prisoners. The Russians have perfected it. As you can imagine it's a hellish invention in the wrong hands. Angel's are very much the wrong hands. As I said, I'm leaving the ship. All love. G.'

(*Pause. She looks up.*)

Oh dear.

(*Lights out on* MRS PINFOLD.

Lights up on PINFOLD *in his cabin and on the others, who form a circle round him.*)

GONERIL: You can't go, Gilbert. They won't let you off the ship.

ANGEL: You mustn't go, Gilbert.

PINFOLD: Mr Pinfold to you. And I am leaving the ship.

GONERIL: We'll give you hell for this, Gilbert.

MOTHER: We'll get you and you know it.

2ND YOUNG GIRL: We'll get you.

FOSKER: We'll never let you go. Your passport expired last week.

MOTHER: You haven't got the money.

2ND YOUNG GIRL: They don't take travellers' cheques in Egypt.

PINFOLD: Shut up! Shut up! Shut up!

(PINFOLD *looks for and finds a copy of a book.*)

ANGEL: You don't understand the importance of the work we're doing. Did you see *The Cocktail Party?* Do you remember the second act? We're like the people in that, a little band doing good, sworn to secrecy, working behind the scenes everywhere –

PINFOLD: (*Reading*) '*Westward Ho!* Chapter One. How Mr Oxenham saw the white bird. The hollow oak our place is, our heritage the sea. All who have travelled through the delicious scenery of North Devon – '

ANGEL: What are you up to, Gilbert?

PINFOLD: I'm going to wear you down with sheer boredom! (*Reading.*) '– must needs know the little white town of Bideford, which slopes towards – '

GONERIL: *Biddy*ford, Gilbert, not Bideford, *Biddyford*! (PINFOLD *continues reading the first page of* Westward Ho! *aloud.*)

ANGEL: You can't leave the ship, Gilbert. You can't. (PINFOLD *reads continuously.*)

MOTHER: You're under observation, Gilbert.

1ST GENERAL: They'll keep you in a home because you're mad, Gilbert. (PINFOLD *continues reading.*)

2ND GENERAL: Mad!

FOSKER: Mad! (*One after the other they repeat the word 'mad' with greater and greater frequency.* PINFOLD *continues his reading, struggling against them, slowly wearing them down.*)

ALL: Gilbert, for God's sake stop!

ANGEL: Leave the bloody ship! (*Blackout.*

Lights up on MRS PINFOLD, *reading a second letter.*)

MRS PINFOLD: 'I have arrived by aeroplane but I had a disappointment leaving the ship. I thought I should get out of range of those psychoanalysts and their infernal Box. But not at all. As I write this letter they keep interrupting. There must be some way of cutting the 'vital waves'. I think it might be worth consulting Father Westmacott when I get back. He knows all about existentialism and psychology and ghosts and diabolic possession. Sometimes I wonder whether it is not literally the Devil who is molesting me. All love, G.'

A cable. I must send a cable to Colombo.

(*Blackout.*

Lights up on PINFOLD, *reading a telegram.*)

PINFOLD: (*Puzzled*) 'Implore you return immediately' . . . ? What can be wrong with her? Can she be ill? Has the house burned down? Perhaps she's concerned on my account. But surely I've said nothing to cause alarm.

(*Lights up on* GONERIL *and* ANGEL *in the upper area.*)

GONERIL: You hate your wife, don't you, Gilbert?

ANGEL: You don't want to go home, do you?

GONERIL: You dread seeing her again, don't you, Gilbert?

PINFOLD: (*Defiantly*) I wish to send a telegram: 'Returning at once. Just off to Mass. Love.'

(*A choir sings. The sound of the Mass begins and continues.*)

GONERIL: Oh, Gilbert, it's all nonsense. You don't believe in God.

ANGEL: There's no one here to show off to, Gilbert.

GONERIL: No one will listen to your prayers – except us.

ANGEL: *We* shall hear them.

GONERIL: You're going to pray to be left alone, aren't you, Gilbert?

ANGEL: Aren't you?

GONERIL: But only we will hear you and we won't let you alone.

ANGEL: Never, Gilbert, never.

(GONERIL *laughs.*)

What is it?

GONERIL: Have you seen to whom the Church is dedicated? St Michael and the Angels!

(*They both laugh. Lights out on them.*

PINFOLD *kneels.*

MARGARET *enters and also kneels.*)

PINFOLD: Margaret . . .

MARGARET: Gilbert.

PINFOLD: Are all the others with you? Or is it just Goneril and Angel?

MARGARET: There never were any others, Gilbert. Oh darling, you are slow on the uptake. What you heard was my brother. He's really awfully good at imitations. That's how he first got taken on by the BBC.

PINFOLD: (*Hopelessly lost*) I think I'm beginning to understand.

MARGARET: Oh Gilbert, you don't understand. We're only trying to help you.

PINFOLD: Who said I needed help?

MARGARET: Don't be cross, darling; not with me anyway. And you did need help, you know. Often their plans work beautifully.

PINFOLD: Well you must realise by now that it hasn't worked with me.

MARGARET: Oh no. It hasn't worked at all.

PINFOLD: Then why not leave me alone?

MARGARET: They never will now, because they hate you. And I never will, never. You see, I love you so. Try not to hate me, darling.

(*Both respond in Latin to the Mass.*)

PINFOLD: Margaret, are you a Catholic?

MARGARET: In a way.

PINFOLD: In what way?

MARGARET: That's something you mustn't ask.

(*They rise to recite the Creed.*)

Pray for *them*, Gilbert. They need prayers.

PINFOLD: I can't. I can't.

(*Lights out.*

Roar of an aeroplane.

Lights up on four aeroplane seats. PINFOLD *and* MARGARET *sit in the front two,* ANGEL *and* GONERIL *behind.*)

TANNOY: Ladies and gentlemen, we have just crossed the English coast at Clacton-on-Sea. Weather conditions in London are cold and raining.

ANGEL: (*Urgently*) Gilbert, listen to me. We've got to come to some arrangement. Time's getting short. Gilbert, old boy, do be reasonable. I want to apologise. I've made a mess of the whole Plan.

PINFOLD: You certainly have.

ANGEL: It was a serious scientific experiment. Then I let personal malice interfere. I'm sorry.

PINFOLD: Well, keep quiet then.

ANGEL: That's just what I want to suggest. Look here, let's do a deal. I promise on my honour we'll none of us ever worry you again. All we ask in return is that you don't say anything to anyone in England about us. It could ruin our whole work if it got talked about. Just say nothing and you'll never hear from us again.

PINFOLD: I'll think it over. I'll let you know when I reach London. But you're in a panic now, aren't you, at the prospect of getting into trouble with the BBC?

MARGARET: Not the BBC, darling. It isn't them that worry him. They know all about his experiments. No. It's Reggie Graves-Upton. The Bruiser. *He* must never know. Gilbert, you must never tell anyone, promise, especially not The Bruiser.

PINFOLD: And you, Meg, are you going to leave me alone too?

MARGARET: Oh, Gilbert dearest, it's not a thing to joke about. I've so loved being with you. I shall miss you more than anyone I've known in my life. I shall never forget you. It will be a kind of death for me. But I know I have to suffer. I'll be brave. You must accept the offer, Gilbert.

ANGEL: Well, what's your answer?

PINFOLD: I said London.

ANGEL: Is it a deal?

TANNOY: Ladies and Gentlemen, we are approaching London airport. Fasten your seat belts and no smoking – Thank you.

ANGEL: Well, is it a deal?

PINFOLD: The answer is: no.

ANGEL: (*Horrified*) You can't mean it! Why, Mr Pinfold, Sir, why?

PINFOLD: Because I don't accept your word of honour.

ANGEL: All right, Gilbert, if that's the way you want it –

PINFOLD: Don't call me 'Gilbert' and don't talk like a film gangster.

ANGEL: (*Lamely*) All right, Gilbert. You'll pay for this.

(*Lights out.*

Lights up: PINFOLD's *study at Lychpole.*

MRS PINFOLD *enters and gazes on* PINFOLD, *who enters, as do* ANGEL, GONERIL *and* MARGARET.)

MRS PINFOLD: You *look* all right.

PINFOLD: I am all right. I'm sorry not to be more demonstrative but it's a little embarrassing having three people listening to everything I say.

GONERIL: How you hate her, Gilbert. How she bores you.

ANGEL: Don't believe a word she says.

MARGARET: She's very pretty, and very kind. But she's not good enough for you. I suppose you think I'm jealous. Well, I am.

PINFOLD: (*To* MRS PINFOLD) I'm sorry to be so
  uncommunicative but you see these abominable people keep
  talking to me.
MRS PINFOLD: Most distracting.
PINFOLD: Most.
  (*Pause.*)
MRS PINFOLD: (*Gently*) You know, Gilbert, you've got it all
  wrong about this Mr Angel. As soon as I got your letter I
  telephoned the BBC and enquired. Angel has been in
  England all the time.
GONERIL: Don't listen to her.
ANGEL: She's lying.
PINFOLD: Are you absolutely sure?
MRS PINFOLD: Oh yes. Here's a letter to prove it.
PINFOLD: (*Taking the letter*) I – I simply don't know what to make
  of this.
ANGEL: I may as well tell you the truth. We never were in that
  ship. We worked the whole thing from the studio in
  England.
PINFOLD: They must be working the whole thing from a studio in
  England.
MRS PINFOLD: My poor darling, no one's 'worked' anything.
  You're imagining it all. Just to make sure I asked Father
  Westmacott as you suggested. He says the whole thing's
  utterly impossible. There just isn't any sort of invention by
  the Gestapo or the BBC or the Existentialists or the psycho-
  analysts – nothing at all, the least like what you think.
PINFOLD: A Box?
MRS PINFOLD: No Box.
ANGEL: } Don't believe her. She's lying! She's lying . . . !
GONERIL:
  (*They run off, their voices dying away.*)
PINFOLD: You mean that everything I've heard said, I've been
  saying to myself? It's hardly conceivable.
MARGARET: It's perfectly true, darling. There isn't anyone. I
  don't exist, Gilbert. There isn't any me, anywhere at all . . .
  but I do love you, Gilbert. I don't exist but I do love . . .
  Goodbye . . . Love . . . I do love . . . I do love . . .

(*She runs off, her voice echoing and dying away. Silence.*)

PINFOLD: They've gone. In that minute. Gone for good.

MRS PINFOLD: I hope that's true. (*Pause.*) Father Westmacott gave me the name of a man he says we can trust.

PINFOLD: A loony doctor?

MRS PINFOLD: A psychologist – but a Catholic, so he must be all right.

PINFOLD: No. I've had enough of psychology. (*Pause; then half to himself:*) I've endured a great ordeal and, unaided, emerged the victor. There is a triumph to be celebrated, even if a mocking slave stands always beside me in my chariot reminding me of mortality. (*To* MRS PINFOLD.) Have a fire lighted in here. I'm going to do some writing.

(MRS PINFOLD *exits.* PINFOLD *turns, goes to his table and sits down. He begins to write.*)

'The Ordeal of Gilbert Pinfold. A Conversation Piece. Chapter One: Portrait of the Artist in Middle Age . . .'

(*The lights begin to fade. Only* PINFOLD *is illuminated. All around him is shadowy. Out of the darkness, very dim and shadowy,* MARGARET *appears and seems to look over his shoulder at what he writes. He is oblivious to her.*)

'It may happen in the next hundred years that the English novelists of the present day will come to be valued . . .'

(*He continues to write.*

The lights fade to blackness.)

AFTER THE LIONS

For
Michael Elliott

CHARACTERS

MAJOR DENUCÉ
SARAH
PITOU
MADAME DE GOURNAY

There are also TWO MILITARY ORDERLIES who double as the
OLD CARPENTER and the YOUNG CARPENTER, and one woman
who occasionally stands in as SARAH's double.

The action takes place mostly in Sarah's rented villa in Andernos,
near Bordeaux, 1914–15, and at the battle-front.

ACT ONE:
Winter

ACT TWO:
Spring

After the Lions was first presented at the Royal Exchange Theatre, Manchester, on 18 November 1982. The cast was as follows:

MAJOR DENUCÉ	John Cording
SARAH	Dorothy Tutin
PITOU	Russell Hunter
MADAME DE GOURNAY	Sheila Reid
OLD CARPENTER/WOUNDED SOLDIER	Tom Harrison
YOUNG CARPENTER/MILITARY ORDERLY	Richard Gallagher
THE WOMAN	Wendy Gerrard
Directed by	Michael Elliott
Music by	Alexandra Harwood

A NOTE ON THE PLAY

After the Lions is intended as a companion piece to my other play with a theatrical setting, *The Dresser*, and I shall give them the collective title of *Plays Theatrical*. A third may be added in time but I do not wish to imply anything as grand as a trilogy; it is simply that, in the course of my work over the past few years, the theatre has been my principal preoccupation and it has emerged as a fitting, not to say inescapable, background for themes and variations which I have wanted to explore.

Sarah Bernhardt is an historical figure and so, I suppose, *After the Lions* is an historical play. But I have not attempted to write a chronicle in the traditional sense. I deal with one incident towards the end of her life because that incident seemed to me to express another aspect of the subject matter with which *The Dresser* was concerned. I plead guilty, therefore, not, I hope, to distorting history, but to interpreting events and motives where necessary.

Fortunately for me there is no great detail concerning the periods immediately preceding and following the amputation of Sarah's right leg. We know that doctors in Paris refused to operate; we know that at the outbreak of the Great War she removed to a villa near Bordeaux; we know she was accompanied by her secretary, Pitou, and her maid-cum-companion Madame de Gournay; we know, too, that an Army doctor, Major Denucé, agreed to remove the leg above the knee. Wilfred Owen, serving with the British forces in France, sent a picture postcard of Le Grand Théâtre, Bordeaux, to his cousin, Leslie Gunston, dated 23 February 1915.

'. . . You may be interested to know that Sarah Bernhardt has gone through the operation all right. The doctor (Denucé) was the same who 'miraculised' upon one of my boys here. I pass by where Sarah lies daily.'
(From *Wilfred Owen, Collected Letters*, London, 1967.)

Of her convalescence, her unsuccessful struggle to walk with an artificial limb, her efforts to return to the stage, there is only fragmentary evidence. She did, however, indeed visit the French soldiers at the front shortly after her operation.

Little is known of the private lives of Pitou, Madame de Gournay and Major Denucé. In biographies of Sarah, Pitou is always mentioned. He is invariably described as 'faithful', 'meticulous' and 'fussy'. He is written about only in relation to his famous employer and emerges as a devoted servant in keeping with the known, documented facts. But the dramatist has licence to invent and embroider where the scarcity of fact bleaches the more vivid human colours.

Even so I feel duty-bound to acknowledge my debt to several authors who have written about Sarah Bernhardt and whose insights have quickened my imagination: James and May Agate, Lysiane Bernhardt, Reynaldo Hahn, Marie Colombier and Maurice Rostand. Sarah Bernhardt's autobiography, *My Double Life*, was, of course, invaluable. *Sarah Bernhardt* by Maurice Baring (London, 1933) was of particular importance to me. I am, however, especially indebted to Joanna Richardson whose fine biography *Sarah Bernhardt* (London, 1959) brilliantly illuminates the actress's character and talent, and whose delightful shorter work, *Sarah Bernhardt and her World* (London, 1977) was, for its text and splendid pictures, the most helpful of all.

R.H.

Liss, August 1982

ACT ONE

Winter.
The drawing room of SARAH'*s rented villa, 'fin-de-siècle', over-*
decorated: Oriental carpet, Mexican sombreros, feather parasols,
trophies of lances and daggers, a host of Buddhas, Japanese monsters,
Chinese curios, ivory work, bronzes, jackals' and hyenas' heads,
panthers' paws. There is a silk-lined coffin, a desk with a telephone,
chairs, a divan covered in skins, a table with a phonograph, a camera
with a cloth and a magnesium flash.
The sound of sea.
Lights:
SARAH *is seated in a wheelchair, her right leg bandaged and extended.*
She is heavily made up and wears a bright red wig. She is attended by
MME DE GOURNAY. MAJOR DENUCÉ *is replacing his stethoscope in*
a medical bag. PITOU *watches a little apart from the others.*

DENUCÉ: Above the knee.

SARAH: So be it.

DENUCÉ: You are certain? Above the knee.

SARAH: Since there is nothing else to be done, why ask my
opinion? Will you make the necessary arrangements without
delay?

DENUCÉ: Wish I was convinced.

SARAH: Convinced or not, do as I ask.

DENUCÉ: These last weeks have had some experience of
amputation. In months to come no doubt more. Youngsters,
of course, bullet wounds and gangrene, results not always –

SARAH: Is it my age?

DENUCÉ: Certainly a factor.

SARAH: Major, I am asking you to remove my right leg for one
reason and one reason only: so that I can return to work. Not
to prolong my life, but to allow me to work. I must *act*. I
must go to the battlefield, I must comfort our brave soldiers
at the front. I must work.

DENUCÉ: The risks –

SARAH: If I die, so be it, but my only chance of ever acting again is to have my leg cut off. Two doctors in Paris have already refused. They wept at the thought of maiming me, I, the divine Sarah – (*A stab of pain.*) I need a man of steel. A soldier. You are my last and only hope. Telephone the hospital. Make the arrangements.

DENUCÉ: Consider consequences. One leg. Artificial limb not easy. Sticks. Crutches.

SARAH: Yes, but after the amputation I hope people will say it's better to see Sarah with one leg than not at all –

DENUCÉ: As what? Forgive harshness. One leg. See you as what?

SARAH: In the theatre it's not the illusion of sight that matters, but the kindling of the imagination. Second-rate actors may be beautiful, athletic, even look the part, but I can give you the very essence of a life in my own terms. I created the role of a sixteen-year-old boy, the Duke of Reichstag, the eaglet, when I was fifty-six years old. I never had a more authentic triumph.

DENUCÉ: True. Saw you. Such grace. Extraordinary.

SARAH: When I act it is my spirit which shines through. And I have an unquenchable spirit.

(*She weeps.* PITOU *draws* DENUCÉ *aside.*)

PITOU: Pathetic old hag, isn't she? Speaks in quotations from her press-cuttings. I've been her secretary for years. She gets loopier and loopier. I've seen it happening. Chop the damn thing off. Give us some peace.

(SARAH *recovers a little.*)

SARAH: I dare to believe I'm capable yet of great things, and I am fortified in the face of this awful affliction by my art. But I cannot exercise my art in pain. Take away the pain.

DENUCÉ: Can't guarantee success.

SARAH: Our professions are remarkably similar.

DENUCÉ: Do my best.

SARAH: Do better. Work miracles.

DENUCÉ: Grave responsibility. Can't even guarantee that afterwards you'll stand upright.

SARAH: Then I shall have plays written for me in which I sit on a throne.

(*Pause.*)

DENUCÉ: This evening. To Bordeaux. Ambulance at six.
Operation tomorrow, a.m., early.

SARAH: Thank you. And may I ask you one more favour?

DENUCÉ: Anything. Ask. Do.

SARAH: Stop talking like a telegram.
(DENUCÉ *laughs*.)

DENUCÉ: Comes from training dogs. Hobby. And Army, of
course. Short, sharp commands. Habit. Apologies.

SARAH: Accepted stop. Must ask further question stop. Regards
Sarah.

DENUCÉ: Not used to being teased.

PITOU: But you like it, don't you, you like it. Here, doggy-doggy-
doggy, here doggy-doggy, good boy, good boy. Down.

SARAH: (*To* DENUCÉ) Pitou. He's been my secretary for years.
He's perfectly pleasant when we're alone, and he makes me
laugh, but he's becoming –
(*She winces with pain*.)

PITOU: Beg, beg.

SARAH: (*To* DENUCÉ) There is something that worries me deeply.
Pitou, shut your ears.
(PITOU *sticks his fingers in his ears*.)
Will I be shaved?

DENUCÉ: What?

SARAH: Shaved, shaved, you know very well what I mean. A
young actress once told me that being shaved was more
unpleasant than the operation itself, but then I think it was
something other than her leg that was being removed.

DENUCÉ: Shaved! See what you mean. No. Not shaved. Not
necessary.

SARAH: All right, Pitou.
(*She mimes to him to remove his fingers and he does so*.)

PITOU: What a ridiculous thing to ask a doctor. I'm sorry. I
couldn't help hearing. What does a doctor know about such
matters? You ask a priest whether or not you'll be saved.
(SARAH *stares at him uncomprehending, laughs, but then winces
with pain*.)
(*To* DENUCÉ.) Not many people can make her laugh. I once
made her laugh in Toronto. That's quite a feat, making

someone laugh in Toronto. She gave me an acting lesson.
Horror. Passion. Laughter. Tears. Very comic.

SARAH: Pitou, be quiet. This is serious.

PITOU: So are horror, passion –

SARAH: (*Interrupting*) Is there anything else for which I should be
prepared? I don't like to be surprised.

DENUCÉ: You'll be asleep. Anaesthetic.

SARAH: I know that. I didn't think you intended to allow me to sit
up and watch while you sawed through the bone.

PITOU: He's an army doctor, you never know.

SARAH: What a wonderful experience this will be for me. The
main action of the drama occurs while I'm asleep. Very
unusual. I hope you have a steady hand.

(*A pause,* DENUCÉ *begins to cry.*)

DENUCÉ: Can't do it, can't do it, can't –

PITOU: Oh my God, not another one. You should've gone to that
English doctor. The English don't cry.

DENUCÉ: Cannot cripple a goddess.

SARAH: How touching.

DENUCÉ: Saw you first as Marguerite Gautier. I was twelve.
Thirty years ago.

SARAH: Not so touching.

DENUCÉ: Don't ask me to amputate.

(*He weeps.*)

PITOU: Yes, a man of steel.

SARAH: (*to* DENUCÉ) Come to me.

(DENUCÉ *goes to her and kneels. She comforts him.*)

DENUCÉ: Apologize. Unprofessional. Unmanly. Unsoldierly.

(*He weeps.*)

SARAH: We must all play our part. Your role is to amputate my
leg. All your distinguished colleagues tell me you are a fine
surgeon. I came here especially to find you. This is not the
sort of house I would normally inhabit. You should have
seen the decorations. Some people's taste is extraordinary.
And will it be easier for you to know that I shall be grateful?
The pain invades my waking and sleepless hours. Nine years
of pain. Sometimes I have wanted to wrench the leg from its
socket with my bare hands.

DENUCÉ: Your portrait above my bed. Next to Salomé.

SARAH: Salomé?

DENUCÉ: First pet. Black labrador.

(PITOU *laughs, makes a note.*)

You stricken. You. Of all people.

SARAH: You'll tell your grandchildren: I gave Sarah relief from
pain by removing her leg. And it's been a much admired leg.
(*A stab of pain.*) Poets have written odes to the way I walked.
'Queen of the Attitude', I was called. Were it not so swollen
now, so ugly and diseased, once removed it would make a
fine exhibit for a side-show: Sarah's leg, sawn from her body
by Major Denucé. Don't cry. You are doing me a great
service. Isn't this typical? The story of my life. I am the one
in pain, yet I am called upon to comfort others.

PITOU: Typical. I don't ever remember you doing it before.

SARAH: (*To* DENUCÉ) There, there. (*She takes his hands*.) A
surgeon's hands, a magician's hands. How beautiful they
are, how –

(*A terrible silence.*)

Filthy! They're filthy! Look at the nails, they're black with
grime. Call yourself a doctor? Get away from me. I've never
seen such dirty nails in all my life. Don't dare touch me.
Have you been patting your dogs? Pitou, see that he washes
his hands.

(*At speed, overlapping*:)

PITOU: At once, immediately, come along –

DENUCÉ: Let go of me –

SARAH: He must wash his hands –

PITOU: Come along, you heard what she said, soap and hot water
for you, my boy –

DENUCÉ: My hands are not dirty –

SARAH: The germs, I'll die of septicaemia –

DENUCÉ: A bruised nail, not dirt –

SARAH: Go and scrub those revolting fingers clean –

PITOU: A bath, you must have a bath. (*Calling.*) Run the bath,
run the bath! Here, boy, here, boy, here –

DENUCÉ: (*To* PITOU) Let go of me!

SARAH: (*To* MME DE GOURNAY) Take me away. I can't bear this, such blackness –

PITOU: Into the bath immediately, clothes and all, good boy, good boy –

(MME DE GOURNAY *wheels* SARAH *off quickly. The instant she is gone,* PITOU *lets go of* DENUCÉ, *relaxes, sits, makes a note in his notebook.*)

DENUCÉ: (*Enraged*) Nearly struck you. Hard. Hate to be touched.

PITOU: You know what I think? I think she's insane. What worries me is, is it catching?

DENUCÉ: Don't like being grabbed. Don't like being touched.

PITOU: One has to humour her.

DENUCÉ: A bruised nail, that's all.

PITOU: She always exaggerates.

DENUCÉ: In the mess. Cracking walnuts with a hammer.

PITOU: Insane. No wonder she's on the list of hostages the Germans want to take if they enter Paris. We had to get out. The government insisted. That's why we're here. And do you know the reason? When the Germans invited her to appear in Berlin, they asked what her terms were. She replied: Alsace-Lorraine. Asking for trouble. I wish they would take her hostage. No one would pay the ransom.

DENUCÉ: Lost a button. (*He looks for it.*) Gold button with regimental coat-of-arms.

PITOU: Why do we bother with her? Do you know the main attraction of this area? A sand-dune. When the wind blows, the sand gets in your hair, in your mouth –

DENUCÉ: Can't go round improperly dressed.

PITOU: And it could all have been avoided, if only I had been more vigilant. I blame no one but myself. And her.

DENUCÉ: Help me look.

PITOU: For want of a mattress a leg is lost.

DENUCÉ: Don't understand a word you say –

PITOU: Then I'll explain.

DENUCÉ: Ah. Found it. (*He picks up the button.*)

PITOU: Did you ever see her as Floria in *Tosca*?

DENUCÉ: No.

PITOU: Rio de Janeiro, the night of 9th October, one thousand, nine hundred and five years after the birth of Our Lord, Jesus Christ. Disaster. Nine years ago, nine years of disaster. *Tosca*, she as Floria, the last act, the last scene. She is on the battlements, pacing and passionate. 'Yes,' she howls, 'I killed your Scarpio, killed, killed, do you hear?' They send an officer. He returns. 'Yes,' he says, 'Scarpio is dead.' And then Spoletta looks up at her on the ramparts and shouts, 'Ah! Devil! I will send you to join your dead lover!' She is still for a moment. She looks down on them. She speaks. 'I go willingly.' She cries. And then, so quickly, seeing is believing, in one spectacular leap, she throws herself off the platform and falls to her death – to great applause, of course. God knows how many times she made that leap, landing – unseen by the audience – on a great mound of mattresses. A famous leap. Floria's leap. On that night, 9th October, 1905, in Rio de Janeiro, there were no mattresses. Someone had forgotten to set them. She landed on the hard floor on her right knee, her cry of pain drowned by the tumultuous cheers. Nine years ago. Nine years of increasing pain. Why didn't I check the mattresses? Why didn't she?

DENUCÉ: Accident. Inexplicable. Shall I make the arrangements?
(DENUCÉ *goes to the telephone.*)

PITOU: 'I go willingly.' Ironic. Haunting. We have a phonograph record of her in *Tosca*. I play it often, God knows why. Always in moments of stress. Over and over again. (*He laughs.*) 'I go willingly.'
(DENUCÉ *lifts the telephone and taps the receiver.* SARAH *wheels herself in;* DENUCÉ *immediately replaces the receiver.*)

SARAH: I apologize. My courage is skin-deep. In my head a sudden black and awful chasm opened. Before me flashed brief but vivid images, playing cards riffled by a conjuror. A knife, hacked flesh, pulsing blood, a face masked, my dismembered limb lying beside me, the knee level with my eyes, a dead lover, a still-born child. Always I have tried to harness my terror to gain repose, but in that moment I faltered. My fear insulted you. I am through the blackness now. I want nothing but to be free of pain, and to face the future. I will be calm and practical. I shall go willingly. Please make the arrangements.

(MME DE GOURNAY *wheels* SARAH *towards the exit, but* SARAH
stops her.)

(*To* PITOU.) Send a telegram to my son, in Paris – 'Maurice
my darling. Tomorrow they are cutting off my leg stop.
Spread the word stop. Sarah is looking for left-legged parts.
Love Mama.'

(MME DE GOURNAY *wheels her out*. PITOU *whistles tunelessly*.)

DENUCÉ: You annoy me.

PITOU: We must all play our part.

(DENUCÉ *goes to the telephone and lifts the receiver*.)

DENUCÉ: (*Into the telephone*) Hospital Bordeaux urgent. (*To*
PITOU.) Extraordinary woman.

(PITOU *takes up a sheet of folded newspaper and begins to cut a
pattern*.)

PITOU: She's not a goddess, you know. She's an old, sick woman,
nothing special. Shall I tell you something about the Divine
Sarah? She is not divine at all. She is of the earth, earth-
bound. She is her own *axis-mundi*.

(*He continues to cut the newspaper*.)

Snip-snip, snip-snip. We are talking about a mad woman.
Have you noticed the coffin? Do you know what she does?
She lies in that coffin, a black muslin veil covering her face,
she lies in her coffin to learn her lines. Have you ever heard
such madness? And that's not the only reason she lies in the
coffin. Once, at night, I came by chance into the room and
she was not alone. You wouldn't think there's room for two
in a coffin, but she could make love in a wash basin. And
probably has.

DENUCÉ: (*Into the telephone*) Doctor Vandal. Denucé. Confirm
surgery. a.m. Good.

(*He replaces the receiver*.)

(*To* PITOU.) Operation tomorrow, 0700. All arrangements
made.

(PITOU *unfolds a string of paper men and snips off the leg of one
of them.*

Blackout.

In the darkness, voices are heard from a phonograph:)

OFFICER: 'Scarpio is dead!'

(*Angry shouts.*)

SPOLETTA: 'Ah! Devil! I will send you to join your dead lover!'

SARAH: 'I go willingly.'

(*A brief pause, then the sound of the phonograph hissing and clicking.*
Lights.
The hissing and clicking continue. MME DE GOURNAY *is seated, using scissors to cut a black silk stocking just above the knee. She does this to two or three stockings, then begins to stitch the upper piece together, discarding the longer part.* DENUCÉ *is adjusting the strap of an artificial limb.* PITOU *is at the phonograph, staring into space.*)

DENUCÉ: Stop that noise.

(PITOU *removes the arm from the record and switches the phonograph off.*)

PITOU: The cheers drowned her cries.

DENUCÉ: No more, if you please. Don't want her upset. Delicate moment this.

(PITOU *goes to a table piled with bills and correspondence. Somewhere a hand-bell rings. All are alert.* MME DE GOURNAY *hurries off.* DENUCÉ *quickly hides the leg and tries to look casual.*)

PITOU: Yes, a delicate moment this.

(*He whistles tunelessly.* MME DE GOURNAY *returns.*)

MME DE G: She'll be another few minutes. She says she wants to make an entrance.

PITOU: Of course.

(DENUCÉ *uncovers the limb and works on it again.*)

MME DE G: She's an inspiration, a wonderful woman. So brave, joking all the time, talking of the future, of visiting our brave soldiers in the front line – (*She stops; goes close to* PITOU.) – I think I shall have to give in my notice. I'll never be able to cope. I'm a maid not a nurse. I'm squeamish. I faint easily. My knees go to water. She talks about her stump. I – (*To* DENUCÉ.) Oughtn't she to have a trained nurse? I can't change dressings, bandages. The smell, the responsibility, the sight of it. I can't bear the word 'stump', it conjures up such a lamentable picture. I feel I shall faint.

PITOU: (*Quietly*) I wish you would.

(MME DE GOURNAY *returns to cutting and stitching stockings.*)

MME DE G: I believe I've been misled.

PITOU: Why should you be different from anyone else? (*To* DENUCÉ.) You won't get paid for this, you know. She's bankrupt.

DENUCÉ: Yes. You said.

PITOU: Just thought I ought to warn you. At least we'll halve the bill for shoes. She's done for. And if the newspapers are anything to go by, we're all done for. I haven't been paid for eight months, two weeks and four days. And I'm her secretary. I'm the one who does the paying so you can imagine how short we are if I haven't paid myself. (*He laughs.*)

DENUCÉ: Want her to take two steps today. That's all. Two.

PITOU: Two steps do not make a waltz.

DENUCÉ: Extraordinary healing power. Stump already like leather –

MME DE G: Please don't –

SARAH: (*Off*) Stand back. I'm advancing at full tilt.

(DENUCÉ *quickly hides the leg. All three stand in expectation.* SARAH *enters on two crutches. She wears a dressing gown. She is triumphant and out of breath, but looks magnificent.*)

There! I have written a poem to commemorate this occasion. (*She hobbles to a plinth or pedestal, hands her crutches to* MME DE GOURNAY *and balances herself.*)

Ode to a maimed goddess by Sarah B. aged – (*She mumbles comically.*) It's very short.

'Do not weep for Sarah B.

Wipe your eyes and you will see

An actress whom the world will beg.

To act again upon one leg.'

(*Silence.*)

I realize it's not Racine but there's no need to look quite so critical. I will not have sad faces. A new life has been given to me and I intend to make the most of it. I am free of pain almost for the first time this century. I shall act again. I shall visit the battlefield. My powers of magic are restored. I will

once more inspire and cause men to forget their earthly
existence. (*To* DENUCÉ.) Have you got my new leg?
(DENUCÉ *uncovers the leg.*)
Why were you hiding it from me?
DENUCÉ: Thought sight of it would shock.
SARAH: Shock? A wooden leg shock? My dear, if you'd ever
played Sydney, Australia, on a Monday night you'd know
what shock is. (*She examines the leg.*) Amazing. Much
prettier than the makeshift one you fitted in the hospital. Not
as shapely as the real thing but less troublesome, one hopes.
How is one to give the illusion of gliding, I wonder? When I
am finished as an actress, I have only one ambition: to be a
concierge. One is always sitting. Well, come along, Major,
proceed. Fit the damn thing and launch me. Turn your
back, Pitou, or leave the room.
(PITOU *turns his back but from time to time peeps and makes a
note in his notebook.* DENUCÉ *and* MME DE GOURNAY *help*
SARAH *to sit. They gather round to fit the limb. While the fitting
is taking place:*)
Pitou, send a telegram to Mrs Campbell in London: 'Leg
removed. Stop. Very Happy. Stop. Love Sarah.' And send
another to Edmond in Paris. 'You have written a play for a
man with a long nose stop. Why can't you write one for a
woman with one leg stop. Love Sarah.'
(*She cries out in pain.*)
DENUCÉ: Too tight?
SARAH: The pressure –
DENUCÉ: (*To* MME DE GOURNAY) Loosen bottom strap –
(MME DE GOURNAY *has to turn away. She puts her smelling
salts to her nose.* DENUCÉ *does whatever is necessary to* SARAH'S
leg.)
(*To* SARAH.) How does that feel?
SARAH: Like a wooden leg.
DENUCÉ: Comfortable?
SARAH: That's a ridiculous question.
DENUCÉ: Not painful.
SARAH: No. Not painful.
DENUCÉ: If you'll allow me.

(*He lifts her up.*)

SARAH: How strong you are.

DENUCÉ: Now. Ready?

SARAH: As ever I shall be.

DENUCÉ: Right. We begin. Lift the leg.

(SARAH *tries.*)

SARAH: I can't, nothing happens, I – what did you tell me in hospital?

DENUCÉ: Imagine crossing legs. Right over left. Remember? You did well.

(SARAH *tries again. The leg moves under the dressing gown.*) Good. Good.

SARAH: It's the oddest sensation, like trying to turn the pages of a book with one's teeth.

DENUCÉ: Again. Several times.

(*While she raises and lowers the leg several times under the dressing gown:*)

SARAH: It was most mysterious. I continued to feel pain in the leg for six days after it had been amputated. Not the pain of the operation, but the pain of my tubercular knee, as if it were still there. I didn't dare tell you, Major. I was terrified. I believed I would be forever haunted by that excruciating ache, like an animal gnawing at my nerves and tendons, a spectral pain in my amputated leg. Then, on the seventh day, it rested. I dared to look down for the first time at my stump, saw what you'd left me, and the sensation receded, like a slow, stately exit to thunderous applause. I cursed my imagination and welcomed reality. I touched the stump to confirm the truth of dismemberment. I said to myself over and over again, 'There is no leg, only a stump, no leg, only a stump, only a stump, only a stump –'

(MME DE GOURNAY *faints.* DENUCÉ *goes to revive her.* PITOU *laughs.*)

Isn't that typical? I'm the one in distress and she faints.

PITOU: But then you are not squeamish.

SARAH: Is that usual, Major?

DENUCÉ: Oh, yes. Even medical students faint –

SARAH: No, no, I mean imagining pain in a leg one no longer

possesses.

DENUCÉ: Have known it. Not every patient has the experience.

PITOU: Not every patient has the imagination.

MME DE G: (*Coming to*) I am so sorry, so terribly sorry –

SARAH: I have no sympathy with people who faint. If I fainted
every time I heard or saw something unpleasant I'd be
perpetually comatose. How you were ever a dancer puzzles
me. Such a physical profession. Is it true that dancers' toes
bleed like squashed tomatoes and that they dip them in
methylated spirits to harden them?

MME DE G: I never did.

SARAH: That is no answer. How long must I go on raising this
piece of wood under my dressing gown? It looks quite
obscene.

(*She laughs, and although the laugh is dangerously near to
hysteria, it is infectious. PITOU and DENUCÉ laugh too.
MME DE GOURNAY gets herself a glass of water. The laughter
stops. Silence.*)

DENUCÉ: Want you to stand now.

(*With difficulty, DENUCÉ and MME DE GOURNAY help SARAH
to her feet. They keep hold of her.*)

SARAH: A remarkable piece of wood. I am again upright. Let me
see if I can manage alone.

(*They let go of her. She sways but keeps her balance.*)

DENUCÉ: Bravo.

SARAH: But how shall I ever move? I can't stand on a stage
motionless like this all night. I can't move.

DENUCÉ: Patient. Be patient. Takes time.

SARAH: I haven't the time. I want to walk now. I must be able to
walk through the ranks of our army. I must stand before
them, a symbol of all they are fighting for.

PITOU: (*To DENUCÉ*) She means it, you know, she means it.
Mad, quite mad.

SARAH: I must walk unaided today. I shall will myself to succeed.
Teach me, Major, how to walk.

DENUCÉ: (*To MME DE GOURNAY*) Cushions. (*To SARAH.*) Now,
exactly as when sitting down. But imagine kicking a ball with
right leg.

SARAH: Splendid. I have never kicked a ball in my life but now I will proceed to imagine it.

(*She tries to take a step. Nothing happens.*)

Of course, I have seen a ball being kicked. One winter, in England, outside Manchester, when I was visiting my friends the Agates, I was driven in my carriage down winding lanes, the naked branches of the trees my guards-of-honour. It was bitterly cold and I was wrapped in furs. Presently, we came upon a field with two teams of men ranged against each other, disputing possession of a ball. We paused to watch. They were covered in mud. For more than half an hour, with wondrous skill, they kicked the ball this way and that. I adore cricket, it's so terribly English. Well, Major, I'm imagining that I am playing cricket but nothing seems to be happening.

DENUCÉ: Kick the ball.

(*She tries; still nothing happens. She forces a laugh.*)

Kick the ball, woman!

(*She is stung by his tone of voice. Eyes closed, with enormous will, she tries. The others are all trying too, their legs twitching with effort.* SARAH *moves, almost falls.* DENUCÉ *rushes to take her hands.*)

SARAH: Don't hold me. Keep your distance.

(DENUCÉ *steps back. Again the act of will. With great effort, she starts to move, barely takes a step then falls.* PITOU *is the first to reach her, the others a second later. She lies absolutely still. They get her to the divan.*)

Undo the leg. I'm suffocating.

(*She faints.* DENUCÉ *revives her.*)

MME DE G: (*To* PITOU) She is allowed to faint.

DENUCÉ: (*To* MME DE GOURNAY) Get the chair.

(*She goes.*)

SARAH: For Jesus Christ's sake, remove the leg.

(DENUCÉ *removes the limb.* SARAH *moans softly with relief, then whimpers quietly. Silence.*)

I must earn money somehow.

DENUCÉ: First time. Only first time.

SARAH: You know nothing. How can I walk on that monstrosity?

I can only limp, and I shall never limp. Throw it away, make splinters of it, sell them as souvenirs, there'll be an income in that – I'm so hot – I'm burning – don't speak to me – I don't want sympathy or encouragement or good advice – I shall never walk again – I'm fainting –

(MME DE GOURNAY *returns with the wheelchair while* DENUCÉ *revives* SARAH.)

DENUCÉ: You will walk. You will work.

(SARAH *turns on him savagely.*)

SARAH: I'm a cripple.

(*Silence.*)

I don't want to die before I'm dead.

PITOU: (*Quietly*) Who does?

(*He whistles tunelessly. Pause.*)

DENUCÉ: Had hoped to find better time to say this. Off to front tomorrow. Must take my leave. Wanted to know you'd managed first steps. Wanted to know you'd walked. Extremely sorry. Army doctor. In peace time, mostly malingerers. In war, God knows. Unlikely chance put you in my care. Great honour. High point. Please. Try again. Please. Walk. Comfort to me in battle, thought of you restored.

(*Silence.* DENUCÉ *turns and goes quickly.* SARAH *waves* MME DE GOURNAY *away and she too goes. Pause.*)

SARAH: Any offers?

PITOU: No.

SARAH: Nothing at all?

SARAH: What will become of me? What was the purpose of all that pain?

(PITOU *turns his back on her, makes a note.*)

If I'm to be denied plays, I must continue to act. I must act. People will still want to hear me. And see me. Won't they? I shall recite. I will give concerts, scenes, speeches from my most famous roles. I can still give the very essence of life – The Eaglet, The Lady of the Camelias – I can still – help me, Pitou, help me – lying on a bed, why not? Marguerite Gautier, the final scene, I can still – the curtain rises – I am discovered reclining in white, camelias at my breast –

279

(*She falls into the dying attitude of Marguerite Gautier.*)

'I am dying, Armand, but I am so happy and my joy conceals my death. You will speak of me sometime, won't you?'

(*The light changes. A solitary violin plays a sentimental theme.*)

'Armand, give me your hand. I assure you it's not difficult to die. I'm not suffering any more. It seems as though life were pouring out of me. I feel so well. I never felt so well before. I'm going to live! Oh, how well I feel!' (*She 'dies'.*)

PITOU: (*Ineptly*) 'Marguerite! Marguerite! Marguerite!' (*He 'screams'.*) 'She's dead! My God, what's to become of me?' (*He 'weeps'.*

Lights return. SARAH *looks at* PITOU.)

SARAH: It's a whole new career. Isn't it? (*Pause.*) Pitou?

(*Silence.* PITOU *whistles tunelessly.* SARAH *stares into space. Blackout.*

In the darkness MME DE GOURNAY *screams in pain. Lights.*

PITOU *has been writing out cards and filing them but has stopped at the sound of the scream.* MME DE GOURNAY *enters, clutching her arm and deeply upset.*)

MME DE G: I am giving in my notice.

PITOU: Who screamed?

MME DE G: I'm leaving. I should like to be paid.

PITOU: So should I –

MME DE G: I want what I'm owed. I want it now. I want no more excuses. I'm not staying here a moment longer.

(*She sniffs her smelling salts.*)

PITOU: Why did you scream?

MME DE G: She struck me with her walking stick –

PITOU: Hard?

MME DE G: I'm in pain.

PITOU: You must have done something to annoy her.

MME DE G: She's become violent and dangerous and – (*Breaking down.*) – disgusting.

PITOU: You're sure it wasn't a playful tap?

MME DE G: Look, look at the mark. There's a welt.

PITOU: There'll be another one if you don't control yourself. What happened?

MME DE G: All I said was that I refuse to accompany her. I don't
    want to go to the battlefield. I don't want to see any more
    limbless, helpless human beings. I haven't the stomach.

PITOU: And she struck you.

MME DE G: She just sat and stared in black silence. So I said the
    whole idea of going to entertain the troops was ludicrous.

PITOU: And then she struck you?

MME DE G: I said she wouldn't inspire the soldiers, she'd
    demoralize them.

PITOU: And she only struck you once?

    (*Somewhere a handbell rings.*)

MME DE G: That sound drives me mad. I go to bed hearing it, I
    wake up hearing it, I hear it in my nightmares. And by the
    time I've answered it, she'll likely be asleep. I hate her. Who
    does she think she is? She spills her food, takes no care of
    herself –

    (SARAH *wheels herself in. She looks old and neglected.*)

SARAH: (*To* MME DE GOURNAY) Didn't you hear me ringing?
    Get out of my sight.

    (*She waves* MME DE GOURNAY *away with her walking stick.*
    MME DE GOURNAY *runs off.*)

    That woman is a disaster. Do you know what she said? She
    said I'd demoralize the soldiers, that I'd lose France the war.
    (*She lapses into gloom.*)

PITOU: I have to be harsh with you. Your behaviour is less than
    first rate. Allow me to say that a little effort is required. You
    talk of going to visit our brave soldiers, of inspiring them,
    but you do not have the bravery to inspire yourself.
    (*No response.*)

    Very well. Do not go to the front. I shall send a telegram to
    Major Denucé informing him the visit is cancelled. For my
    own part, I shall breathe a sigh of relief. I am not addicted to
    travel. I long for a life without movement.
    Shall I cancel the visit?
    (*No response.*)

    We must make other plans. Shall we return to Paris?
    (*No response.*)

    Shall I make you laugh? Horror, passion –

(*Half-heartedly he simulates the emotions. No response.*)
Evidently not. So be it. Then I must ask you to do as you're
told, allow yourself to be treated like a recalcitrant child.
And to that end I must ask you not to strike your servants.

SARAH: Strike? Strike? Whom did I strike?

PITOU: Madame de Gournay says you struck her. She showed
me a mark –

SARAH: Struck her? I? Did she say that I struck her? She is a
congenital liar. I simply made a dismissive gesture with my
walking stick and she happened to get in the way. She is
terribly accident-prone. It is the story of my life. I have
always been maligned.

PITOU: She has given in her notice.

SARAH: Good.

PITOU: She wants to be paid.

(*Silence.*)

SARAH: What will become of me? (*Pause.*) Why have I suffered
all this pain? For what? What has been the purpose?

PITOU: The purpose was, I thought, to rid yourself of pain.

SARAH: I have rid myself of a leg. I have rid myself of
possibility. I am weak, dreadfully weak. I have so little
energy.

PITOU: You have enough to make dismissive gestures with your
walking stick.

(*Silence.*)

SARAH: Infirmity is terrible for actors.

PITOU: It's pretty bad for audiences too.

(*Silence.*)

SARAH: I want to talk to you intimately. I regret not doing so
more often but we are seldom without company. And you
have always been different when we're alone. Will you
listen to me without banter?

(PITOU *whistles tunelessly.*)

Listen to me.

(PITOU *stops whistling.*)

I will give recitals. I will play my most famous scenes. And
I must go to the battlefront. I must give the soldiers respite.
That is a duty, an obligation. But I am haunted by a

dreadful, silly anxiety which plunges me into darkness. The anxiety is this: how will I travel?

PITOU: How will you travel? As you've always travelled, I suppose. By motor car, I suppose, by private train, I suppose, by ocean liner, I suppose –

SARAH: Yes, but how will I change platforms at railway stations? I am old. I have so little strength. How will I mount gangways? One can't be wheeled up flights of stairs. My crutches exhaust me. They make my armpits throb with pain. I would have to be carried, but how, by whom? I'm frightened of becoming a piece of useless baggage labelled 'Not Wanted on Voyage'.

PITOU: My point of view precisely.

SARAH: There must be some way of transporting me. At the back of my mind an idea hovers, a memory, a ceremony, a great crowd –

PITOU: Allow me to say, the time has come for a quiet life. The war won't last long, if the newspapers are anything to go by. Why not return to Paris, and there remain? Stationary. A fixed point. A monument. Immovable. Immortal. And once settled, you may think of doing one piece in one theatre for one hundred years. No movement. No more travelling.

SARAH: No more travelling. (*Pause.*) If only I could recall. Glory. A shaft of sunlight.

PITOU: It's winter now.

SARAH: I despise old age.

PITOU: Allow me to say –

SARAH: Don't lecture me. Make me laugh rather. I haven't laughed for weeks. I want so much to laugh. Make me laugh.

PITOU: Whenever you say that, I feel as though I've just sucked on a lemon.

(*She smiles faintly.*)

SARAH: Humour me. Dispel the gloom. I know you think I'm mad. You always have. Humour me, Pitou.

PITOU: I offered. The moment has gone. Let us play our game instead.

(*He collects up two sets of white pieces, which he sets out on a board.*)

SARAH: Please. Horror. Passion. Laughter. Tears.

PITOU: No, no, no.

SARAH: You were so comical as Armand. 'Marguerite, Marguerite, Marguerite!' Please.

PITOU: No.

SARAH: Please, Pitou. Horror. Humour me. Pitou, please make me laugh. Show me your friendship. Make me laugh. Laughter's a sign of friendship.

PITOU: No.

SARAH: You're a miserable wretch. You're trying to make me kill you, but I won't do it. (*Pause.*) I never laughed as much as I laughed in Toronto. Horror, passion, laughter, tears. For an old woman thrown on the refuse heap. Horror, Please, Pitou.

(*Reluctantly, he tries to simulate the appropriate expression. She smiles affectionately.*)

No, no, bigger the gesture. Yes, yes, but open the mouth wider. Wider. Like this. (*She demonstrates.*) You're hopeless. Now, passion.

PITOU: I can't do passion.

SARAH: Of course you can. Let your hands play over your body. (*She demonstrates.*) Don't be a spoilsport. Show me passion. (*He shows half-hearted passion. She begins to laugh a little.*) You see how difficult it is to act? You're dreadful, really dreadful. Laughter, now, come, let's laugh.

(PITOU *tries ineptly.* SARAH *lets out a splendid, tinkling laugh. They both laugh now,* PITOU *falsely,* SARAH *convincingly.*) (*Abruptly.*) Tears. Cry.

(PITOU *tries to cry.* SARAH *laughs genuinely.*)

Weep, weep, my dear, weep.

(PITOU *tries.*)

Weep. You're such an amusing man –

(SARAH *lets out a glorious wail.* PITOU *tries to imitate her. She laughs. They both weep.* MME DE GOURNAY *runs in.*)

MME DE G: What is it, what's happened, have the Germans entered Paris?

SARAH: Can't you see we're in the middle of a conversation?

MME DE G: I'm so sorry, so terribly sorry.

SARAH: You are the most insensitive creature. (*To* PITOU.) I was
   just beginning to enjoy myself. What does she want?

PITOU: (*To* MME DE GOURNAY) What do you want?
   (MME DE GOURNAY *steels herself*.)

MME DE G: My wages.

PITOU: (*To* SARAH) Her wages.

SARAH: She may leave my employ after we return from the front.

PITOU: You may leave –

MME DE G: I do not want to go to the front.

PITOU: She does not –

SARAH: I heard her. Now I understand why she failed as a ballet
   dancer. She has no sense of the higher purpose.

PITOU: Without wishing to take sides, the higher purpose is all
   very well, but there is a small matter of the lower reality.

SARAH: What reality? My only interest is to defeat reality.

PITOU: I'm pleased to hear it, because I'd be interested to hear
   your plans for defeating your lack of money, your abundancy
   of debt and your imminent bankruptcy.

SARAH: *Et tu, Brute*.

PITOU: You have had no income for months. You live on your
   credit and you have no credit. You are penniless.

SARAH: Money is irrelevant.

PITOU: Money is irrelevant only to those who have it, among
   whom you are not presently numbered. You must sell your
   jewels.

SARAH: Never.

PITOU: You must do something. This is certainly no time to be
   charitable, however worthy the cause. Forget about our
   brave soldiers. Make only one major journey. Return to
   Paris. Give your recitals, open a school of acting, horror,
   passion, whatever, but let us come to rest.

SARAH: I must go to the battlefield. Artists are the torchbearers of
   civilization.

PITOU: It's difficult to hold up a torch while standing on one leg.

SARAH: If one has been privileged as I have been privileged, one is
   beholden to repay.

PITOU: Beholden, I see, beholden, and are we lesser mortals who
   only have two legs also beholden? Beholden to die in penury,

to starve, to be weighed down by – we have lives, too, you know.

SARAH: (*To* MME DE GOURNAY) He's showing off again – leave us –

PITOU: No, this concerns her. She doesn't want to go, I don't want to go, only you want to go, and you are unable. How will you present yourself to the Army? Will you crawl through the trenches? Will you walk their ranks on crutches – ?

(SARAH *is suddenly consumed with impotent rage. While she talks she hurls things at* PITOU, *or uses her walking stick to smash anything that is near.*)

SARAH: Parasites. Why do you hate me so much? What have I done that you should hate me?

PITOU: Hate you? Stop that – hate you? – I've given you more than half my life – don't – we could get money for that – (*To* MME DE GOURNAY.) She's having a brainstorm –

SARAH: The two of you suffocate me in hatred. You begrudge me every breath I take. (*To* MME DE GOURNAY.) And you are a catastrophe.

PITOU: We'll have nothing left.

(SARAH *stops her destruction. She takes off her wig and flings it aside. Her hair is white beneath.*)

SARAH: I am old and poor and defenceless. I need support, not loathing. They have cut off my leg. I cannot even go to the lavatory alone.

(PITOU *picks up the pieces of a broken object and tries to fit them together.*)

PITOU: (*Distressed*) I wonder if we can claim for willful damage on our insurance.

SARAH: I am an actress. I have to travel. My physical presence is my passport. I have lived in dread all my life of being incapacitated. They say you must have gift and talent, but health is – (*She breaks off.*) Send a telegram to Harry Houdini in the United States. 'Houdini, you do such wonderful things stop. Could you bring back my leg for me? Signed Sarah.'

PITOU: You're not serious?

SARAH: I have never been more serious in my life. He does the
impossible and I want the impossible.

PITOU: As who does not?

(*Silence.*)

SARAH: Wheel me back to my grave. I may as well die.

PITOU: Shall I send for a priest?

(SARAH *is suddenly alert.*)

SARAH: The Pope.

PITOU: The Pope?

(*He makes a gesture behind her back to indicate total insanity.*)

SARAH: The Pope, the Pope, His Holiness the Pope –

PITOU: I doubt he'll come at such short notice –

SARAH: Stop behaving like a clown. The Pope. I remember now,
the ceremony, wait, listen, let me think, he has a word for it,
what does he call it?

MME DE G: (*Quietly*) Purgatory.

SARAH: In Latin, in Latin –

PITOU: I've lost the thread of this conversation –

(*Pause.*)

SARAH: *Sedia gestatoria.*

PITOU: Sounds like a bad Italian actress.

SARAH: All Italian actresses are bad. Pen and pad.

(PITOU *gives her a pen and pad. She begins to sketch rapidly.*)
Don't you remember how the Pope entered St Peter's? We
were there. I was at the very front.

PITOU: I was at the back.

SARAH: A portable throne. He was carried on the shoulders of his
Swiss Guard, seated on the *sedia gestatoria*. Such glory.
Sunlight. Why can't I be carried on a portable throne? My
own *sedia gestatoria*? I will be lifted by strong, handsome,
young warriors so that all the army, the hosts of Gideon, may
see me. Find a carpenter. Have him construct this for me to
sit on.

(*She gives* PITOU *the sketch she has made and begins to wheel
herself out.*)

(*To* MME DE GOURNAY.) On my dressing-table put boot-
black and unctions.

MME DE G: What about your wig?

SARAH: I do not want to tell you again: it is not a wig, it is a transformation. Wigs are vulgar. (*As she goes.*) And they say something to the Holy Father as they carry him, something to do with glory. What is it they say as they carry him?

MME DE G: Am I to take you for your walk?

SARAH: That is the last thing they say.

(*She laughs and wheels herself off.*)

PITOU: What do they say about glory? I'll tell you what they say. They say the glory passes. *Sic transit gloria mundi*.

MME DE G: And I thought I was so privileged. My acquaintances thought so too. How privileged you are, they said. One particular friend observed I would not be a maid but a lady-in-waiting, attendant to an empress, the most famous, beloved and glamorous woman in the world. Glamorous. The smell in her room is degrading. In the mornings, when I enter with her tray, I retch. I have always been rather fastidious, but she has no self-respect. She is not greatly enamoured of washing. She wears the same under-garments for three or four days.

(PITOU *stuffs his fingers in his ears*. MME DE GOURNAY *raises her voice.*)

She snores. I can hear her snoring in my room through the wall. She snores with her mouth open, jaw sagging, tongue lolling. I have to go in and whistle to make her stop. I have to whistle!

(PITOU *whistles tunelessly*. MME DE GOURNAY *shouts at him.*)

She farts! She is old and cruel and dirty. The divine Sarah smells of stale scent and not the odour of sanctity.

(*Pause.* PITOU *removes his fingers.*)

PITOU: In future, do not be coarse. I will not have talk of her nether garments.

MME DE G: She's so – so ordinary.

PITOU: Yes, but the gods whisper in her ear and not in ours.

MME DE G: I thought taking the job would be an inspiration. I've never had the slightest encouragement for anything I've done in my life. My ex-husband said I could do nothing right. But I'm not someone to be disparaged. My father was Superintendant of the Municipal Baths in Lyons. He wasn't rich but at least he had the prestige of the title. I am as much of a person as she is.

PITOU: Yes, and to a Turk Mozart is noise. Do you want your wages? Or will you stay? In this house the persons who are servants never leave. They are dismissed.

(*He takes out his wallet, counts out some notes and offers them to her.*)

MME DE G: I've nowhere to go.

(*The handbell rings.*)

PITOU: Time for her walk. The garden is looking particularly bleak at this time of year. The trees bare, the soil frost-hard, and the wind ice. The sand is blowing off the dune and the sea rages.

MME DE G: What am I to do?

PITOU: You are to hear gun-fire and your eyes will smart with the smoke of battle. And when you are old you will be able to say you served her in peace and in war, and that will make you extraordinary. Wouldn't it be paradise if the world were just?

(SARAH *wheels herself in. She has a play text in her hands.*)

SARAH: (*To* MME DE GOURNAY) Why do you never come when I ring? Are you punishing me? Is it that you enjoy seeing me helpless? I need my spectacles. Where are they? Find them.

(MME DE GOURNAY *looks for* SARAH's *spectacles.*)

(*To* PITOU.) I have been so encouraged by the thought of my portable chair, I am alive with excitement. I have had such a splendid idea. I shall do a speech from *The Eaglet* for the soldiers. The one on the battlefield. 'And all the arms – the bloody arms, I see' –

(MME DE GOURNAY *brings* SARAH *her spectacles.* SARAH *puts them on and consults the text.*)

If necessary I shall read it.

(*She searches the text.*)

Yes, here. (*To* PITOU.) Find me the cloak I wore. In the chest. The white cloak. (*To* MME DE GOURNAY.) Help me.

(MME DE GOURNAY *helps her. She assists* SARAH *to a plinth which* SARAH *leans on.* PITOU *brings her the cloak and helmet.*)

Around my shoulders. I shall wear it over a very plain grey dress. Drape it for me.

(MME DE GOURNAY *and* PITOU *help* SARAH *with her cloak*.)
I've lost the place – yes – here – I shall need my glasses – do you think it's ridiculous me playing a sixteen-year-old boy? Tell me honestly, is it ridiculous?

(*She looks at them for some reaction but gets none. Abruptly she launches into the speech; she starts by reading it but soon lays down the text, and removes her glasses*.)

    'And all their arms, the bloody arms I see
    Arms without hands, the stumps outstretched to me.
    Oh young soldier, with your ashen face,
    Forgive me, Oh forgive me! Pray you, grace!'

(*Lights change. The distant sounds of war*.)

    'Look not upon me with your murdered eyes,
    Accusing me, Ah no! Spare me your cries.'

(*The sounds of war louder*.)

    'My agony has put their woe to rout.
    The groans are stilled. And oh, I hear a shout!
    Where on the grassy plain woe loomed so large,
    Lo, phantom heroes lead a phantom charge!

(*A great cry*.) Glory!'

(*She stands frozen. The sound of war dominates.*
Blackout.
The sounds of war fade to become distant. Torrential rain dominates.
Dim light.
Like a strange eastern caravan, SARAH's *procession crosses the stage: first,* PITOU, *under an umbrella; then,* SARAH (*a double*), *seated on her portable throne, carried by* TWO MILITARY ORDERLIES. *She, too, is sheltered by an umbrella, as is* MME DE GOURNAY, *who brings up the rear.*
The sound of cheering. The rain is incessant.
The procession crosses and exits. The cheering fades. 'The Nightingale Song' is played on a solo harmonica. A pause, then PITOU *re-enters, running under his umbrella*.)

PITOU: I've found him! I've found him! Over here! Over here!

(*A sudden light on* DENUCÉ. *He lies propped up on a stretcher or a bed, his head bandaged. He stares blankly. There is a brazier near him. The* TWO ORDERLIES *carry on* SARAH, *followed by*

MME DE GOURNAY. PITOU *leads them to where* DENUCÉ *lies.*
There is much shaking off and closing of umbrellas, warming of
hands. SARAH *quickly removes her gloves and takes hold of*
DENUCÉ's *hands. He does not respond.*)

MME DE G: The smell of pus is disgusting.

PITOU: They call this place The Morgue. Used to be a school. Now
they bring the dying here.

SARAH: Be quiet. He'll hear you.

PITOU: He'll hear, but he won't understand.

MME DE G: I'm going to vomit.

(*She retches.*)

SARAH: (*To* PITOU) Take her out. Leave me alone with him. Call
me when the soldiers are ready.

(PITOU *and* MME DE GOURNAY *go with the* TWO ORDERLIES.)

Major, do you know who I am?

(*A solo* TENOR VOICE *now sings 'The Nightingale Song'*
accompanied by the harmonica.)

TENOR: 'Nightingale, nightingale, do not sing tonight,

My men are weary from battle,

Let them rest before they fight.

Nightingale, nightingale, keep a silent watch,

Give my soldiers a blessed sleep,

At dawn again they march.'

(SARAH *listens for a moment.*)

SARAH: Give me a sign you know who I am. You did me a great
service. They tell me the shell exploded almost on top of you,
and that you're lucky to be alive. Speak to me. Give me a sign.
Say that you know you are lucky to be alive, and that you want
to live.

(*Pause.*)

Wherever I have gone today I have heard that song, but I
cannot catch the words. (*She listens.*) When I was a child, a
difficult, wayward child, I once said to a Mother Superior, 'I
didn't ask to be born.' She slapped me very hard, asked God's
forgiveness and slapped me very hard again. I shall slap you in
a moment.

(*Pause.*)

Surely you remember me. I made you wash your hands. I am

senile and gaga now. I am an old and crippled woman. No worse: I am an old and crippled actress. But the secret is I'm still that difficult, wayward child within. Two beings. I called my autobiography *My Double Life*.

(*Pause.*)

Give me a sign. Show me the life within.

(*Pause.*)

A man I once loved told me we are duty-bound to live. He was cruel and gave me pain. But the pain, he said, was a sign of life. Better to suffer than to die, he said. He was a playwright. His plays were full of death and despair. Art has a lot to answer for. If life is so awful, why do we cling to it so? Speak. Give me a sign.

(*The song continues to be played on the harmonica. The rain is incessant.*)

What is needed is courage and will. I've had the riches of the earth, fame and adoration and reward. But you must survive without your name writ large, without helpers, without fanfares. Nevertheless. Show me that you want to survive.

(*Pause. Distant guns.*)

Listen to these words. I've never known anyone who wasn't moved by these lines. Except the Australians.

(*Gently she turns* DENUCÉ'*s head so that he looks at her.*)

   'O France, when thou art prone and bound,
   Beneath the tyrant's ruthless heel,
   A voice from the deep caves shall sound
   And rive thy chains of steel

   The exile watching wave and sky
   Shall raise a voice that men shall hear
   Like words that in a dream drift by
   Above the darkened sphere.'

(*Above the rain comes the sound of soldiers, like an expectant audience in a theatre.*)

   'O'er newer races Time doth weld,
   They like a thundercloud shall break;
   And if the quick in sloth he held,
   The ashamed dead shall wake.'

(DENUCÉ *looks blankly at her. The soldiers begin to clap and stamp their feet. They chant, 'Sa-rah! Sa-rah! Sa-rah!'*)
You are not alone. You are alive. You must not want to die. Take strength from me. See in me a body bereft but a spirit indestructible. But I also need encouragement. Give me a sign.

(*No response.* PITOU *and the* TWO ORDERLIES *come to her.*)

PITOU: Two thousand men stamping and calling your name. It won't be long before they tear the place apart.

(*Pause.* SARAH *nods to the* TWO ORDERLIES. *They are about to lift her when* DENUCÉ *suddenly makes a short grunt that sounds either like 'ache' or 'wake'. He reaches out a hand, which* SARAH *grasps.* DENUCÉ *grips her tight and seems to smile.* SARAH *also smiles. The soldiers' shouting turns into a chant: 'Sa-rah! Sa-rah! Sa-rah!' The sound grows and grows continuously. Blackout.*
The chant turns into wild applause and cheering.
Lights.
SARAH *stands in a pool of light, supporting herself between the* TWO ORDERLIES. *She drinks in the ovation, acknowledging the cheers.*
Blackout.)

ACT TWO

Spring. The villa.

SARAH: (*In the dark, very loud*) I never had a more authentic triumph.

(*Lights.*

SARAH, *lying full stretch on a chaise-longue and looking glamorous, is on the telephone.* MME DE GOURNAY *is cutting out clippings from newspapers and pasting them in a scrapbook.* PITOU *is busy with the camera that has a cloth and a magnesium flash attachment.* MAJOR DENUCÉ, *head bandaged, is knitting with difficulty. He has recovered physically but requires all his concentration to co-ordinate. Often he wears a lost, distant look and, from time to time, a vacant, foolish smile.*)

(*Into the telephone.*) A triumph, a great triumph. Two thousand men stamping and shouting my name: Sa-rah, Sa-rah, Sa-rah!

DENUCÉ: Sa-rah, Sa-rah, Sa-rah –

SARAH: (*Continuing on the telephone*) What? Carried. Carried. On a portable throne. A throne. *Throne.* (*To* MME DE GOURNAY.) The Major's dribbling. (*Into the telephone.*) You would have been proud of your poor old mother, Maurice. I recited and talked and made them laugh. They lost themselves and I lost my voice. And have you seen the newspapers?

(*She snaps her fingers.* MME DE GOURNAY *brings her the scrapbook.*)

'Sarah Enlists', 'Sarah Goes to War' – too disarming. I brought cheer to the soldiers and reminded the world of my existence. The offers will come flooding in, you'll see. No. Just the servants and Major Denucé. My surgeon, the man who did the dreadful deed. I've brought him back here to recuperate. He was shock-shelled or whatever they call the scars of war. What do you mean, caviar? Surgeon, dear, surgeon! (*She listens.*) How much? Of course. Immediately.

294

Don't worry. But Maurice, why is it that you never
telephone? Why don't you visit your poor mother? Hello,
Maurice, Maurice, hello.
(*She replaces the receiver.*)
We've been cut off. In more ways than one. Pitou.
(*She beckons* PITOU *to her.*)
Send Maurice ten thousand at once. He is in need.

PITOU: So are we.

SARAH: Send it. (*To* DENUCÉ.) I was talking to my son, Major. His
father was a prince. I feel so well. Soon, soon, those good-
for-nothing playwrights will put pen to paper. Sarah can still
work wonders, they will say, and they will chivvy their dull
brains into creating vehicles for me. Vehicles in which I sit.

PITOU: The camera is ready.

SARAH: I'm so happy today. It's wonderfully warm. I do believe
spring is here at last. I can smell the pine trees. The sea is
calm and soothing. But I am restless. I feel Venus is in the
ascendancy. I want to travel.

PITOU: May I ask a favour? Will you allow me to be
photographed with you? Playing our game.

SARAH: Of course.
(*He helps her to stand.*)
My dear little Pitou, you are really very beautiful.
(*He helps her towards a plinth on which is set a sort of game of
draughts.*)
Your jacket is disgusting. With all the money I give you, you
can at least be clean.

PITOU: Which you give me? Which you promise me, you mean.
How am I to send money to your son? We have no money.

SARAH: Oh, you're so pedantic.

PITOU: Will you sell your jewels, your precious stones?

SARAH: No. Never. They are all I have.

PITOU: (*To* MME DE GOURNAY) I will show you how to take the
photograph.

MME DE G: I've never taken a photograph before.

PITOU: It's quite simple.

SARAH: I feel nineteen again. (*Pause.*) Well, twenty.
(PITOU *puts* MME DE GOURNAY's *head under the cloth.*)

MME DE G: Everything's upside down.

SARAH: I feel I have a future.

PITOU: (*To* MME DE GOURNAY) There is nothing to it. Any fool can take a photograph.

(*He shows her how the camera works.*)

SARAH: The future, yes, the future. Silence! I am about to issue a proclamation. (*She hums the opening bars of the 'Marseillaise'.*) The future lies in moving pictures. I shall make films. Films are modern sorcery. In films, I shall walk, sit, stand and run. Future generations can judge me.

PITOU: Eleanora Duse is making a film.

SARAH: She was always headstrong.

(PITOU *takes up his position at the plinth. He and* SARAH *use pointers to push the pieces in their game of draughts.*)

PITOU: This is the first time we have been photographed together.

SARAH: (*To* MME DE GOURNAY) Will you hurry please? I can't balance here forever.

MME DE G: (*From under the camera*) Why are all the pieces white?

SARAH: That is a secret. Photographs should always be mysterious, charged with unexplained drama. Photographs, like life, should be full of feeling. Passion, Pitou.

PITOU: I am better at acting enigmatic.

SARAH: In that case, I shall give out an aura of intellectual wistfulness.

MME DE G: But how do you know which pieces are yours?

SARAH: Take the photograph. Not everything can be explained.

(MME DE GOURNAY *takes the photograph. The magnesium flash explodes.* DENUCÉ *cries out.* PITOU *goes to him.*)

PITOU: It's only a photograph, Major. We'll take one of you in a moment.

(DENUCÉ *holds* PITOU's *hand tightly.*)

SARAH: We must do the solos now, Pitou.

(MME DE GOURNAY *helps* SARAH *into the wheelchair.* PITOU, *with difficulty, pulls away from* DENUCÉ *and goes to the camera.*)

Concentrate on the eyes. I can convey more with my eyes

than most playwrights can with an entire scene. (*To* MME DE GOURNAY.) Put on some music, bright and sparkling. From a ballet. That'll make the choice simpler for you. And let us be quick, Pitou. Capture this gaiety. Important the public believe me truly restored. Publicity is all illusion.

(MME DE GOURNAY *winds up the phonograph and puts on a record. From the phonograph* SARAH's *voice is heard.*)

VOICE: 'Why? Do you want to know why, Armand? Because there are moments when I lose myself in that dream.'

SARAH: Why have you put that on?

MME DE G: A mistake, I'm sorry —

VOICE: 'Because there are days when I am weary of the life I lead and imagine another, because in the midst of my turbulent existence — '

SARAH: (*To* MME DE GOURNAY) Give it to me.

(MME DE GOURNAY *brings the record to* SARAH, *who breaks it.*) People will say that was recorded after my death. You've spoiled my mood.

MME DE G: I'm terribly sorry.

SARAH: I am exhausted now. No more of this. Pitou, go and see if there's any post. I want letters, plays, poetry, offers.

PITOU: The solos —

SARAH: Go and see if anyone wants me.

(PITOU *goes.*)

DENUCÉ: Pitou, Pitou —

MME DE G: He's going for the post. (*To* SARAH.) He's very attached to Pitou. They hold hands.

DENUCÉ: Wants me to remember. Hurts to remember.

SARAH: Yes. Memory is painful. I hate the past. My voice then, those words 'my turbulent existence' suddenly evoked a hideous mirage of memories. My life has been shot with thunder and lightning. Yes, it seems now that my life was fiction, a dream. The true substance was the time I spent upon the stage acting, and in rehearsing when I was not acting, fourteen, fifteen hours a day. Looking back that is all that seems to matter now. The whirlwind of dates, the titles, the gleaming swords, the fireworks, the men of genius and the clever men, the honours, smiles, prayers and tears, they do not count. My voyages round the world, up and down the provinces of every country, my bankruptcies, my vast fees and fortunes, the despair, the joy, all these do not count. I was the greatest lover in the world. Kings and princes competed for my favours. I earned and lost millions upon millions. Oscar Wilde laid an armful of lilies at my feet. I enslaved cities. In London 100,000 admirers filled three volumes with their signatures on my birthday. The streets of New York were blocked by my admirers. The Prince of Wales allowed me to dress him as my dead lover in *Fédora* and he lay upon the stage so that he could say he played a scene with me. Everything I did or said was repeated, written down, distorted. I think of that part of my life and a great clamour arises: applause, sobs, whistling trains, steamers screaming in the fog, a patchwork of all countries, a babel of all tongues, shouts of enthusiasm, a great litany of worship. To the world I was earth, air, fire, water. Vapour producing vapour. My marriage, lovers, passions, are like my sculpture, my painting, my playwriting: these were the sideshows. But the star attraction, the profound fact of my life was that I acted on a stage. I want to act now. I must act again. My reality is the creation of illusion. I hate the past. Memory is a curse.

DENUCÉ: Sa-rah, Sa-rah, Sa-rah –

SARAH: Stop that. It makes you dribble. Call me when Pitou returns.

(MME DE GOURNAY *starts to wheel* SARAH *off.*)

I can manage. Stay with the Major. What are you teaching him to knit now?

MME DE G: A pair of socks.

SARAH: That is in very bad taste.

(SARAH *exits.* MME DE GOURNAY *resumes the work with the newspaper cuttings.*)

DENUCÉ: Spring now, no more rain, hate the rain, and the mud. Can't keep the wounds dry. Woke from a dream.

MME DE G: You weren't asleep.

DENUCÉ: Glory, she said. Thunderclouds –

MME DE G: Stop that now. You're talking nonsense again. Do your knitting. You mustn't upset yourself.

DENUCÉ: Her voice –

MME DE G: Concentrate on what you're doing.

DENUCÉ: Want Pitou.

MME DE G: As soon as he gets back.

DENUCÉ: Want me to tell him the story.

MME DE G: Yes, yes, very nice –

DENUCÉ: Teaches me to make things –

MME DE G: So do I –

DENUCÉ: Snip, snip, snip, snip –

MME DE G: Go on with your knitting.

(*He knits. She cuts out and pastes.*)
There's a war on, and they have nothing else to write about but an old woman giving recitations. And she only did it because she wanted the publicity. The soldiers come second. Didn't you hear her? 'I reminded the world of my existence.' Well, of course you heard her. Impossible not to. I don't know why she bothers with the telephone. They'd have heard her in Paris without one.
(PITOU *comes running in, brandishing an unopened envelope.*)

PITOU: Where is she? We've had a letter. A New York postmark. An offer, I've no doubt. I'm almost too frightened to open it. My hands are trembling. (*He tears it open.*) Yes, yes, from New York! (*He reads, bursts out laughing then stops abruptly.*) This is a disaster. (*He puts the letter in his pocket.*) Say nothing.

MME DE G: About what, what is it?

PITOU: Say nothing.

(PITOU *paces.* DENUCÉ *sings a snatch of 'The Nightingale Song'.*)

MME DE G: That's right, Major, you sing, he laughs, and I cut out pieces from the newspaper to paste them in a book. (*She reads:*) 'Troops cheer our greatest actress', 'An inspiring visit.' The newspapers are full of catastrophe but you sing, he laughs, and I cut out items favourable to my employer. (*She reads:*) 'She is a woman whose courage is infectious.'

PITOU: I wish you'd catch some of it.

(*Somewhere the handbell rings.* MME DE GOURNAY *shudders; after a moment she rises and goes.* PITOU *sits by* DENUCÉ.)

So, Fido, how's the knitting coming along? Must keep the
boys at the front warm.

(DENUCÉ *takes hold of* PITOU's *hand*.)

Please, Fido, you must stop doing that. People will talk. Let
go, there's a good chap. Please. (DENUCÉ *keeps a tight hold*.)
Well, I suspect we all need a bit of comfort. As a matter of
fact, I welcome a bit of hand-holding. I have a very
unpleasant task to perform. We've had an offer. But what an
offer. I suppose I have to tell her. Whether I do or not, she'll
find out.

(MME DE GOURNAY *wheels in* SARAH. DENUCÉ *immediately
lets go of* PITOU's *hand and half stands, smiling devotedly at*
SARAH.)

Down boy, down boy, down.

SARAH: What's all this about a letter from New York?

PITOU: (*To* MME DE GOURNAY) I told you not to say –

SARAH: Read me the letter, Pitou.

PITOU: (*To* MME DE GOURNAY) Why not take the Major for a
walk? (*To* DENUCÉ.) Fido, go for a walk.

(DENUCÉ *grabs hold of* PITOU's *hand*.)

SARAH: I want to hear what's in the letter.

(PITOU *nods sharply to* MME DE GOURNAY, *who goes*.)

PITOU: Leave us; down boy, down. Stay. Stay.

SARAH: Why are you so cruel to him? Read me the letter, Pitou.

(PITOU *tries to free his hand then pulls away from* DENUCÉ.)

PITOU: That's a good boy.

(PITOU *takes out the letter*.)

SARAH: Is it an offer?

PITOU: Yes.

SARAH: I knew it, I knew it. All this publicity was bound to bear
fruit. Read it to me, read it to me. What sort of offer?

PITOU: From America.

SARAH: Yes, yes. They adore me in America.

PITOU: A tour.

SARAH: Wonderful. I long to cross the ocean again.

PITOU: One problem. (*He reads:*) 'Because of the present
hostilities, transfer of funds to France is nigh impossible.
You would have to finance your own journey and we would

refund you on arrival.' We have not the funds to be refunded.

SARAH: You've become fairly preoccupied with money. This tour: major cities?

PITOU: And others.

SARAH: What others?

PITOU: Here's the pertinent passage. (*He reads:*) 'But all these dates are conditional upon the aforementioned circus offer which we strongly recommend, for we believe we could negotiate a very high fee. She would, of course, appear in what is called the star spot, that is to say, after the lions and before the elephants.'

(*A long silence.* SARAH *is absolutely still. Very slowly she wheels herself off.*)

DENUCÉ: Don't go –

PITOU: My point of view precisely.

DENUCÉ: Snip-snip, snip-snip. Please.

(*Pause.* PITOU *takes up a double sheet of newspaper, folds it carefully, then picks up the scissors and begins to cut.*)

PITOU: Snip-snip, snip-snip, snip-snip-snip.

DENUCÉ: Snip-snip-snip, snip, snip-snip.

(DENUCÉ *smiles.* PITOU *finishes cutting then unfolds the paper which he has cut into a row of joined figures in the shape of elephants.* DENUCÉ, *smiling, applauds slowly.*

Lights fade to blackout.

In the darkness, voices are heard from the phonograph:)

OFFICER: 'Scarpio is dead!'

(*Angry shouts.*)

SPOLETTA: 'Ah! Devil! I will send you to join your dead lover!'

SARAH: 'I go willingly.'

(*The sound of the phonograph hissing and clicking, and of a solitary slow hand-clap.*

Lights.

PITOU *is at the phonograph.* DENUCÉ, *wearing a silly smile, applauds slowly.* MME DE GOURNAY *enters.* PITOU *stops the phonograph.*)

MME DE G: I never thought anyone could cry so much. She seems to be crying her life away, as though the tears were dousing the embers.

PITOU: I swear that's a quotation. Racine? Phaedra. She's been talking to you, I can tell –

MME DE G: She even embraced me. I resisted at first but then gave way. It was the first time she ever seemed to need me. She buried her face in my neck. My collar is still wet. 'A circus, a circus, God help me, a circus,' she said. 'I must have sinned. I'm being punished.'

(PITOU *laughs*.)

PITOU: Excellent, splendid, wonderful. That's that. I'll make arrangements for our return to Paris. The last journey. Thank God. We shall all die in our beds. And about time.

(*He does a little dance of joy.* SARAH *wheels herself in.* PITOU *is still. Silence.*)

She is no longer crying.

SARAH: Bring me my jewels.

(PITOU *is suddenly alarmed*.)

PITOU: Why? What for?

SARAH: You know why.

PITOU: Do nothing rash. Pause. Consider. What you need is a play. And who knows, there may be a playwright at this moment –

(SARAH *explodes with real venom*.)

SARAH: Don't mention that word playwright to me. It's not so long ago that they were beating a path to my door with their crass melodramas. On their knees they came, pilgrims to the shrine, begging me to read their grubby little manuscripts, praying to the good God that I should condescend to speak their unspeakable lines. I have put vast fortunes into the pockets of playwrights. Where would they be without me? I guaranteed production, I guaranteed success. Don't mention playwrights to me. They do their work, if you call it work, and then they lose interest. And we actors have to perform night after night, year in, year out, while playwrights disport themselves in Monte Carlo. And do they visit us? How often have you seen a playwright in a dressing-room? And if they do make an enquiry after their puppets, you may be certain it is only to ask whether or not the house was full. Royalties, that's all that interests them. Playwrights are not artists, they are businessmen.

PITOU: Nevertheless, you cannot do without them –

SARAH: And ask them to cut a line, a precious word, and one would think one was asking Our Lord to revise the Sermon on the Mount. Don't speak to me of playwrights. And where are they now I am alone and in jeopardy? Where? Not one has the wit to write me a part in which I sit or stand. (PITOU *tries to interrupt*.) Playwrights! God help us when audiences pay to see plays instead of actors in plays. They are nothing without us. Playwrights need actors. Playwrights are pimps.

PITOU: Granted, but they are also a necessary evil.

SARAH: Circus acts can do without them.

(*Silence.*)

PITOU: So it's the circus, is it?

SARAH: Bring me my jewels.

PITOU: It's a high price to pay.

SARAH: You do not know the half of it.

PITOU: I hate the circus.

SARAH: You are not alone. I hate tightrope walkers and bare-back riders. I have never laughed at clowns. A circus is cruelty to animals, and they are asking me to be an animal-act, a one-legged human who spouts poetry. I hate cruelty to animals. I regret playing Lady Macbeth in a leopard skin. I always got a laugh on 'Out, out damn'd spot.'

PITOU: Let me send a cable: 'Your offer totally unacceptable –'

SARAH: Give me my jewels –

PITOU: Why? Why? Why?

SARAH: Better a circus than a charitable institution for cripples.

PITOU: You're certain of that, are you?

SARAH: I have been trying to imagine what it'll be like. One would have to wait outside the tent, listening to the roar of the lions and the cracking of whips. One would hear too, the circus band, all trombones and euphoniums, like a constipated gorilla straining for relief.

PITOU: Yes, yes, and think of the smells.

SARAH: Yes, animal manure and human sweat. But perhaps the elephants would trumpet a protest. At having to follow me. I adore elephants. They are the only beasts on this planet who instinctively understand that life is unbearably funny and unbearably sad. That is why they look the way they do. They know the meaning of humiliation.

MME DE G: May I add my voice?

PITOU: Is your collar dry?

MME DE G: I had a dream last night of childhood. My father took me once to a circus, the only time I've ever been. And what impressed me most was the trapeze artist, a young woman with bright red hair. She was thrown between two men, somersaulting, cavorting, twisting and turning. She had muscular legs. I remember. I dreamed of her last night. I saw her falling from a height and there was no safety net.

SARAH: That is your dream, it has nothing to do with me. Dreams are always personal.

PITOU: You will not be reproached for declining the offer.
(*Pause.*)

SARAH: I want you to photograph me. Solo. Let it be harsh and cruel. Let it reveal acceptance. Let it show me staring into the camera, confronting my own image. The world has become impervious to mutilation. So must I. I have been supported by crutches, by self-deception, by gazing lovingly into distorting mirrors. No more lies. No more lip-service to survival. That does not mean I shan't, from time to time, suffer panic or despair, or harbour thoughts of self-destruction, or need comfort, or escape into a fantastical garden of sweet scented flowers. But I determine from this moment to use reality, to take affliction into my being and transform it into triumph. With my will I shall use truth and terror to fuel my fragile presence. Let the photograph be life-like. I am. I shall be.
(*Silence.*)

PITOU: You are an actress, not an act.
(*Silence.*)

SARAH: Give me my jewels.
(PITOU *goes to a cupboard and unlocks it.*)
Madame de Gournay?

MME DE G: Yes?

SARAH: Thank you for comforting me.

(PITOU brings SARAH *her jewel box.*)

(*To* MME DE GOURNAY.) Come. Sit by me. We will sort the jewels.

(PITOU *returns to* DENUCÉ.)

PITOU: Fido, I'll teach you to cut patterns out of newspapers.

SARAH: We will sell enough to settle my debts, and to buy one first-class passage on an ocean liner. And two in steerage.

PITOU: I have lost the day.

SARAH: We must rid ourselves of sad jewels, of sombre stones. Jewels ought to be happy. Sell these diamonds. I detest diamonds. Hard and unfeeling. To feel. That is paramount. Diamonds remind me of those who smile with eyes of bayonets. Sell them.

PITOU: Instead of bits and pieces, allow me to say it would be better to rid oneself of one grand possession.

SARAH: I have already done that. I have lost a leg,

PITOU: I mean the villa at Belle-Île.

SARAH: Never. I would rather lose all I have than sell Belle-Île. One day, Madame de Gournay, I shall take you to Belle-Île.

MME DE G: Is it very beautiful?

SARAH: At night, when the Furies plague me, I think of Belle-Île and I am comforted. Terrible to become attached to a single spot on this earth, to cliffs and sea, and the wild, bleak skies. No. Sell the diamonds. And the amethysts and bloodstone and garnets. But not Belle-Île. Keep the burnt topaz. It's deep and variegated, and much finer than yellow diamonds. It was given to me by a king.

(*She tries not to cry.*)

MME DE G: And these pearls?

SARAH: No. Not the pearls. I adore pearls. This one was slipped into my hand by a man on the railway station in Vienna. I tried to thank him, but he scuttled away and disappeared into a third-class carriage. How curious people are.

PITOU: Yes. How curious.

(*He laughs.*)

MME DE G: Perhaps he couldn't afford the pearl. Perhaps it was a sacrifice.

SARAH: The word is very unjust. Thank God. Pitou, take my

photograph. I have done what had to be done.

(*She shuts the jewel box.* PITOU *goes to the camera.* SARAH *takes up pen and pad.*)

And you're to have this made. Remember, in a circus people sit in a circle so I must be protected on all sides. Find carpenters. Get the Major to help. It will be good for him. We will rehearse.

PITOU: You are determined.

SARAH: I must learn my lines.

(PITOU *takes the photograph. The magnesium flash explodes.* DENUCÉ *cries out and begins to shudder.*)

MME DE G: The Major –

SARAH: Get his medicine –

(MME DE GOURNAY *goes for his medicine.* PITOU *runs to* DENUCÉ.)

PITOU: It's all right, it's all right –

SARAH: Give him his sedative –

MME DE G: He'll never swallow it –

PITOU: Leave the spoon, give me the bottle. Hold him.

(SARAH *wheels herself to* DENUCÉ, *takes his face in her hands and holds him tightly.*)

SARAH: Now.

(PITOU *feeds* DENUCÉ *from the bottle.*)

Swallow, no matter how bitter. (*To* MME DE GOURNAY.) Something to take away the taste.

(MME DE GOURNAY *finds a sweet and gives it to* DENUCÉ. SARAH *holds him until he is calm.*)

MME DE G: He remembers the horror.

(PITOU *simulates his expression of horror.*)

SARAH: It would be better if we were born each day afresh. Without memory. Constantly I remember my roles, beings divided from me, quite separate, independent creations, yet more real than – (*She breaks off.*) It is the same for him. He is a man divided. His reality is not of the present. The cure is unity and acceptance. (*Pause.*) What do doctors of the mind know? Suffer the sick to come unto actors.

(*She smiles at* DENUCÉ, *who is more or less calm.*

MME DE GOURNAY *helps him to a chair and settles him.*)

MME DE G: He's calmer now.

SARAH: I must work. I must study, I must lie in my coffin, I must, as they say, put together my act. My next trick will be impossible.

(MME DE GOURNAY *wheels her off.* PITOU *watches them go.*)

PITOU: Insanity, I suppose, should engage our compassion. *Sic transit gloria mundi.* Doesn't she know one should never pull an elephant by the tail? Once, I remember –

DENUCÉ: Told me her name. Sssss . . .

PITOU: What?

DENUCÉ: Bombardment number three sector continuing. A sign. Slapped. Slapped me. Twins. Double Life.

PITOU: Yes, yes, her memoirs – why? –

DENUCÉ: Didn't ask to be born. Blackness and gun smoke. Awful noise. Lost my button. Awful pain. (*He touches his head.*) Silence. No feeling. A sign.

(PITOU *begins to take notes.*)

She and I, alone. Her voice. A great distance. Sunless regions. Piercing darkness. Voice of gold. Felt her hands, saw her eyes, blazing gems, heard my heart, a pounding gun. Thought I'd entered a room. Saw someone I'd lost, someone I'd loved, someone from whom the world divided me. A child spoke. Saw Phaedra, Marguerite Gau – , Napoleon's son, Duke of – Duke of – Two lost children. Words. Unfamiliar. Stirring. Other worlds. No sense of being. Only glory. Glory. Gave a sign. No one there. A shaft of sunlight. (*He hums 'The Nightingale Song'.* PITOU *continues to write for a moment, then stops.*)

PITOU: These are the mysteries. We have a grave responsibility. 'You should've seen her,' we'll say, and the youngsters will shrug and answer, 'We've seen better.' (*Pause.*) We are nothing without her.

(*He is consumed by sudden and dreadful rage.*)

She's an old hag!

(DENUCÉ *smiles and continues to hum.* PITOU *goes. Blackout. Lights.*

MME DE GOURNAY *is stitching a black doublet, trimmed with*

gold. SARAH *lies in the coffin, softly murmuring her lines*. PITOU
enters. MME DE GOURNAY *gestures for him to go*.)

MME DE G: She's learning her lines –

PITOU: Leave us.

MME DE G: But she said –

PITOU: Leave us.

(MME DE GOURNAY *goes*. PITOU *paces energetically, working
himself up*.)

I'm not going to apologize for disturbing you, because I feel
obliged to make one last effort to dissuade you from leaving
these shores. I am against a long transatlantic crossing.
You'll be exhausted before you arrive. If you arrive. The
Bosche is no respecter of persons or personages. His
torpedoes are merciless. Do I make myself clear? I am
against going to America.

(*He calms down a little*.)

So what's the alternative? A return to Paris, a stately life of
honours, admiration and work. What work, you ask? A play,
I reply. Don't get excited. You will not have to wait
indefinitely.

(*He takes out his notebook*.)

I am now ready to inform you that I, Pitou, am about to put
pen to paper. I am going to write you a play. (*Pause*.) All I
need is encouragement. As who does not? (*Pause*.) It is the
story, not of your past, but of your present. If I tell you that
my play begins with Major Denucé's words – (*He consults his
notebook*.) 'Above the knee,' you will understand.
Throughout you will be in a wheelchair or helped to stand by
loving – by attentive attendants. I have been keeping notes,
recording things said and done over these past months. (*He
reads:*) 'Then I shall have plays written for me in which I sit
on a throne.' Well. Here we are. And why not? You will
order Denucé to wash – I'll die of septicaemia, such
blackness – and we will see you trying to walk, visiting the
battlefields, carried in your chair. We will see you inspiring
the wounded and dying. I have thought of a marvellous
scene, two marvellous scenes with the Major. We will see
him stirred by your presence. We will hear in his own words

what that meant – (*He reads:*) – 'She and I, alone. Her voice,'
and so on and so forth. I have all the notes. And you will ask,
'What will become of me? What was the purpose of all that
pain?' But here let art command reality. If it pleased you we
could collaborate. Let us write a different final act. No
circus. But my play with a happy ending. Our play.
(*He sits near the coffin.*)
Do not sell your jewels. If it's the money that's worrying
you, allow me to say that I have been prudent. I have made
investments. I am in receipt of a modest income. To which
you are welcome. (*Pause.*) I apologize for being forever
abrasive. Once you said I was a different person when we
were alone. This is because – (*Pause.*) Allow me to say.
(*Pause.*) There is no need to reply now, but – (*Pause.*) I
should like nothing more in this life than to care for you until
– (*Pause.*) I am fully aware that I am not the most
presentable of men, but I have such for you – such – I have
profound feelings. (*Pause.*) I am your servant. (*Pause.*) I
would not regard it an insult if, for one reason or another,
you did not deem it fitting to use my name. Sarah Pitou is not
– (*Pause.*) Once I came into your room. You were lying as
you are now. Do you remember? Were you alone in this
coffin? Was I imagining? (*Pause.*) I am able to put from my
mind your present disability. I see you as I first saw you –
overwhelming and divine. I am your servant.
(*He leans very close to the coffin, whispers, and seems about to
climb in on top of her.*)
Shall I? Shall I?
(*He waits for an answer.* SARAH *snores.* PITOU *rushes out.*
SARAH *continues to snore.* MME DE GOURNAY *returns, sits and
resumes her stitching.* MME DE GOURNAY *whistles.* SARAH
stops snoring.
Blackout.
Hammering.
Lights.
The OLD CARPENTER *and the* YOUNG CARPENTER *are at
work on the platform.* DENUCÉ *is putting finishing touches to the
painted ballustrade.* MME DE GOURNAY *wheels in* SARAH.)

309

MME DE G: Look at what the Major's painted. He has a gift.

SARAH: Good, Major.

DENUCÉ: All done.

SARAH: It's very fine and just what I wanted. You should give an exhibition in Paris. It's meant to be a ballustrade, not can-can dancers on a foggy day. But it's excellent. It will serve our purpose.

MME DE G: And these are the men who made the platform. They're from the village.

(*The* TWO CARPENTERS *bow. They are horribly embarrassed and overawed.*)

OLD MAN: Honoured.

SARAH: Show me how the platform runs.

(*The* OLD CARPENTER *nods to the* YOUNG CARPENTER. *They pull the platform this way and that.*)

Splendid. Now you must fit the ballustrade.

(*The* OLD CARPENTER *nods to the* YOUNG CARPENTER, *who takes the ballustrade from* DENUCÉ *and begins to fit it around the platform so that the stool and most of the pillar are concealed.*)

OLD MAN: Would you sign this.

(*He offers her a photograph.*)

SARAH: Joan of Arc. A favourite role. Did you see me play the part?

OLD MAN: No. It's just that my mother was born in Domrémy.

SARAH: My interpretation of Joan of Arc is not meant to remind you of your mother. Never mind. Fit the ballustrade.

(*Having signed the photograph, she returns it to the* OLD CARPENTER, *who helps the* YOUNG CARPENTER *fit the ballustrade.*)

MME DE G: It's nearly time.

SARAH: I am nervous. Why should I be so frightened? Perhaps it's the presence of those two men. One stranger constitutes an audience. I can hardly catch my breath. Will I remember? Do I know the lines? I have played the part a dozen times but still I – (*She stops.*) Where will you sit?

MME DE G: Here?

SARAH: Good. And the Major?

MME DE G: By the phonograph.

SARAH: The men must complete the circle. Is my make-up all
right?

MME DE G: Perfect.

SARAH: You must forget I'm old.

MME DE G: Of course.

SARAH: Having to say that betrays my lack of confidence. I feel as
though all over again I'm making my debut.

MME DE G: I feel nothing but excitement.

SARAH: And, Major, you must make no noise while I speak.
Promise?

DENUCÉ: Promise.

SARAH: And no dribbling.

DENUCÉ: No.

SARAH: We must all lose a sense of ourselves.

MME DE G: We will. We will.

SARAH: What is Pitou up to? Why do I put up with him?

MME DE G: He's preparing a speech, an introduction. Shall I tell
Pitou to begin?

SARAH: Very well. And take off the platform so I can prepare.
And do not say, 'Break a leg.'

MME DE G: (*To the* TWO CARPENTERS) Take the platform off
please. She will tell you when to bring it on.
(*The* TWO CARPENTERS *pull the platform off.*
MME DE GOURNAY *winds up the phonograph, selects a record
and places it on the turntable.* DENUCÉ *has come to her.*)

DENUCÉ: Dance, dance.

MME DE G: No, no, no. I was never very good.

DENUCÉ: Yes. Dance. Please.

MME DE G: No. I was in the corps-de-ballet, never a soloist. I was
not naturally turned-out. Now go and sit down.
(As DENUCÉ *goes to his chair he catches sight of the unseen*
SARAH.)

DENUCÉ: Crossed herself.
(*He demonstrates.*)

MME DE G: Go and sit there. (*She calls:*) Are you ready?

SARAH: (*Off*) Ready.
(MME DE GOURNAY *calls to* PITOU:)

MME DE G: We're ready! We're ready!

(MME DE GOURNAY *and* DENUCÉ *take their seats.* PITOU
*enters. He wears white tie and tails and the false nose of a clown.
He makes clawing movements and roars like a lion. He gives a
hand-cue to* DENUCÉ, *who puts on the record – something by
Offenbach.*)

PITOU: Lady and gentleman! Welcome! Welcome to Sarah's
Circus. Admission free, children and invalids half price.
Tonight you are privileged, nay uniquely privileged, to
witness before your very eyes, the eighth wonder of the
world – I am your guide into uncharted territory, that
country where – (*He lowers his voice:*) – the divine queen-
goddess is determined to continue her life as though neither
time nor the surgeon's knife has scarred her. (*He raises his
voice again:*) For, she belongs, lady and gentleman, to that
tribe who crawl from their dens at night, who prowl and
strut and stalk their prey in darkness and like moths are
drawn to bright, bright light. I mean of course, the Theatre
tribe, for our queen-goddess is an actress, Queen of the land
of illusion, the kingdom of dreams. Tonight, and on
succeeding nights, until the oceans turn to sawdust, you are
privileged to witness the rehearsal of an amazing act –

SARAH: (*Off*) Get on with it, Pitou.

PITOU: Now you hear the roar of the lions and smell the filth of
animals. And you are entitled to ask with the poet, 'Is man
no more than this?'

(*The phonograph runs slow.*)

Take it off, take if off!

(DENUCÉ *stops the record.*)

Lady and gentleman, I give you the only, the one and only –
thank God – the one and only Sarah Barnum!

(DENUCÉ *applauds and stamps his feet.*)

MME DE G: Not yet, Major, not yet.

(*The* TWO CARPENTERS *pull in the platform. On the platform
sits* SARAH, *cloaked and hooded,* PITOU *pulls her into the centre,
then goes to the camera and covers himself with the cloth.* SARAH
stands, holding on to the truncated pillar with one hand.)

SARAH: Ladies and Gentlemen, I give you a speech from one of
my greatest roles: Hamlet, Prince of Denmark.

(*She throws off her cloak. She is dressed in an inky black doublet and wears a boyish wig.*)

    'O, what a rogue and peasant slave am I!
    Is it not monstrous that this player here,
    But in a fiction, in a dream of passion,
    Could force his soul so to his own conceit,
    That from her working all his visage wann'd,
    Tears in his eyes, distraction in 's aspect,
    A broken voice, and his whole function suiting
    With forms to his conceit? and all for nothing!
    For Hecuba!
    What's Hecuba to him, or he to Hecuba,
    That he should weep for her? What would he do,
    Had he the motive and the cue for passion
    That I have? He would drown –'

(*She makes a great sweeping gesture, knocks over the ballustrade so that she is fully revealed for the first time, balancing on one leg, holding on to the truncated pillar. The* YOUNG CARPENTER *laughs but the* OLD CARPENTER *gives a severe look to silence him. Her concentration is disturbed by the accident, but she continues hesitantly:*)

'He would drown – he would drown the stage with tears – cleave, cleave, the general – the general ear with horrid speech, make mad the guilty – make mad the guilty – confound the ignorant – appal the free – Yet I! Yet I! Yet I!'

(*She cannot remember. But she stands in a glorious pose.*
MME DE GOURNAY *is lost in wonder.* DENUCÉ *smiles his vacant smile and begins to applaud slowly. The* YOUNG CARPENTER *watches open-mouthed; the* OLD CARPENTER *wipes away tears. Under the camera cloth,* PITOU'*s whole body shakes with weeping; or he could be laughing.* SARAH *stands perfectly still, maintaining the pose on one leg, arm raised, head held high, triumphant.*
The lights fade.
Blackout.)

THE GUESTS

This play was written for television and first presented by ATV on 10 December 1972, directed by Valerie Hanson.

The part of the WOMAN was played by Margaret Leighton.

A flat near Olympia, London. The stage is divided into three main acting areas. The largest of these areas is the living room/dining room with two armchairs and a sofa, a small dining table laid for five, a sideboard. Next there is a bedroom area with a bed and bedside cabinet; last, and smallest, the kitchen area with a gas cooker and a rickety chair. Books are piled everywhere except in the living area.
There is a front door.
It is winter and cold.
Darkness.
A light on the WOMAN's *face: she is seated on the bed, gazing at herself in a hand mirror, frozen. Then, she begins to powder her face with a grubby piece of cotton wool: the light grows. She is in her mid to late forties and is wearing a chiffon blouse and a slip. Although she makes some effort with her appearance, she does not altogether succeed. Lost in thought, she reaches for a necklace and puts it on. She rises, and is about to move when suddenly she looks down and sees she is wearing a slip: she stifles a gasp and runs a nervous, uncertain hand across the creased material. In slight panic, she looks round for her skirt, moves books off the untidy bed and rummages through the bed clothes, finds the skirt and hurriedly slips it on. Quickly she goes from the bedroom where the light fades.*
Light hits the dining table, laid for five. The WOMAN *steps into the light and gazes at the five places. Then, she takes up four place cards and puts one at each of the places as though this requires a great effort of concentration and some determined physical action. This done, she moves away and the light grows to reveal the living room area. She warms her hands by an electric fire which has artificial coal and flame effect. Slowly, very slowly, she becomes deadly still. Silence. Then, suddenly, as if she hears something she snaps into life, but nervously, a little frightened. She gathers her courage, crosses to the front door and opens it to the extent of a short chain. She peers through the crack. Her face lights up*

THE WOMAN: It is you!

    (*She closes the door, undoes the chain and then opens the door wide.*)

Agnes! Tom! How lovely to see you again! Come in . . .
(*She leans forward, lips pursed to kiss. There is no one there. She
is kissing the air.*)
Let me take your coats – (*Mimes taking coats.*) – It's been
raining! (*Mimes hanging up the coats.*) Really? You poor
things! And so cold! (*Laughs. Stops. Registers pleasure.*) Oh
you shouldn't, you shouldn't! (*Mimes taking present.*) But I'm
on a diet – never mind – no, of course not – they're lovely – I
shall put on lots and lots of weight, I simply don't care.
(*Listens.*) Nonsense! I'm spreading like a chestnut tree, look!
(*She displays her figure, then laughs as if at a joke that has just
been made and closes the door.*)
(*As she closes the door.*) Of course you've seen it before, I wore
it to Church. (*Turns.*) Don't stand in the hall – (*Going,
leading the way.*) – Yes, isn't it typical? You country people
are always the first to arrive, but Brenda and Colin who live
just across the road will be late, you'll see. (*Laughs.*) Yes,
yes, as usual, how right you are!
(*She enters the living room area.*)
Tom, you do the drinks, won't you? I'm always accused of
giving everyone too much. Do sit, Agnes, help yourself to
nuts. (*Listens to Agnes.*) No, no, sit where you like, of course
I don't have a favourite chair, you should know that by now.
(*Listens to Tom in the direction of the sideboard.*) The same for
me, thank you, Tom, and not too much tonic. (*Laughs.*) Use
the good glasses. (*Listens to Agnes.*) Just the five of us as
usual. (*Listens.*) I'm so pleased you're here. You've no idea
how I look forward to . . . (*Listens.*) No, nothing special. The
week seems to have flown by what with one thing and
another . . . I washed my hair . . . I read . . . nothing special
. . . (*Looks up and mimes taking a drink.*) Thank you. Cheers,
here's to us. (*Looking up at Tom.*) I must say you're looking
frightfully well – (*Listens to Agnes.*) – He's not! What
nonsense! (*To Tom.*) But whatever for? You're not an ounce
overweight! (*Listens to Tom.*) Doctors! What do *they* know!
You should never listen to doctors – is it a very strict diet?
. . . because I've made – (*Breaks off as if interrupted.*) – well,
just leave what you're not allowed . . . (*Pause.*) You remind

318

me of Peter. You remember how strict he was about food?
He kept me up to scratch, I would have spread like a
chestnut tree – (*Laughs.*) – it's not rubbish – I'd've gone to
seed! (*Smiles.*) Oh, I'm so pleased you're here! Where are
you going, Agnes? (*An embarrassed laugh.*) Oh. I don't think
I put out any guest towels – be a dear, you know where the
linen cupboard is . . . (*Pause as if watching Agnes go. Then
turning urgently to Tom.*) Tom, while she's out of the room, I
must talk to you about . . . (*Stops.*) . . . I simply don't know
what to do, the Bank claim they haven't received last
month's cheque from the Trust! (*Listens.*) That's just what I
said! How could it possibly have got lost? That was exactly –
exactly – (*Listens, nodding fiercely in agreement.*) – exactly – I
knew you'd help . . . (*Pause, again she seems to lose the thread
and stands quite still, then.*) Yes, yes, yes, yes. (*Urgently.*)
Well, can't we break the Trust? It's so restricting. (*Listens.*)
You're a lawyer, Tom, find a way! (*Listens.*) But everything
goes up except my income. Talk to them for me, Tom,
please – (*Listens.*) – Don't – don't – scold me. (*Listens.*) I'm
not extravagant! (*Listens.*) I *know* Trusts are formed not to be
broken – I know, I know, I know, *all right!* (*A gesture ending
the conversation.*) Forgive me, I don't mean to sound . . .
(*Listens.*) You're not serious. (*Listens.*) Can you see me as a
landlady? With *lodgers*? (*Listens.*) No-no-no-no, it's not
possible, I couldn't face it. I couldn't take in strangers – no –
if I had a young nephew or niece – a student, that'd be quite
different, that'd be family – family are reliable but not . . .
strangers, no. Am I being tiresome? I complain and yet I
won't do . . . (*Pause.*) . . . You see, I was brought up to pay
my bills – not to live on credit – that's why I can't bear these
money worries any longer – I can't bear – one has to pay
one's way . . . (*Pause: shudders.*) . . . Lodgers . . . (*Pause.*)
My father was a very reliable man . . . that's where I get it
from . . . he disliked credit . . . not Mummy . . . she was
terribly extravagant . . . but then she had the money . . .
Brenda's extravagant . . . (*Listens.*) Perhaps when I was very
young, but not later, not when I was old enough to see
things, I didn't get on with Mummy . . . she wasn't clean . . .

that's where Brenda gets it from. Brenda takes after Mother.
I take after Father. (*Pause, angrily.*) It's so like her to be late!
You can't trust Brenda! (*Pause, her eyes narrow.*) Tom . . .
confidentially . . . truthfully . . . did Agnes . . . ever say – or
even hint – that Brenda was . . . having an affair with Peter?
(*Listens, then more fiercely.*) Did they ever go to bed together,
that's what I'm asking?! (*Pause.*) Deep down, I have this
feeling . . . (*Listens.*) Isn't that just Agnes being loyal, loyal to
Peter, just because she doesn't want to slander her own
brother? You see, she was so upset when Peter left me . . .
unnaturally upset . . . I thought . . . she must know
something about . . . Brenda and Peter . . . (*Listens.*) Agnes
deserves a man like you. You're so good. (*Suddenly turning.*)
Agnes, I've been flirting with your husband! I know you
won't mind. You can rely on me. I'm not the sort who
prefers other people's husbands . . . not like Brenda . . . Pour
me another gin, Tom, I – I spilled mine.
(*She goes abruptly to the fire and warms her hands. The action is
rather elaborate and uncontrolled. Then she crosses to a chair and
sits.*)
Disgraceful! It's after eight and they only live across . . . look
at the time . . . do you know what she told me, what Brenda
told me? Tom, listen to this, listen to what Brenda told me
the other day – (*Stops, mimes taking a drink.*) – oh, thank you
– oh, don't smoke your own, there's some in the box – what
was I saying? (*Listens to Agnes.*) Oh yes. Brenda told me –
only the other day – she said that almost always, when
they're dressing to go out, that's when Colin finds her most
attractive and starts to touch her and . . . (*Coyly.*) . . . things
. . . you know . . . one touch leads to another and . . . funny
time to enjoy marital bliss when you're dressing to go out . . .
and Colin a doctor, he ought to know better . . . (*Listens to
Tom and bursts out laughing saying next line as if she is repeating
Tom's joke.*) 'No wonder they lead such a busy social life!'
(*Continues to laugh then stops abruptly.*) Yes. They go out all
the time. (*Rises.*) I can see the front door from my bedroom
window. Hardly a night . . . (*Laughs.*) . . . 'such a busy social
life'. (*Eyes narrow, suspicious, hunted.*) Why are you two

looking at each other like that? (*Pause.*) Are you up to
something again? (*Despairing.*) You promised me you
wouldn't ... (*Alert.*) You've been in touch with Brenda,
haven't you? With Brenda and Colin, you've talked to
them, talked to them, haven't you, haven't you? (*Pause, she
is very still, imploring.*) Let's for once, oh please, just once,
have a quiet evening ... (*Lost, long pause, snaps back.*)
Tom, open the wine for me, you'll find it in the kitchen ...
two bottles for five persons? (*Calling to Tom.*) The opener's
in the top right hand drawer ... The top right hand
drawer, by the sink! (*To Agnes.*) Men are so helpless.
(*Pause.*) Helpless. (*Urgently.*) Agnes, promise me you
haven't spoken to Brenda and Colin, promise me there's no
... I can't say the word but you know what I mean.
(*Listens.*) I can't say it, but you know what I mean!
(*Listens.*) Yes, you do, you do! All right, then, I'll say it ...
conspiracy! Don't look so shocked, it's a perfectly ordinary
English word, conspiracy, to get together behind my back –
in church ... I remember, was it last week we went to
church? In the pew behind me whisper, whisper, whisper,
not your prayers. No, just whispers, whispers behind my
back. Everyone heard you, that's why I had to say 'Stop it!'
You can't imagine how humiliating, everyone looking at me
... Don't try to be clever. You were *not* saying your
prayers! That's what conspiracy means – behind my back!
Yes, yes, yes, yes, I know what you're thinking – (*Sudden
sharp laugh.*) – one may describe a conspiracy not only when
it is imagined, but also when it happens to be *true*! (*Listens.*)
Why don't you look at me when you speak? What are you
afraid I'll see? What is it between you and Tom? (*Pause.*) I
trust *you*, Agnes. (*Pause.*) Of all people, true or false, I
trust you. (*Listens, then as if interrupting.*) You *are* being
evasive – my own good? What nonsense, when did anyone
think of my good, except me? Don't lecture me, Agnes,
yes, yes, yes, yes, yes – I do *not*! (*Looks away as if Tom
re-enters.*) Oh, on the table, one bottle at each end. (*Pause.*)
Where *is* everyone? (*Pause.*) Well, what shall we talk about
then? (*Listens.*) Yes, awful. (*Listens, then wearily.*) Oh, the

usual. One day is very like the one before and the one to come. (*Trying to concentrate*.) Thought there was something I wanted to say . . . what was it . . . something important . . . (*Pause*.) . . . something I did . . . (*Listens*.) No, no, I never have enough time for that, there's always so much, no something else – I know what it was! I visited mother's grave yesterday! Of course silly of me to forget. It's the first time I've been to the cemetery for over five years. I suddenly had the urge. It was as if, as if – it sounds fanciful, so don't take this amiss – but it was as if she was calling me . . . stupid really. (*Pause*.) I saw such a strange thing, an old woman, foreign obviously, all in black, you know how foreigners wear widow's weeds, funny little black caps and thick woollen stockings . . . she was tending the grave next to mother's – I noted the name on the headstone, Dennis Smith, died 1940, aged eighty-one. This woman, this little old, foreign woman dressed in black from head to foot, I thought she had fainted because she was leaning up against the stone, but d'you know what she was really doing? She was talking, quite chattily, quite happily, gossiping away to Dennis Smith, died 1940, aged eighty-one, talking in her foreign tongue, not in English, talking a foreign language to Dennis Smith. Aren't people strange? (*Listens*.) Oh yes, I pay a small annual sum and they keep the grave quite . . . tidily. (*Listens*.) Hmm? No. Nothing. As if a stranger was buried there. Impossible to imagine her lying beneath the earth, rotting . . . rotted . . . impossible. (*Pause*.) I wish she'd told me she was going to die. (*Pause*.) I only went because of this – this urge, but standing there, looking down at the gravel chips, I felt – don't think me awful – I felt . . . indifferent.

(*She begins to pace up and down, stalking to and fro*.)

Peter would never allow me to visit the cemetery. He said it was indulging the superstitious side of my nature. (*Tearful*.) I should never have thrown him out, never, I shouldn't have listened . . . (*Pause*.) I just simply couldn't keep up with him. I did try, you know, but I can't, I simply can't retain anything. Proust and Lawrence, Rebecca Woolf and Orwell

. . . I'm not clever and that's all there is to it. (*Pause.*) I'm
pretty . . . (*Pause.*) . . . pretty stupid, Peter said . . .

> 'If all good people were clever,
> And all clever people were good,
> The world would be nicer than ever
> We thought that it possibly could.
> But somehow, 'tis seldom or never
> The two hit it off as they should;
> The good are so harsh to the clever
> The clever so rude to the good.'

I only remember the lightweight things now. (*Pause.*) Where
are Brenda and Colin? Do you know what she said the other
day on the telephone? She said 'I'm as God made me!' You
know what she meant by that, don't you? (*Listens, laughs.*)
Oh Tom, you're such a scream! 'Such a busy social life!'
(*Suddenly.*) Was that the bell? (*Pause.*) I distinctly heard . . .
did you hear the bell, Tom? There! I told you. I'll just let
them in . . .
(*She is half way to the front door when she stops dead.
Pause, lost.*) . . . Should I? It was so awful last week . . .
(*Inner terror growing, urgently to Tom and Agnes.*) Agnes,
Tom, promise me something . . . don't let's become . . .
serious . . . tonight . . . please . . . don't let's . . . (*Calling.*)
Coming! (*Listens to Tom.*) What? Yes, how clever of you, yes,
yes, more water than whisky for Colin, more water than . . .
(*As she goes.*) . . . they're so terribly late!
(*She reaches the front door, but pauses, as though trying to
overhear what Tom and Agnes are saying.
She seems for the first time genuinely terrified, but with an
awkward jerk of the head, frees herself of the fear, dabs at her
hair, and opens the chain and the door.*)
(*Gives 'kisses'.*) No, of course not, it's only just gone eight.
Give me your coats – (*Stops, disapproving.*) What a daring
dress! And your hair! Is that the latest colour? Quite the
fashion plate . . .
(*She hangs up the coats and is about to shut the front door when
she becomes perfectly still.*)
Someone's there.

(*Silence. Flustered, she continues to stare out at the landing. She is listening to Brenda. Then –*
To newcomer whom we shall call the man.)
Do come in, please forgive my sister – she's so vague – how silly of me – Brenda, you should have said, no, of course, we can manage an extra one – no trouble at all. (*Listens.*) They're in the drawing room, do go in. Tom'll give you a drink, I shan't be a second.
(*She pauses for a moment, wearing a fixed, frozen smile, but suddenly is forced to stifle a sob and keep herself under control. She passes a hand through her hair, reassumes her 'hostess' smile and goes into the living room area, standing as if listening with approval to her guests.*) What a gay party! Have you done the introductions, Brenda? Have you introduced your friend? (*Smiles.*) Good. Dinner won't be long. (*Listens.*) No, no, please don't move, I'll perch here – next to Colin . . . (*She sits on the arm of a chair, a low insinuating tone.*) I know why you were late, Colin dear. I know what you've *just* been doing. You're blushing! (*To the others.*) Colin's blushing; for a doctor you're frightfully gauche. (*Looking down at him.*) You're going bald, Colin. Your hair's falling out, comes from too much dressing before dinner! (*Laughs.*) Blush, blush, blush. (*Pause.*) Have you heard from Peter? (*Pause. Her attention is distracted*) Oh, Brenda, you're dreadful, if a doctor can't – (*Breaks off: troubled.*) I must lay an extra space – place – place . . .
(*She goes to the dining table, distractedly moves knives and forks, wanders to the sideboard for the extra cutlery, takes also a half bottle of wine – of which half is already drunk – and returns to the table.*
Startled.) Agnes – please – I can manage, really I can, don't bother. (*Listens.*) Hmm? No. He'll sit by me. On my right hand. You on my left. Brenda next to Tom, and Colin . . . I can't work it out. I'll start again. Six people. I'll be at the head, of course – (*Slight panic rising.*) Then our new friend to my right, that's proper, isn't it? You on my left – you're older than Brenda, aren't you? Yes you on my left. That leaves Colin – now, he mustn't be next to his wife, must he?

So – Tom sits next to Brenda and Colin sits . . . next to Tom!
The men can't be together can they? No. You do it, Agnes, I
can't . . . get it right. (*Whispers viciously.*) Look at her! Look
at her! She's practically popping out of her dress! Pushing
herself, insinuating like a snake – I wouldn't have a friend
staying in my house if I were her husband! Just look, just
look, it makes me want to vomit! (*Stops. . . . Far away.*) She
had a knack of sitting with her legs apart as though she were
a duchess . . . (*To Agnes.*) . . . Daddy used to say that . . . I
was always the more lady-like, in fact, the more . . . in front
of others . . . more gentle, genteel, I suppose. There is
nothing more despised in this world than good breeding.
Peter taught me that. He would have liked me to be more
catholic in my tastes . . . more . . . lewd. (*Flustered laugh.
Calling to Brenda.*) Brenda – unravel yourself, dear, and give
me a hand with dinner – no, Agnes, Brenda will help.
(*Smiles: waits.*) Come along, Brenda.
(*Pause. Face clouds with fear. Panic which she manages to
control. Then –*
Sternly.) Brenda! (*Pause.*) I hope everyone likes
beef . . .(*She marches into the kitchen area, and opens the oven
door.*
Muttering.) I think it's burnt . . .
(*From the cooker she withdraws a frozen TV dinner of beef etc.
Dried out, unappetising. The sight of it distresses her. She begins
to mutter but not as if there is someone else there, but rather as one
quite accustomed to being alone.*)
No one'll notice – what's it matter? – who cares? – what can I
do? just put it on a tray – food is food – keeps you going –
time was – fuel, that's all, fuel – (*Finds tray.*) – There. Who'll
care? I don't care. I just want to (*Suddenly flaring.*) Who is
that man? (*Listens.*) Don't lie to me! D'you think I haven't
got eyes in my head? D'you think I can't see? You've done it
again, you've done it again, *little bitch!* I know you! What are
you after, this flat? Or my paltry six pounds a week? Trusts
are made not to be broken, understand that, not to be – ! (*As
if Brenda has interrupted her.*) He's not! He's not here by
chance! He's not here by chance! (*Calling gaily.*) We're

coming! Yes, we're all starving! (*Intense.*) Why do you hate me, Brenda? Why? How can anyone be so cruel?

(*Long pause. Stillness. She begins to mutter again as if the fantasy world is slowly disintegrating.*)

(*Looking at the tray.*) Can't help it, can I? Forgot I'd put it on – not a crime – no one has to eat it – only me – I have to – doesn't matter – tastes like leather – (*Snaps back.*) *I know who he is!*

(*She goes back into the living-room area, and puts on her hostess smile.*)

Here we are! Do sit everyone. Agnes'll tell you where. (*To the man.*) No. You're beside me . . . (*Smiles coyly.*) Do start, everyone, don't let it get cold. (*She begins to eat. Again the highly imagined world she has created disintegrates, but now in a different way, she chatters ceaselessly, without waiting for replies or reactions. It is a sort of grotesque monologue, like a puppet out of control, jerky, uncoordinated, breathless, nodding, smiling, laughing, giving the impression of speeded up film, while all the time eating rapidly, and gulping wine.*)

Is that so? How funny? Just like her! Did you? Why? Pass the salt! Have some wine! Where was she going? How ludicrous! What for? Like a beanpole! Too sweet! In the middle of the shop, whatever next! Cold and damp what a thing to say, to a military chaplain, as if anyone, anyone who'd ever been to church would respect rank! Laughable! Utterly laughable! Cheers! *Gloria in excelsis* as my father used to say before sleep. How can illegitimacy run in a family? Out of the question? Maggots? Please, we're at table. Dear little worms, eating everyone up, including Mummy! But that's swearing! French *what*? Oh, French *leave* I see, cheers! (*Laughs. Stops. Pause.*)

(*She suddenly rises and almost runs to the sideboard, opens a drawer, takes a pencil, returns to the table and very carefully marks the level on the wine bottle label. She becomes calmer again, but continues to chew the last mouthful, staring into space. At last a smile crosses her face, a playful, teasing smile as she turns to the empty chair on her right hand.*)

So you're here quite by chance, are you? (*Listens.*) Really, you expect me to believe that, do you? (*Listens.*) I will *not* tell you. I will tell you nothing except . . . I know why you're here. (*Pause. To Colin.*) Colin, you're drinking too much as usual, and Brenda, if you lean any further forward we'll all be able to see your navel. (*To the man.*) Tell me about yourself, how did you meet Brenda and Colin? (*Listens.*) Just like that. Casually. The one they brought last week they met aboard ship . . . or at the Boat Show . . . it doesn't matter. (*Listens.*) Oh, you don't know about that. Hmmm. You're a very bad liar! (*Urgently.*) Isn't it true that Brenda and Colin brought you here for one reason and one reason only? Isn't it true that Agnes and Tom are in on it? (*Pause.*) I may not be clever, but I do know when people are lying! I do wish they wouldn't whisper, I like to catch what they're saying. (*Pause.*) Look! You look: in a moment or two. Colin will sidle up to Agnes, and Brenda will make eyes at Tom. (*Angrily.*) Dirty little bitch! Everything is sex, sex, sex, sex, sex, that's all she thinks of. (*Pause, then quite chattily.*) I expect I'm the first person you've ever met who was born in Ipswich! Our father was something in the city. Mummy never knew exactly what he did. Nor did we. She couldn't tell us, because she didn't know . . . and didn't care. She had the money. Left it to me. Six pounds a week, clear after rates, gas, *etcetera*, *etcetera*, and every penny losing its value. Do you think there'll come a time when six pounds is worth nothing? Brenda says I ought to be grateful. She got nothing in the Will. She wasn't paid off. (*Eyes darting.*) Look, look, what did I tell you? Look: Brenda and Tom, Colin and Agnes, look at them, so blatant! (*Long pause.*) I was led to believe it would be quite different until I married Peter. He was rather – rather rough for an intellectual. And what do you make of that? What conclusions do you draw from that? (*Swivels round.*) Stop pretending to dance! *There isn't any music!*

(*She looks from one to the other, giving the impression that they are surrounding her, closing in on her.*)

Look at them, look at them . . . do you wonder I accuse them of conspiracy?

(*She backs away, stumbles over a chair and catches her balance
on the dining table. She grabs hold of the wine bottle,
brandishing it about, as she addresses the man.*)
I suppose you're going to be a party to this, are you? You'll
lend your hand to this – obscenity! You know what they're
at, don't you – I can explain thank you, Brenda – they want
my paltry six pounds a week and this flat, this roof over my
head! And there's only one way they can get their hands on
it, isn't there, short of *killing* me. (*Listens to what is being said
with growing panic: she is frantic.*) Don't believe a word Colin
says, he's just a general practitioner, he doesn't know about
such things! (*Turns to the man.*) You need three doctors to do
it, three not two, three! Three! (*Listens in terror.*) You're
lying, you're a bad liar!
(*She drops the wine bottle and runs to the sideboard, opens and
closes drawers until she finds a small booklet of the type issued by
H.M. Stationery Office. She begins to page through it.*)
You need three doctors, three. (*Suddenly still.*) Please,
please go away. (*Continues to page through booklet furiously.*)
Here, here! What did I tell you? Part Four! Look, I've
marked it, look in ink, I've marked it, Section Four.
Compulsory Admission! I was right, listen, Part Four,
section three! (*Reads at speed.*) 'An application for admission
for observation shall be founded on the written
recommendations in the prescribed form of two medical prac
. . . (*Stops.*) . . . two medic . . . two . . .' (*Angrily.*) What date
is this? It's out of date! 1959! They've changed it, haven't
they changed it? Two? You need three, not two! (*An
anguished cry.*) *Peter*!
(*In desperation she glances round, as if for help, then seizes a
knife from the table holding it before her as though to defend
herself.*)
Nobody's going to put me away, *nobody*!
(*Sudden petrified stillness. Gradually, she begins to cry, almost
inaudible at first, then building to a harsh and painful sob.*)
Peter, Peter, Peter, *PETER*!
(*Sobbing continues for a brief moment, then stops abruptly. She
looks up, becomes aware of her surroundings and, almost with*

*horror, sees the knife in her hand which she lets fall as though
contaminated. She shivers with cold and moving at speed trots to
the bedroom, rummages on the bed, finds an old coat and puts it on,
returning to the living room area, but stops, seeing the wine bottle,
she goes down on her hands and knees: picks up the bottle.)*
(Muttering to herself.) That's odd . . . amazing really . . . not
broken. Huh. Not even cracked. *(She examines the pencil
mark she made.)* Not a drop . . . lost. *(She sings tunelessly.
Hums a little longer, then stops abruptly.)* Later, I'll do the
washing-up later.
*(She is about to rise when she sees, lying on the floor, the copy of
the Mental Health Act, 1959. She touches it as though it might
move, then, as if she cannot bear the sight of it, she stands and
runs into the kitchen, opens the gas oven, lights the gas and sits
before it warming herself.
Pause.)*
(Quietly.) I'm sorry if I behaved badly. *(Pause.)* I'll join you
when I'm feeling . . . I'll be all right . . . in a moment . . . just
leave me . . . alone.
*(She huddles herself for comfort, and talks into the oven as
though Brenda is inside it.)*
Tell them I'll be in in a moment, Brenda. *(Listens: then
firmly.)* No. That's just putting it off. We're going to have it
out once and for all. I don't want anyone to go home.
(Pause.) Don't touch me . . . thank you. *(Hums a little.
Pause.)* You've said your piece, you've given me your
assurances, and I don't believe a word you say. Do I make
myself clear? Do I make myself crystal clear? I do not believe
you. Is that – rational – enough for you? Is it a statement you
regard in any way as ambivalent? Do you detect any
symptoms of – illness in my conviction that I know you to be
a congenital liar? I do not believe a word you say, Brenda.
You brought that man, that electrician, you brought him
here for one reason and one reason only; to certify me
mentally ill. Is that clear enough for you, crystal clear
enough? To certify me, for him and Colin to submit written
recommendations in the prescribed form, the *two* of them,
the *two* medical practitioners. Well, let me tell you, I shall

fight the two of them tooth and nail. I shall fight them through the courts, to the highest court, I'll find a really unbiased judge who's on my side! There! I cannot speak plainer than that! (*Pause.*) And I'll tell you this: they won't accept Colin's evidence, they won't, and d'you know why? Because he's your husband and they won't let relatives put relatives away. They won't let you benefit, d'you understand? The State is very, very careful about such things. The State does not encourage relatives to lock each other up!

(*She bangs the oven door shut and rises. She begins to go towards the living-room area.*)

(*As she goes.*) – you live like a queen with your little doctor husband and you never think of me! In and out of bed, in and out, that's all you think of! Well, I've got the State on my side –

(*She is in the living-room.*)

– the whole State! (*Stops. Looks around.*) A nice kettle of fish, a nice how-d'you do, hmmm? All one's family, all these relatives, ganging up, yes, ganging up, *conspiring*, I don't care what it sounds like, *conspiring*! (*Near to tears.*) Tom, can't I take out an injection against them, can't I restrain them? (*Pause.*) And you, our electrical friend, you've very little to say for yourself, what have you to say? Aren't you ashamed of yourself, well, aren't you? (*Listens: then turns to others. Desperately.*) Don't listen to him! How dare you! These are my guests! It's not for you to tell them to leave! *I'll* tell them when to leave! *They're my guests*! (*Panic.*) Don't go, please, Brenda, Tom, Agnes, Colin, don't go. I promise I'll be nice, we'll play Bridge, we won't talk about me, we'll talk about other things – don't leave me alone with him – just the four of you, as it always was – *I'm not well enough to be left alone* – I've been hasty! (*Going towards front door.*) Don't go! Don't!

(*As though struggling, she opens the front door.*)

– don't leave me alone with him, you know what he'll do, he'll – he'll – we may never see each other again! I apologise! I take back everything I said! I didn't mean a word of it! Say there'll be other times! (*Closes the door and spins round.*) How dare you tell them to leave? How dare you! You come here, uninvited, not so much as – (*Becoming very disturbed and irrational.*) – as – as – as – a – a – curtsey or a bow or anything like that. You just barge in with your electrical equipment bulging, *I don't want you here!* I never wanted you here in the first place, is that understood? I want Brenda and Tom and Colin and Agnes, that's who I want! (*Near to tears.*) Can't you see I'm getting better?

(*She goes into the bedroom. She falls on to the bed.*)

Go away, go away!

(*Lies still for a moment, then pulls the pillow over her head to shut out the sound.*)

I'm not listening, I'm not listening.

(*Pause. She spins onto her back, staring at the ceiling.*)

They're regular visitors, they're my guests, you can't suddenly turn on people you've known for years and tell them never to come again, you can't, it's not as easy as that. It isn't polite to break all the rules of hospitality on one night. And they only mean to be helpful, you know, to keep me . . . (*Listens.*) Once a week and that's the truth. I don't invite them every night. Good God who could afford to entertain every night? (*Listens.*) No. I don't. You'll have to ask them, – (*Sitting up.*) – call them back and ask them, ask them why they abuse my hospitality so. (*Listens. Then as if speaking while he is speaking.*) Don't start on Peter, please, leave him out of this, we're divorced, is nothing sacred to you? (*Vehemently.*) Don't speak ill of Peter! (*Pause.*) He's been my strength, my pillar. When men like you, horrid little electricians like you have wanted to put me away, who kept me out, who prevented it, who fought for me tooth and nail? Peter, that's who! *Peter kept me out!* (*Listens: mocking.*) Oh, you do make it sound attractive. Just go in and give myself up, shall I? That's what you advise, is it? Green walls and goldfish, plastic window panes and stainless steel bedpans with blunt edges. I've seen it all! (*Listens.*) When? Hmmm. I shall have to think. (*Suspicious.*) Why do you want to know? When did I see it, when did I see green walls? (*Very*

staccato.) End of war. Summer. Mummy died. Here in this room, on this bed. Only child, me. Father dead, mother, all dead. Missed her. Missed Mummy. (*Pause, then business-like*.) A bad attack of grief. (*Tetchy*.) Don't hover! If you want to sit down, move some books.
(*Pause. She picks up hand mirror*.)
Peter said I had lovely eyes. That's what first attracted him to me, he said. I couldn't keep up with him, you see. Do you think he married me for my money? In those days, six pounds a week was rather fancy. Mother kept us both and saved. A tidy sum. Brenda can have the flat when I'm six foot under or . . . (*Pause*.) New neighbours all the time, impossible to know, they get smarter and smarter, oh, the neighbourhood's gone up by leaps and bounds – (*Looks up at ceiling*.) – and there's a dreadful man upstairs summons the boys in blue from time to time, but they are my friends and call me 'miss'. (*Pause*.) One must hold on to what one's got. What one's got, is all one has. (*Listens*.) You're very persistent. Peter, Peter, Peter! I don't want to go into all that – it's much too – too – (*Listens*.) Oh, you are inquisitive, stock-in-trade, is it? All electricians are inquisitive, trying to find the short-circuit, are you? (*Listens*.) I don't like the way you say that. You seem to imply that I don't always tell the truth. (*Listens: agitated*.) They call me 'miss' because – because – (*Rises*.) – because that's the polite form of address. (*Listens*.) How should I know why they don't call me *madam?* Very, very stupid! You expect me to know the answer to questions that I can't possibly – can't, will not, they call me 'miss' and that's all there is to it! (*Sudden realisation. She crawls across the bed to him*.) You're getting at Peter, aren't you, you're trying to imply that we lived in sin, you're preoccupied with sin, aren't you? (*Pause*.) What was that noise?
(*She goes to the window and, like a prying neighbour, looks out through the curtains*.)
It's foggy out. Or are the windows dirty? You should never have made me divorce him. (*Listens: becomes agitated*.) All right, not you, someone else, the man they brought last

month, last week, yesterday, the day before, I don't know, some man, another electrician . . . (*Crying*.) He made Peter leave me. It was awful . . . a terrible, terrible scene . . . we'd been married for such a long time. (*Listens*.) In St Clements Dane, on a June day in 1951, I wore white, and a veil, and Tom gave me away! (*Listens*.) *I don't know why they call me 'miss'!* (*Long pause*.) Yes, I do. I know very well why. (*Turns, holding up her left hand. Smiles*.) Spinster of this parish. (*Pause*.) That's why they call me 'miss': because we were divorced. Last week. Last month. There you have it. That's why they call me 'miss'. The Special Branch know everything. (*Listens*.) I don't want to tell you, I've been through it so many times . . .

(*She goes to bedside table, and takes out several packs of cards all similar, but makes a very careful choice of one particular pack and goes out into the living-room area.*
She sits on the floor, shuffles the cards and begins to play patience.)

This helps me to arrange my mind, helps me to think clearly. (*Concentrates on the game*.) Where were we? (*Her face clouds with alarm*) The ace of clubs . . . (*Plays the cards*.) It must come out, it must . . . (*Listens*.) Peter. Yes. We met in . . . (*Plays*.) He was a biochemist, which is rather a difficult thing to be: you have to be rather tall, I believe – (*Breaks off*.) – The Queen of Hearts, it must come out, it must! (*Excited*.) I'm winning. It's come out, you'll see, I shuffled right and it'll come out, shuffle, shuffle, shuffle! (*Pause*.) That's what you do, isn't it, shuffle the cards at random, *electrically*! Yes, a meteorologist, that's what Peter was: fair as straw, full sensual lips, and extraordinarily agile fingers. Should have been a pianist, or a fiddler, something dexterous. (*Plays at the cards with intense concentration but growing panic*.) You're losing! It won't come out! (*To the man*.) I *am* telling the truth. He was a metal-worker, *he told me*! (*She throws the cards into the air and watches them fall*.) If I choose the eight of clubs, I won't tell you anything! (*She chooses a card at random, holds it up: four of spades. In a rush:*) I led a very protected life, we all did in those days, air raid shelters and

gas masks, we were protected from every sort of danger. You see, before the war, well bred people were quite common, if you'll pardon the expression. There was absolutely nothing nasty in the world – except the war of course. (*Listens.*) I was a student at the time, a student of . . . (*Face clouds over.*) . . . no need to go into that, no need . . . (*Pause.*) I used to be so clever. Three languages. I was good at languages. But then they rearranged the . . . (*Pause.*) No. That was after Mummy died. (*Pause.*) The vicar was no help at all. (*Pause.*) He found me, as a matter of fact, two weeks after Mummy's funeral, quite alone. At first, he thought I was light headed, but he was wrong. (*Laughs.*) That's when I saw the green walls and the goldfish bowls. I believed I was just passing through, but I was mistaken. (*Confidentially.*) I can hide pills in my navel, you know. (*Pause. Gathers up the cards with much energy.*) That's when I first met the electricians. Talk about a shock. (*Shuffles the cards.*) Shuffle, shuffle, shuffle . . . where have all the facts gone, and those foreign words, millions of them? I can't remember a bloody thing! It doesn't do to give well bred people shocks. (*Lays out another patience. Pause.*) They just let me out, you know, just like that. I don't like what they've done, I do not want it to happen again. I said to myself: *this won't happen again!* (*Plays the cards.*) Where are all the twos? There are no twos? (*Pause.*) I came back here, to this place, here, alone. (*Pause.*) I sold all my dictionaries. No use to me. Sold every last one. (*Pause.*) I need protection, I thought. Someone must help me to stop that happening again. That's when I met Peter. (*Irritated.*) Not a two in sight! (*Leaves the cards, and rises.*) He was waiting for me when I came back from the hospital, standing there, half in, half out of the bedroom, typical! (*Listens.*) Just listen and don't interrupt. It isn't easy for me. I'll make it as clear as I can. Please. Don't speak.
(*She begins to pace.*)
I looked everywhere for someone to protect me, someone kind. Difficult, you know, very difficult to find. (*Laughs.*) I believed I was being followed, they were out to kidnap me, you see, oh I believed it, quite, quite, loony, at least fifteen

amps gone! I told them, I went to the nearest hospital and I
told them they want to kidnap me. Why don't you go to the
police, they asked. Because the police are in on it, too, I
said. (*Sits.*) I saw the look in his eyes, this chief electrician,
sparks flying! So I came back here and there he was:
waiting for me: Peter! I never thought of looking for him
here. We were married at once, no priest, nothing silly like
that, he didn't believe in it, nor did I, anything to please,
yes, Peter and I were married here ten minutes after our
first meeting. And they stopped following me. And Peter
and I lived a normal, happily married life, in this place, and
I went out to work to keep him, because he was too clever
to work and I had become too stupid to do anything else. I
was Mr Greenaway's receptionist, not Greenway,
Green*a*way, he was very particular about that. What did
who look like? (*Rises, agitated.*) What did Peter look like?
He had two eyes and a nose and a mouth, and that was
enough for any man and any woman! Peter introduced me
to everyone, and I had relatives, next-of-kin, his sister,
Agnes, and her husband Tom, and my own sister Brenda
and her doctor-husband Colin. I didn't even know I had a
sister until I met Peter. He was the whole world to me! I
told him to leave, I didn't need him anymore – I just kept
my friends, my relatives, my immediate family, Agnes,
Tom, Brenda, Colin, asked them once a week to a little
dinner . . . and now you've sent them away. (*Pause.*) I enjoy
having them. I look forward to it. (*Long pause. A kind of
litany.*) I know I've got to manage on my own . . . Perhaps
next week . . . But I'm not quite ready yet . . . to be left . . .
Next week . . . (*Listens.*) I promise not to ask them back.
(*Pause.*) Brenda brings out the worst in me. (*Pause.*) Agnes
the best. (*Pause.*) I never have a very clear picture of Colin
. . . Tom has a moustache. (*Listens.*) I promise. I won't
invite any of them again. (*Pause.*) Perhaps Peter could die.
(*Pause.*) I think I can manage on my own. (*Listens.*) They
kept me out, you see. If it wasn't for them, I'd have gone
back in long ago. They – they protected me. (*Listens.*) No,
no, I'll stand by my promise: I'll never invite any of them

ever again . . . I know I've got to manage on my own . . .
(*She turns to the man.*) But you'll come, won't you, next
week, you'll come . . . won't you?
(*The light fades so that only her face is illuminated.
Darkness.*)